NTC's
Dictionary
of
ADVERTISING

NTC's
Dictionary
of
ADVERTISING

Second Edition

Jack G. Wiechmann

First Edition Edited
by Laurence Urdang

National Textbook Company
NTC a division of *NTC Publishing Group* • Lincolnwood, Illinois USA

7-95

24320973

Library of Congress Cataloging-in-Publication Data

Wiechmann, Jack G.
    NTC's dictionary of advertising / Jack G. Wiechmann. —2nd ed.
        p.   cm.
    ISBN 0-8442-3486-9
    1. Advertising-Dictionaries.   I. Title.   II. Title: Dictionary
of advertising.
    HF5803.W54   1992
    659.1'03-dc20   91-29459
                                                            CIP

Published by National Textbook Company, a division of NTC Publishing Group
4255 West Touhy Avenue
Lincolnwood (Chicago), Illinois 60646-1975, U.S.A.

2 3 4 5 6 7 8 9 0 VP 9 8 7 6 5 4 3 2 1

As always,
to my family

◆ Preface ◆

When NTC Publishing Group asked me to edit the second edition of their Dictionary of Advertising, I said "Sure, piece of cake." Then they told me to add 1,000 new terms and definitions to the 4,000 already offered in the book. Where would I find 1,000 words?

Although I thought I was in trouble, the funny thing was that I easily added that number. The advertising people I approached for suggestions couldn't have been more considerate and helpful. Then too, advertising is an industry that is ever-changing, and that includes its vocabulary. I soon discovered that my problem wasn't how to add enough new terms but rather how to keep the length of the book under reasonable control. Undoubtedly, you will think of words that belong but are missing or wonder why some others are there at all. Don't worry. Just send your suggestions to the publisher. There will be a third edition some day.

Some words you may never have heard of before, like "quad," "kerning," "vertigrate," and "mackle." Our objective, of course, has been to serve a variety of users, from secretaries concerned with spelling and grammar, to students seeking a basic understanding of the terms, to more experienced professionals concerned with accurately distinguishing between the meanings of one word and another.

The vocabularies that form this dictionary include those used in marketing planning, copywriting, art direction, graphic supply, print production, commercial production, media planning, research analysis and buying, marketing and advertising research, merchandising and promotion planning, publicity and public relations, advertising finance, and client service.

Included are special meanings of ordinary words, words unique to a single specialty, names of devices, services and organizations, and extensive cross-references for abbreviations, acronyms, and synonyms. Reference has been made to industry organizations, and syndicated research firms, since their influence on the basic terminology of the business has been pervasive.

Finally, while this is the most comprehensive collection of its kind prepared to date, it is intended only to serve as a supplement to a basic English dictionary. It cannot be considered perfect or complete. The vocabulary of the advertising industry changes much too rapidly, grows far too quickly, and tends to adapt ordinary words and expressions to its own needs.

I trust you will find as much pleasure in using this volume as I have had in compiling it.

Jack G. Wiechmann
Guilford, Connecticut
September 1992

◼ Acknowledgments ◼

Without the constant guidance, support, and patience shown by Anne Knudsen and Karen Shaw at NTC Publishing Group this project would never have been completed. I am deeply grateful to them. I also appreciate the help offered by so many advertising executives, some now retired. They have shared much of their time and knowledge of the industry in order to help me put together as complete an advertising dictionary as possible.

I am particularly indebted to James Dunham, who saw enough potential so long ago to let me write my first ad; to Arthur C. Kammerman, who taught me the excitement and joy of putting the right words in the right places to make something good happen; and to Philip A. Bossert, who has never let me forget that "there is no circus until you can smell the peanuts."

Among many others, I owe much to Jack Bertram, Lee Elliot, Bill Gale, Ed Graceman, James R. Gregory, John Hill, Allan Kelly, Alfred Lippmann, Jim Michaelson, Robert Montgomery, Douglas Olson, George O'Rourke, Byron Radaker, Gus Richter, Bill Silverman, William Smolkin, John Stahlin, Ellie Tibaldo, Robert K. White, Lynn P. Wiechmann, Richard J. Wiechmann, and Tom Wilzinski.

Nor should I forget Mary Muenkel, Vice President and Director of Information Services at BBDO. She and her staff helped greatly in gathering much pertinent information.

I would be remiss if I did not pay special tribute to Laurence Urdang, his associates, and the management of Tatham-Laird & Kudner Advertising for all the thoughtful planning, research, and labor that went into the first edition of this dictionary. Their efforts have made my job that much easier.

In like manner, the work of R. Terry Ellmore in preparing *NTC's Mass Media Dictionary* has aided me immeasurably in tracking down some of the more recent advertising terms and their definitions.

Finally, special thanks to my wife, Betty, for her never-ending patience and encouragement during the year-and-a-half it took to compile this dictionary.

A See *angled*.

AA See *advertising agency*, *author's alteration*, *average audience*.

AAAA See *American Association of Advertising Agencies*.

AAAA spot contract A standardized contract specifying the terms of purchase between an advertising agency and a spot television supplier; model format prepared by the American Association of Advertising Agencies. See *time contract*.

AAF See *American Advertising Federation*.

A & M See *art and mechanical*.

A and M See *art and mechanical*.

AANR See *American Association of Newspaper Representatives, Inc.*

AA rating See *average audience rating*.

AAW See *Advertising Association of the West*.

ABA See *area-by-area allocation*.

abandonment The release of a trademark by a manufacturer through nonuse or sale.

ABC See *Audit Bureau of Circulations*.

ABCD counties Classifications of counties by population size as designated by the A.C. Nielsen Company. See *county size*.

abeyance order A spot television order for commercial time not available at time of purchase.

ABMS See *Audit Bureau of Marketing Services*.

above-the-line cost A budgeted expense in television production (e.g., producers, directors, cast, script). See *below-the-line cost*.

ABP See *American Business Press, Inc.*

abscissa The horizontal coordinate of a graph. Also **x-axis**. See *ordinate*.

A-B split A division of a list of individuals into two groups for a survey, control group, or test group by selecting every other name on the list.

abstraction A composition in advertising graphics with recognizable human, animal, or inanimate figures represented as generalized or geometric forms.

ACA See *Association for Communication Administration*.

ACB See *Advertising Checking Bureau*.

access 1. Users' right of entry to services such as cable television, telephone lines, or a computer system. 2. The availability of media time to various persons and groups, such as retail establishments or political candidates. 3. See *daypart*.

access to media A right claimed by individuals to purchase advertising air time or print space. This access is not guaranteed by law, except for legally qualified candidates for public office.

accordion fold A zigzag, accordion-like fold in an advertising brochure or insert, permitting it to be extended to its full size with a single pull. Also **accordion pleat**.

accordion insert An advertisement attached in a periodical after printing that has an accordion fold.

1

accordion pleat See *accordion fold.*

account 1. A general term for the business relationship existing between an advertising agency and its clients. 2. A client of an advertising agency. 3. A contract between a broadcast station and an advertising agency or advertiser for the purchase of time. 4. A customer of a supplier or vendor, as one purchasing goods or services for advertising production.

account conflict The opposing interests that occur when an advertising agency accepts competing clients.

account executive (AE) 1. An advertising agency or marketing organization employee responsible for maintaining liaison with designated agency clients and for developing and controlling client advertising plans. Also **account manager, account representative, contact executive.** 2. A salesperson, especially in Canada, who sells media space or time.

account group The advertising agency team coordinated by the account executive that services a specific account or accounts.

account manager See *account executive.*

account representative See *account executive.*

account supervisor An advertising agency employee responsible for overseeing the work of one or more account executives and for maintaining liaison with supervisory staff in the client's advertising department. See *management supervisor.*

Accuracy in Media (AIM) A citizens' watchdog group.

ACD See *associate creative director.*

ACG See *Address Coding Guide.*

ACI See *Advertising Council, Inc.*

A.C. Nielsen Company A leading market research and marketing services firm.

A county See *county size.*

across the board The scheduling of a television or radio program or commercial each day at the same time, usually Monday through Friday.

ACT See *Action for Children's Television.*

act break The interruption of a radio or television program by commercials, station breaks, and so forth.

action device A feature used in advertising to motivate responses in prospective buyers by requiring some particular action, such as affixing a stamp to show which periodicals are being ordered.

Action for Children's Television (ACT) A citizens' group lobbying for the elimination of commercials in television programming aimed at children.

active buyer A buyer who has made recent purchases, often in response to advertising.

active member A member of a book (or other merchandise) club who has not completed the original commitment and remains obliged to purchase the required items.

active subscriber A subscriber who continues to receive books, newspapers, magazines, etc.

actual A radio or television program based on a real event.

ACV All commodity volume. See *distribution.*

AD See *art director, assistant director.*

ad See *advertisement, advertising.*

Ad-A-Card™ A perforated tear-off coupon attached to advertisements in selected Sunday newspaper comics and supplement sections.

ad agency See *advertising agency.*

ad alley The section of a composing room used for display ads. Also **ad side**.

ad copy See *copy*.

Ad Council See *Advertising Council, Inc.*

adcut See *logotype*.

add-on sales In retailing, additional purchases made at the time merchandise is ordered, often on the recommendation of the salesperson.

add-on service A function that inserts names in mailing lists at consumers' request.

address coding guide (ACG) A publication that contains postal ZIP codes, listed by number, block, and district.

address correction requested A printed notice on an advertising mailer requesting the U.S. Postal Service to advise the sender if the addressee has moved.

Addressograph™ A machine that prints addresses from letterpress plates through an inked ribbon. Often replaced by computerized mailing list programs.

Addy Award An award given by the American Advertising Federation (AAF) for excellence in advertising.

adequate sample A sample large enough to minimize chance as a factor affecting the analysis of data obtained from research.

ADI See *Area of Dominant Influence*.

ad interconnect The linking of two or more cable television systems for the purpose of distributing advertising.

adjacency 1. The relationship between radio or television programs that precede or follow each other. 2. Pertaining to the interval between programs, available as commercial time.

adjacency policy A radio or television station's or network's guidelines for separating competing commercials.

adjustment A loss of outdoor advertising service requiring delivery of a similar service of equal value. In other media, called a **make good**.

ad lib A verbal or physical action by a performer without specific reference to a script, score, or the like.

adman A person who works in the advertising industry. Also **adperson**, **advertising person**.

ad mat A papier-mâché mold of set type, etc., used to produce a duplicate for printing advertising.

adnorm The readership of an advertisement placed in a specific periodical; the term is used by the research firm of Starch & Associates. The measurement is based on experience with the periodical, size of the advertisement, use of color, and type of product, considered as a proportion of the norm established for that type of advertisement. Also **adnorm score**. See *noted, read-most, seen/associated*.

adnorm score See previous.

ad-noter A reader who claims to have noticed an advertisement in a particular issue of a particular periodical; used by the research firm of Starch & Associates. Also **noter**. See *noted score*.

ad-page percentage In Canada, the percentage of readers of the target area for printed advertising who have actually observed the page containing the advertising.

ad-page exposure (APX) The frequency at which readers are exposed to an average advertising page in a periodical.

adperson See *adman*.

ad retention The measure of advertising message recipients' ability to correctly identify their own exposure to advertising.

ad side See *ad alley*.

ad slick A glossy print of an advertisement for approval and reproduction purposes.

advance canvass A series of visits to retailers in a territory to obtain support for a forthcoming promotional campaign.

advance ratings 1. Ratings information released before the publication of a survey report. 2. Nielsen *Station Index* audience estimates available via telephone prior to client receipt of the printed report.

advertise To attempt to persuade people to voluntarily produce a behavior pattern (such as purchasing a product) by presenting them with an openly sponsored, multiply reproduced message, generally delivered via paid periodical or newspaper space, television or radio time, or outdoor boards.

advertised price The price of a product or service as stated in an advertisement.

advertisement A written, verbal, pictorial, graphic, etc., announcement of goods or services for sale, employing purchased space or time in print or electronic media. Also **ad**.

advertiser The entity that pays for the placement of an advertisement.

advertising 1. The process of calling the public's attention to the availability of goods, services, or causes. 2. The process of using advertisements as a means of meeting marketing objectives. 3. The business or profession of producing and placing advertisements. 4. Loosely, an advertisement or advertisements. Also **ad**.

advertising agency (AA) A commercial organization that contracts with advertisers to develop and manage their advertising for a fee or for commission. Also **ad agency**, **agency**.

advertising allowance A payment or provision of a service by a source of products or services to a merchant for advertising the products or services.

advertising appropriation The amount of money budgeted by an advertiser to pay for advertising.

Advertising Association of the West (AAW) A group of West Coast advertising organizations; absorbed into the American Advertising Federation in 1967.

advertising campaign See *campaign*.

Advertising Checking Bureau (ACB) An organization that supplies advertisers and agencies with tearsheets of advertisements run in publications and information to help them assess client and competitor advertising approaches and their impact.

advertising continuity The words written for a commercial or advertisement.

advertising contract 1. An agreement between an advertiser and a communications medium for advertising space or time; usually negotiated by an advertising agency. 2. An agreement between a source of goods or its representative and a retailer that the latter will advertise the goods in return for stated consideration.

Advertising Council, Inc. (ACI) A nonprofit organization supported by the AAAA that produces messages regarded as in the public interest.

advertising cutoff A boundary separating advertisements from news, text, or other advertisements.

advertising department 1. The department of an advertiser responsible for advertising. 2. The department of a newspaper or magazine responsible for advertising; often divided into display and classified units.

advertising director 1. An individual within a company who is responsible for the advertising budget and for the execution of advertising plans. See *advertising manager*.

2. A media executive who coordinates the sale of advertising space.

Advertising Federation of America (AFA) An association of organizations representing various activities relating to advertising. Now part of the American Advertising Federation.

advertising linage The number of lines of advertising carried in a publication in a given issue.

advertising manager An employee of an advertising organization who reviews and approves advertising plans and, usually, execution of advertisements. Sometimes responsible for approving sales promotion plans. Typically reports to an advertising director, communications director, or marketing director.

advertising media The print and electronic media used to convey advertising messages.

advertising mix 1. Advertising plan consisting of more than one medium. 2. The proportion of time or space purchased in different media by an advertiser.

advertising penetration The degree to which people in a market have seen a particular advertisement.

advertising person See *adman.*

advertising promotion The efforts made by the print and electronic media to sell, increase sales, or improve the quality of advertising.

advertising rates The charges made for space or time in media that carry advertising.

advertising representative A person or agency that sells advertising space for newspapers and magazines. See *station representative.*

advertising research 1. The analysis of a product or service to discover its market-able characteristics. 2. The investigation of a market to evaluate buying potential for a product or service. 3. The measurement of an advertisement's potential for success before it is used and actual success after it is used.

Advertising Research Foundation (ARF) An association of advertisers, advertising agencies, advertising media, and researchers whose purpose is to advance advertising research methodology and maintain research standards. It publishes the *Journal of Advertising Research.*

advertising reserve An advertising budget line established without a prior specification for its use, to be used subsequently for unanticipated advertising contingencies.

advertising response coefficient A measure of market demand for a product or service, determined by dividing the percentage of change in sales by the percentage of change in advertising.

advertising schedule The complete listing of advertisements, media to be used, and insertion dates for an advertising campaign.

advertising service The various forms of assistance rendered to an advertiser by the agency and/or media to aid in producing advertising.

advertising specialty An inexpensive item bearing an advertiser's name, used as a promotional gift. See *giveaway.*

advertising strategy The planning and directing of an advertising campaign, including research, creative concept and execution, media selection and use, and marketing.

advertising theme The dominant subject or idea that ties an advertising campaign together.

advertising wedge A product's superior feature(s) that can be referred to in designing a commercial or advertisement.

advertising weight The number of advertising messages used in or planned for a campaign. Also **support**.

advertorial A blend of *advertisement* and *editorial*. A combination of display advertising and editorial comment. Sometimes considered a deceptive form of advertising; in print versions the publisher may head it with the word "advertisement."

advocacy advertising Advertising by a company or industry that takes an editorial position on some subject of public concern, such as the environment, taxes, education, etc.

advt. An abbreviation for *advertisement*.

AE See *account executive, angled end*.

AFA See *Advertising Federation of America*.

affidavit of performance A notarized statement from a television or radio station that commercials or programs were broadcast as scheduled.

affiliate 1. An organization that contracts to supply goods or services, to advertise and merchandise, or in various ways to carry out the policies of a company operated in close association with it. 2. A television (including cable) or radio station that contracts to make a portion of its time available to a network. Also **network affiliate, network station**.

affiliate agreement A contract between a radio or television network and its affiliates that specifies the rights and duties of the organizations involved. Also **affiliation agreement**.

affiliated chain A regional chain of retail stores associated with other, noncompeting stores for the advantage of large-scale purchasing or for exclusive territorial rights to the marketing of certain brands.

affiliated retailer 1. A retailer affiliated with a voluntary chain. 2. A retailer that participates with others in a cooperative wholesale purchasing operation.

affiliated station A television station having a regular affiliation with one of the three national television networks, under which it serves as that network's primary outlet for the presentation of programs in a market.

affiliated wholesaler A wholesaler that sponsors a voluntary chain of affiliated retailers, or that is a member of a voluntary chain of wholesalers.

affiliation agreement See *affiliate agreement*.

affordable method A way to determine marketing budgets based on judgment of what funds remain after other spending and profit goals are established.

AF (of) M See *American Federation of Musicians*.

afterimage An illusory visual image remaining with a spectator after the actual image is no longer visible.

afternoon drive See *daypart*.

AFTRA See *American Federation of Television and Radio Artists*.

agate line A unit of measurement used as a standard in selling advertising space in periodicals. Fourteen agate lines equal one column inch. Also **line**.

agency See *advertising agency*.

agency ad An advertisement furnished by an advertising agency.

agency commission A form of compensation paid by media to advertising agencies for placing business; traditionally a 15% discount on the gross cost of the media billed to the client by the agency. Commissions are now often negotiated between client and agency, depending on the overall media budget.

agency group See *network*.

agency network See *network*.

agency of record (AOR) The agency, chosen to purchase media time and space, selected from two or more agencies serving the same client.

agency-produced program A television or radio program, often a special, assembled as a package by an advertising agency and sold to a station or network ready for presentation.

agency recognition See *recognition*.

agency recommendation See *recommendation*.

agent 1. An individual who negotiates the buying and selling of goods and services without taking title to them. 2. A talent booking representative.

age/sex populations Estimates of population, broken out by various age/sex groups within a county.

aggregation A theory that assumes that all consumers of the mass media are similar.

AGMA See *American Guild of Musical Artists*.

Agricultural Publishers Association (APA) A nonprofit organization of publishers of periodicals edited for farmers' interests.

AGVA See *American Guild of Variety Artists*.

AID See *Arbitron Information on Demand*, *Automatic Interaction Detector*.

AIDA Attention, interest, desire, action. The four-step marketing procedure used in developing some advertising messages: Gain the audience's attention, develop their interest, motivate their desire to purchase, and move them to action.

aided recall A technique for measuring consumer memory of an advertisement or commercials; the interviewer gives the respondent a clue about the advertising being studied. See *unaided recall*.

AIGA See *American Institute of Graphic Arts*.

AIM See *Accuracy in Media*.

air 1. White space in a print advertisement. 2. To broadcast a radio or television program.

airbrush 1. A device for applying paint by means of an atomizer, making possible subtle gradations of tone; used in poster and photographic retouching. 2. To use an airbrush.

air check A taping or recording of a radio or television broadcast, used by a sponsor for evaluation, confirmation, and record-keeping purposes.

air date A scheduled broadcast date for a television or radio program or commercial.

airing The broadcast of a radio or television program, announcement, or commercial.

à la carte agency An advertising agency that works on a fee basis instead of by commission. Also **modular agency**.

alive See *live*.

all commodity volume (ACV) See *distribution*.

All-Inclusive Study An A.C. Nielsen report on audience data containing tabulation of four-week cumulative television audiences, used to estimate reach and frequency and to calculate gross rating points.

all market measurement period See *sweep*.

all news A radio station format that specializes in news reports. See *format*.

all night See *daypart*.

allocation 1. The allotment of limited amounts of an item or items to purchasers. 2. A preassigned quantity of merchandise to be made available to a designated customer.

"all other" circulation The dissemination of a periodical outside city limits and the retail trading zone of its market of origin, as established by the Audit Bureau of Circulations.

allotment 1. A specific number of poster panels offered to an advertiser by an outdoor advertising company. 2. An equitable distribution of advertising space or time for which demand exceeds supply. 3. See *allocation*.

allowance See *buying allowance*.

All Radio Marketing Study 2 (ARMS2) A report conducted in the 1970s by Three Sigma Research that provided data on cross-media audience duplication as related to product usage in selected categories. New York City and Los Angeles provided the sample bases.

All Radio Methodology Study (ARMS) A study of audience rating methods begun in 1963 by the National Association of Broadcasters and the Radio Advertising Bureau, Inc. See *Cumulative Radio Audience Method, Radio's All-Dimension Audience Research*.

all talk A radio station format consisting of two-way conversations between a communicator and the listeners. See *format*.

all up Copy that has been set in type.

alteration A correction or change made in proof after it has been set in type. See *author's alteration, editorial alteration, printer's error*.

alternate bundles run A variety of split run. Different versions of an advertisement are printed in separate phases of the press run of a periodical; the two versions are geographically commingled when the issue is bundled for delivery.

alternate delivery service A mail service that is not run by the United States Postal Service.

alternate sponsorship The purchase of advertising time during a television or radio program by two or more advertisers in turn, day by day, week by week, or program by program, within the same time slot.

alternate weeks (A/W) Scheduling instructions to a medium, especially to a newspaper, indicating advertisements are to appear every other week.

A/M See *art and mechanical*.

AM Amplitude modulation; a method of radio broadcasting using the signal from a source (microphone, tape, record, CD, etc.) to modulate the amplitude of the carrier wave generated by a radio transmitter to produce sound. See *FM*.

AMA See *American Management Association, American Marketing Association*.

AM broadcast band The band of frequencies from 535 to 1705 kilohertz.

American Advertising Federation (AAF) A national association of advertising agencies, media owners, advertisers, and others; it promotes professional and public understanding of advertising's value and supports higher professional standards. Founded in 1967 through a merger of the Advertising Federation of America and the Advertising Association of the West.

American Association of Advertising Agencies (AAAA) A national association of independent advertising agencies; its purposes are to promote advertising generally, to improve the advertising business, and to serve member agencies and their employees. Also **Four A's, 4 A's**.

American Association of Cable Television Owners An organization of members of minority groups who own cable television stations.

American Association of Newspaper Representatives, Inc. (AANR) The former name of the **National Advertising Sales Association**.

American Business Press, Inc. (ABP) An organization of business publishers founded in 1965 through a merger of Associated Business Publications and National Business Publications.

American Federation of Musicians (AF (of) M) A union representing musicians.

American Federation of Television and Radio Artists (AFTRA) A union of actors, singers, announcers, and certain technicians in radio and television broadcasting. Formed by a merger of the American Federation of Radio Artists and the Television Authority.

American Guild of Musical Artists (AGMA) A labor union of singers and dancers.

American Guild of Variety Artists (AGVA) A labor union of comics, magicians, circus performers, etc.

American Institute of Graphic Arts (AIGA) A national organization devoted to the encouragement of the graphic arts.

American Institute of Public Opinion (AIPO) A research firm founded by George Gallup in 1935 that conducts the Gallup Poll. See *Audience Research Institute*.

American Management Association (AMA) A nonprofit organization devoted to education and discussion in the field of business management.

American Marketing Association (AMA) A national organization formed in 1937 for the improvement of marketing practices. It publishes the *Journal of Marketing* and the *Journal of Marketing Research*.

American Newspaper Guild (ANG) A labor union of newspaper, magazine, and wire service employees.

American Newspaper Publishers Association (ANPA) An organization of publishers of daily newspapers in the United States and Canada, founded in 1887.

American Public Transit Association (APTA) An organization of individuals and companies involved in transit advertising.

American Research Bureau, Inc. (ARB) A national measurement service that provides television and radio audience size and composition data for advertisers and advertising agencies. See *Arbitron*.

American Society of Advertising and Promotion (ASAP) A group that provides practical information on all forms of advertising and promotion and works to improve the quality of promotion.

American Society of Composers, Authors, and Publishers (ASCAP) An organization formed in 1914 that licenses nondramatic performances of musical compositions on behalf of its members and collects royalties for them. See *Broadcast Music, Inc.*

American Statistical Association (ASA) A national professional organization of statisticians founded in 1839. Of interest to advertising and marketing researchers are the Business and Economic Statistics section and the Social Statistics section.

American Television and Radio Commercials Festival The annual competition to honor excellence in broadcast advertising. The winners are awarded a golden statuette, the Clio.

AM-FM total A figure shown in market reports for AM-FM affiliates in time periods when they are simulcast.

AMMO See *Audience Measurement by Market for Outdoor*.

amplitude modulation See *AM*.

ANA See *Association of National Advertisers*.

analysis of variance A statistical method of determining the relative input of a number of variables on a specified outcome.

ancillary market. The buyers of products related to the primary product, such as toys, games, posters, etc.

ancillary rights The legal rights granted to an entity to produce items, often used as premiums, that are related to specific motion pictures or television programs or their characters, such as toys, games, posters, and so on.

Andy Awards Awards for print and broadcasting creativity given by the Advertising Club of New York.

ANG See *American Newspaper Guild*.

angled (A) For an outdoor advertising structure, having one end set back more than 6 feet from the other end.

angled end (AE) The outdoor advertising structure that is closest to the approaching vehicle when more than one structure is built in the same facing.

angled single (AS) The outdoor advertising structure that is the only panel visible to approaching traffic. Posters are considered angled single when no other panel is visible within 25 feet along the line of travel; for bulletins, when no other bulletin is visible within 50 feet.

animatic 1. A television commercial produced from semi-finished artwork; generally used for test purposes only. See *photomatic*. 2. Pertaining to mechanical animation.

animation 1. The creation of an effect of movement, life, or human character to a representation of an object, animal, or person. This may be done by means of a series of drawings (**cartoon animation**); a film creating a story or a repeated sequence (**cyclic animation**); the actual movement of drawings in which full movement is not depicted but which relies on key poses and the movement of only those portions of the character that are essential to the motion (**mechanical** or **limited animation**); or the imparting of motion to photographed objects by moving them slightly between frames (**live animation**). 2. Special treatment given to outdoor advertising such as moving units or flashing lights. Commonly used on rotating, permanent, or spectacular bulletins.

animation designer 1. The art director of an animated film. 2. The cartoonist who creates the key drawings in an animated sequence.

animation effects The illusion of movement other than character movements, such as rain, smoke, fire, etc.

animator An artist who uses the techniques of frame-by-frame filmmaking to give drawings the illusion of movement. In studio animation, the person responsible for drawings the moving characters; in independent animation, the animator generally responsible for all phases of production.

ann. See *announcer*.

anncr. See *announcer*.

announcement A radio or television advertising message, noncommercial spot, or brief promotion.

announcement campaign An advertising campaign using only spot announcements.

announcement program A radio or television program designed to carry the commercial messages of different noncompetitive advertisers. See *participation program*, *sponsored program*.

announcer (ann.) (anncr.) A person who delivers messages to an audience by radio or television; may be employed by a station, network, cable system, advertising agency, advertiser, or work freelance.

annual ADT   See next.

annual average daily traffic (annual ADT) In outdoor advertising, the estimated number of passing vehicles for the year, divided by 365 days. Counting is generally conducted by state highway commissions, using mechanical instruments to locations throughout the state in a program of continuous traffic count sampling. Resulting counts are adjusted for seasonal influence, weekly variation, and other variables.

annual discount   A discount given by a print or broadcast medium to an advertiser that purchases 52 consecutive weeks of space or time. Also **annual rebate**.

annual rebate   See previous.

ANPA   See *American Newspaper Publishers Association*.

answer print (AP)   A final film print of a television commercial prepared for review and approval before airing. Also **composite daily print, optical print, pilot print**. See *fine cut*, *rough cut*.

anthology drama   A dramatic television program using a different theme and cast each week, usually with differing content and style. See *series*.

antique finish   See next.

antique paper   A soft, unevenly textured, high-quality paper used mainly for advertising folders, leaflets, brochures. Also **antique finish**.

AOR See *agency of record*.

AP See *answer print*.

APA See *Agricultural Publishers Association*.

APO See *optical answer print*.

appeal   An attempt to persuade prospective buyers of the desirability of a product or

service. Appeals can be based on emotion or on logic; common appeals include prestige, convenience, attractiveness, good taste, etc.

applause mail   Mail expressing approval of or commenting favorably on a television or radio program. Originally used as a crude form of audience survey.

appropriation   In privacy law, the use of a person's name or likeness without his or her permission.

APTA See *American Public Transit Association*.

APX See *ad-page exposure*.

AQH Average quarter-hour. See *quarter-hour audience*.

ARB(I) See *American Research Bureau, Inc.*, *Arbitron*.

arbitary method   A way to determine an advertising appropriation based on a cost estimate made in the absence of objective figures.

Arbitrends   Ratings information released by Arbitron that covers an extended time rather than only one ratings period.

Arbitron 1. The Arbitron Company, formerly called the American Research Bureau. 2. An electronic television monitoring device once used by the American Research Bureau. Arbitrons were placed in television sets of a representative sample of area viewers and sent data on channels being viewed to a central computer. See *Audimeter*.

Arbitron Information on Demand (AID) An Arbitron service that provides client-specified, custom spot television audience measurement data

area-by-area allocation (ABA)   A method of assigning an advertiser's media budget, proportionate to established or potential local sales of the advertiser's product or service. Also **market-by-market allocation.**

Area of Dominant Influence (ADI) A geographic market assignment made by Arbitron, in which a home market receives the preponderance of television viewing from each county. Similar to Nielsen's **Designated Market Area** and Pulse's **Radio Area of Dominant Influence**. See *exclusive market area.*

area probability sample A selection, as for a survey, for which the units are well-defined geographic areas, such as city blocks. Also **area sample.**

area sample See previous.

ARF See *Advertising Research Foundation.*

ARI See *Audience Research Institute.*

arithmetic mean See *mean.*

ARMS See *All Radio Methodology Study.*

ARMS2 See *All Radio Marketing Study* 2.

arousal method A technique for testing advertising effectiveness using a psychogalvanometer, which measures changes in the moisture of respondents' palms. See *galvanic skin response, psychogalvanometer.*

arousal theory The concept that the mass media arouse emotional responses in readers, viewers, and listeners, and thus may change behavioral responses.

arrears The set of lapsed subscriptions to a periodical that are retained temporarily on active subscription lists. Audit Bureau of Circulations requires that arrears must be dropped from circulation figures after three months.

art Any illustration in an advertisement, brochure, leaflet, etc., that is not typeset, including photographs, sketches, and hand lettering. See **artwork.**

art agency An organization that serves as a representative for artists.

art and mechanical (A and M) (A & M) (A/M) Pertaining to the graphic materials required for the production of a print advertisement.

artboard See *board.*

art buyer An employee of an advertising agency or commercial studio who is responsible for commissioning art or photography for advertising reproduction.

art card In television, a graphics card for titles, credits, pictures, etc.; often made from illustration board.

art department The department of an advertising agency or advertiser responsible for the design and execution of layouts, finished art, and mechanicals, and for the purchase of outside art services.

art director (AD) 1. The person in charge of an art department. 2. An employee of an advertising agency, art studio, or other organization who is responsible for developing the general design and supervising the final artwork and mechanicals for the advertisements of one or more clients.

art house See **art service.**

art service A company that specializes in creating advertising artwork and often oversees production. Also **art house, art studio, design house, graphics studio.**

art studio See previous.

artwork A term similar to *art* and often used interchangeably. *Artwork* sometimes implies a finished product or camera ready copy; *art* may be considered more inclusive.

AS See *angled single.*

ASA See *American Statistical Association.*

ASAP See *American Society of Advertising and Promotion.*

asap As soon as possible.

ASCAP See *American Society of Composers, Authors, and Publishers*.

ASI See *Audience Studies, Inc*.

as-it-falls method A technique for assigning media weight to a test market that attempts to deliver the same level of advertising exposure as would be delivered into that market by the advertising campaign being tested. See *correct increment method, little America method, media translation*.

aspect ratio The ratio of picture width to picture height.

assembly dailies Film footage from a day's shooting that is selected and spliced in proper sequence. See *rushes*.

assessment method A way to determine an advertising appropriation based on a specific amount per item sold in the most recent budget period.

assigned mailing dates The dates on which a mailing list user has the obligation to mail a specific list. No other date is acceptable without express approval of the list owner.

assistant art director An assistant to the individual in charge of an advertising agency's art department or, in larger agencies, art group. Often works on a single account at a time.

assistant director (AD) In television, a person whose job it is to assist in implementing a director's instructions.

associate creative director (ACD) An advertising agency employee who devises advertisements; reports to a creative director.

Associated Business Publications See *American Business Press*.

association 1. In statistics, the degree of measurable apparent relationship between two statistical variables as measured by co-variations in the relationship. 2. In psychology, the joining of two ideas or of two words expressing such ideas in the mind of the subject. In **controlled association**, subjects are limited in their ideas or words by their instructions; in **free association**, subjects may express any idea that comes spontaneously to mind, especially as a response to a stimulus. 3. A group of individuals, usually within an industry, who share common interests and goals. Often a professional association with a code of conduct.

Association for Communication Administration (ACA) An organization of college and university communication administrators.

Association of National Advertisers (ANA) The national organization of the advertising business. It is supported by more than 400 major corporations, accounting for 90 of the 100 largest users of advertising. The ANA represents the collective interests of advertisers; performs original research and case studies on major functional aspects of advertising, marketing, and communication; and helps members keep up with successful practices and techniques.

association test A research tool used to discover the degree to which people are able to identify brand names, logos, themes, and the like.

atmospherics The graphic identity of a corporation, as represented by the physical appearance of its publicly visible property, communications, and employees.

attention compeller See next.

attention getter Any visual sign or sound that attracts more than passing notice. Also **attention compeller**.

attention line The words that cause people to be attracted to a product or service. See *AIDA*.

attitude A predisposition to respond to a stimulus in one way rather than another. See *opinion*.

attitude intensity In psychology, the degree of resistance to change in an attitude.

attitude scale A quantitative range used to measure respondents' attitudinal response to a given stimulus.

attitude study A survey of opinions about an organization, product, service, and so on; often made before and after an advertising campaign to measure changes.

audience Persons or households viewing television or hearing radio commercials, or who read a given print medium or advertisement, especially as expressed quantitatively.

audience accumulation 1. The increase in the total audience viewing a television program by including reruns in the count. See *reach*. 2. The total net audience exposed to repeated periodical, outdoor, television, or radio advertising.

audience composition The makeup of a radio or television program's audience, analyzed by such categories as age and sex. See *audience profile*.

audience duplication 1. The overlap of individuals or households reached by two or more media vehicles of the same medium or different media. 2. The number or percentage of households or individuals reached by one program or station that are also reached by another program or station.

audience flow A measure of the change in viewers during and between programs; the percentage of people or households who turn on or off a program, switch to or from another channel, or remain tuned to the same channel as the previous program.

audience fragmentation The division of available viewers into small groups because of the wide diversity of sources of media outlets and programming.

audience-holding index A measure of the degree to which the beginning audience of a radio or television program continues to listen or view until the end.

audience measurement A count of viewers or listeners, expressed as a percentage (a rating) or as an absolute quantity (a number of households or individuals).

Audience Measurement by Market for Outdoor (AMMO) A service that reports reach and frequency by market, showing market sizes with demographic breaks by age, sex, and income.

audience profile The set of demographic characteristics of individuals or households reached during a radio or television program, used to evaluate its suitability for specific kinds of advertising. See *audience composition*.

audience rating See *rating*.

Audience Research Institute (ARI) An audience research organization founded by George Gallup. See *American Institute of Public Opinion*.

audience share See *share*.

Audience Studies, Inc. (ASI) A qualitative research organization that studies audience reaction to commercial products.

audience turnover The average ratio between the cumulative audience and the average audience listening or viewing. For example, 200 persons listened to a particular station at a particular time and day during a 12-week survey, but only an average of 50 persons was listening at any one time; the audience turnover would be 40. See *audience accumulation*.

Audilog A log of programs seen by participating television viewers in a ratings survey conducted by the A.C. Nielsen Company, as prepared by an Audimeter.

Audimeter An electronic device, trademarked and used by the A.C. Nielsen Company, which automatically records television set use and tuning by viewers participating in a ratings survey. See *Arbitron, Audilog.*

audio The medium of electrically transmitted or reproduced sound, especially in the context of television, where the audio signal, supplying the sound, is contrasted with the video signal, which supplies the image.

audio-visual A description of equipment used in radio, television, and as instructional or presentational tools, such as slide and film projectors, opaque projectors, tape decks, and the like.

audit 1. An official examination of the financial or other records of an organization. 2. A count of the number of names on a mailing list. 3. An examination of circulation figures. See next.

Audit Bureau of Circulations (ABC) A nonprofit cooperative association of advertisers, advertising agencies, and publishers of newspapers, business publications, magazines, and farm publications. Its objectives are to issue standardized statements of circulation based on data reported by members; to verify through an audit the figures shown in these statements and to disseminate such data, without opinion.

Audit Bureau of Marketing Services (ABMS) An organization affiliated with the Audit Bureau of Circulations that offers auditing services to various advertising media and other marketing services not offered by ABC.

audited A label given by the Traffic Audit Bureau, Inc., as it verifies records and circulation for the outdoor media according to established procedures approved by its buyer and seller members. Methods are similar to those of Audit Bureau of Circulations and Business Publications Audit of Circulation. Also *authenticated.*

audition 1. A performance by an actor, musician, or other performer to determine his or her suitability for employment in a show, program, or commercial. 2. A test performance of a program to determine its suitability for sponsorship.

audit report An annual statement of the results of an audit by the Audit Bureau of Circulations, printed on white paper. Also **white audit**.

authenticated See *audited.*

authorization A chain headquarter's approval allowing its stores to stock or otherwise promote a designated item.

authorized item In retailing, an item authorized by chain headquarters for distribution or promotion at a store manager's discretion, but not carried in the chain's warehouse.

author's alteration (AA) 1. In proofreading, a correction or change made by or on behalf of an author. 2. An alteration other than one to correct a printer's error. Also **author's change, author's correction**. See *editorial alteration, printer's error.*

author's change See previous.

author's correction See *author's alteration.*

automatic distribution The distribution of goods to retailers by a wholesaler or by chain headquarters without a specific order; usually done on a guaranteed sale basis.

Automatic Interaction Detector (AID) A multivariate technique used to reduce large amounts of data to determine which variables (e.g., demographic or attitudinal) and categories within the variables combine to produce the greatest discrimination in defining a dependent variable, such as product or brand usage.

automatic merchandising The use of vending machines as a means of retail distribution and sale.

automatic ordering In retailing, an arrangement for a standing order to replenish a basic stock item.

avail. See next.

availability (avail.) In television or radio, a period of time offered by a station or network for sponsorship.

available audience In Canada, potential television or radio audience.

available commercial time The amount of commercial time allowed during a specific broadcast period by the code of the National Association of Radio and Television Broadcasters.

average A statistical quantity representing the general or typical significance of a set of values. See *mean, median, mode*.

average audience (AA) An estimate of the households or individuals viewing the average commercial; of obvious importance to sponsors. Widely used by Nielsen, it is an average of the program's audience at minute 1, 2, 3, and so on. It is used by the networks and buyers for negotiation. Also used to compute share and cost per thousand (CPM).

average audience rating (AA rating) A rating based on the number of persons tuned to a program compared with some basic figure, e.g., the number the program is able to reach. Computer by averaging a series of ratings over a specified period, such as the length of a television or radio program or a 15- or 30-minute period. See *total audience rating*.

average daily circulation 1. A statistical estimate of the number of different radio or television households reached by a station on each day of the week. 2. An estimate of the distribution of a daily periodical on an average day.

average frequency The number of exposures of an average household or consumer over a specified period to a series of advertisements through all media carrying the advertisements.

average net paid circulation The average circulation of a periodical per issue, computed by dividing the total number of copies sold for the period being examined by the number of issues during the period. Also **average net paid, average paid circulation**.

average net paid See previous.

average paid circulation See *average net paid circulation*.

average quarter-hour (AQH) See *quarter-hour audience*.

average total audience rating See *total audience rating*.

average valued impressions delivered (AVIDS) In Canada, the sum of the average gross audience for a television or radio program, time block, etc., as estimated at quarter-hour intervals.

AVIDS See previous.

A/W See *alternate weeks*.

away-from-home listening An estimate of listening for which a participant indicates that listening was done away from home, either in a car or some other place.

Ayer's A directory of newspapers and magazines.

baby billboard See *car card*.

baby boomer A person born during the dramatic population growth in the years following World War II and through the 1950s.

baby spotlight A small spotlight used to highlight a specific area or figure. Also **inky, inky-dinky**.

back cover (BC) The outside back page of a magazine, often a premium position for advertisements. Also **fourth cover**.

backer card An advertising poster or card designed to fit on to a display bin or pole.

background (BG) (BKG) 1. In television or radio, the scenery, music, or sound effects supporting the primary message of a commercial. 2. In marketing planning, the context or environment in which advertising and marketing plans are developed and executed.

background effect Sound effect(s) used in the background.

background music See *mood music*.

back matter See next.

back of the book (matter) The section of a magazine, following the main editorial section, containing the continuation of stories and advertisements. Also **back matter**.

backslant In typography, the slanting of letters to the left; the reverse of italic.

backspace To reverse a videotape prior to editing so that the player and recorder are synchronized.

backtime To time a script, music, or other element of a radio or television commercial from the end to the beginning in order to make the commercial end on time.

back-to-back The airing of commercials one directly after the other.

back up To print the reverse side of a sheet after printing its face.

back-up page See next.

back-up space An advertising space purchased in a magazine or newspaper to run an insert; usually equivalent in cost to one black-and-white page. Also **back-up page**.

bait advertising See next.

bait (and) switch advertising The advertising of low-priced products or services as a means to attract customers to the business, where they are pressured to buy higher-priced products or services. Also **bait advertising**.

balop See next.

Balopticon™ A machine that projects still images, usually onto a reflecting surface, for tracing or for pickup by a camera. Also **balop**.

B&W See *black and white*.

bandwagon effect An advertising appeal that urges consumers to identify themselves with a popular product and with other purchasers of the product.

bangtail A type of self-mailer used for placing an order; it often features a tear-off flap.

banner 1. A large paper or cloth display sign for retail advertising, often draped over a wire or cord so as to be readable from both sides. Also **overwire hanger**. 2. A bold headline.

BAPSA See *Broadcasting Advertising Producers Society of America.*

BAR See *Broadcast Advertisers Reports, Inc.*

bar code A series of vertical or horizontal parallel lines, readable by a scanner, containing product and manufacturer information.

barker A short headline in large type placed above the main, smaller-type headline. Also **hammer, reverse kicker**.

barker channel A cable television channel used to air information about programs on the other channels.

barn door Shutter or flap, usually in twos or fours, attached to the front of a stage light source to manipulate the shape of the light beam. Also **flipper**.

bar sheet A form used by directors and animators to plan the movement of art and camera, on which all the elements of a commercial—music, voices, sound effects, visuals—are charted frame by frame in their relationship to time.

barter In television or radio, the furnishing of products or services by an advertiser as full or partial payment for spot broadcasting time or mentions. Also **trade deal, trade out, trade spot**.

barter broker An agent who arranges barters between advertisers and broadcasters. Also **barter house**. See *prize broker.*

barter house See previous.

barter spot A commercial in a syndicated radio or television program sold by the distributor of the program.

barter syndication The distribution of a syndicated television program wherein the station allows the syndicator to sell some of the commercial time within the program.

barter time Broadcast time exchanged for goods or services.

base In advertising research, the number of households from which a sample is drawn.

base count The number of in-tab households used in computation.

baseline A line at the bottom of a display advertisement indicating the theme of the advertisement.

base rate See *open rate.*

basic bus A transit bus in which all the advertising space is sold to one advertiser.

basic cable household A household subscribing to cable television service in a given area.

basic network The principal affiliates of a radio or television network, usually in the major markets, on which air time is sold.

basic price The price at which periodical sells to its ordinary readership under normal conditions. See *advertised price.*

basic rate See *one-time rate.*

basic station A television station included in the basic network.

bastard face See *bastard type.*

bastard measure In typography, a line that cannot be measured evenly in picas or half picas.

bastard size Any size that does not conform to standard sizes in typography or advertising space units.

bastard type 1. A typeface not in proportion to its body size. 2. A nonstandard type size. Also **bastard face**. See *point system.*

battered type Worn or damaged type that is not suitable for printing.

Bayesian analysis In advertising research, a method for assigning subjective probabilities to uncertain conditions, rather than relying solely on objective data obtained from samples or populations.

BBDO Worldwide The international advertising firm of Batten, Barton, Durstine, & Osborn.

BBM See *Bureau of Broadcast Measurement*.

BC See *back cover*.

B county See *county size*.

BD See *brand development*.

BDI See *brand development index*.

beamed program A technique to direct broadcast commercials to a predetermined segment of the audience.

beard 1. An error by an announcer or talent reading a script. Also **flub**, **fluff**. 2. In typography, a part of the type body that slants away from and supports the face.

beauty shot A close-up of a product in a television commercial.

bed Music used as background for an audio PSA or commercial.

beg your pardon A newspaper advertisement correction. The term is outdated.

behavior measurement Research into the actions of an audience, audience segment, or individual.

believability The degree of acceptance as truth of advertising's contents and claims. See *persuasiveness*.

bell curve See *normal distribution*.

below-the-line cost In television production, a cost that is not included in above-the-line items (e.g., set construction, props, transportation, technical assistance, rentals, etc.). See *above-the-line cost*.

benchmark 1. A standard for comparing similar items, such as research findings, the creative elements of campaign, advertising results, etc. 2. A standard for comparing products to determine competitors' costs, quality, etc., with one's own.

benday A printing process that uses a pattern of dots or lines to produce a gray effect. It is used to create shading textures. Named after a New York printer, Ben Day. Also **shading tints**.

benefit That quality of a product or service that supplies satisfaction or need fulfillment to the consumer.

best food day The day on which a newspaper runs editorial on food, thus encouraging advertising by retail grocers and food manufacturers; usually Wednesday evening or Thursday editions. Also **food day**.

best time(s) available (BTA) The time(s) for the airing of radio or television commercials as left to the discretion of the station. See *run of schedule*.

Better Business Bureau An agency supported by a local business community to detect and prosecute frauds and to correct misleading advertising.

BF See *boldface*.

BG See *background*.

bias In advertising research, a systematic error that occurs because the questionnaire or interview appears to lead or encourage the respondent to a particular answer.

bias of nonresponse In advertising research, error caused by respondents differing from nonrespondents with respect to a measured characteristic. See *nonresponse*.

big ticket item Merchandise with a high price and a high markup.

bill See *poster*.

billback (allowance) A discount given to purchasers who provide proof of compliance with merchandising requirements.

billboard 1. A flat, upright structure for displaying outdoor advertising. See *painted bulletin, poster panel*. 2. In television and radio, a brief announcement identifying the sponsor at the beginning and end of a program. Also **program billboard**.

bill enclosure A promotional piece or notice enclosed with a bill, invoice, or statement. Also **bill insert, stuffer**.

billing 1. A charge made to an advertiser by an advertising agency, based on the listed or gross charges of the media from which space or time has been purchased, along with any other costs and fees incurred by the agency. The money spent by an advertiser through an agency. 2. The net charge made by a medium to an agency; the gross charge minus the agency discount.

billing log A listing by a broadcast station of all commercials aired during a broadcast day.

bill insert See *bill enclosure*.

bimonthly A publication issued every two months. See *semimonthly*.

bind-in card A return postcard bound into a periodical for obtaining subscriptions or to respond to an advertisement printed at the point of insertion. See *blow-in card*.

bingo card (*sl.*) See *reader service card*.

bird (*sl.*) A communications satellite

bite off To eliminate a scheduled part of a television or radio show without previous planning.

biweekly A publication issued every two weeks. See *semiweekly*.

BKG See *background*.

BL See *body line*.

black and white (B&W, B/W) Printed in only one color, typically black, on white paper.

black box In advertising research, a device for analyzing audiences or television and radio commercials and programs. See *program analyzer*.

blackface See *boldface*.

black week A week during which national audience measurements are not taken. Also **dark week**.

blanket contract An agreement between a medium and an advertiser covering more than one campaign, regardless of the number of agencies involved. Also **master contract**.

blanket coverage The ability of radio and television stations to reach all locations within a given area.

blanking 1. A white paper border, placed between the panel and the poster, to surround the copy area of an outdoor advertising poster. 2. Impressions on heavy paper or cardboard stamped without color, foil, or ink. Also **blind embossing, blind stamping**.

blanking paper The border framing a poster in outdoor advertising. See previous.

blank line A type slug line containing only white space.

blank out Blank paper used on an outdoor advertising structure to cover the advertising message. See *paint out*.

blank tape See *raw tape*.

bleed (page) 1. To print an illustration so that it goes to the very edge of the page on one or more sides, without a border or margin. 2. An illustration extended to the edge of a page in this manner. 3. The arrangement of an illustration on a page by bleeding; e.g., a bleed on two sides.

bleed-face bulletin An outdoor advertising poster which covers the entire surface of the panel. Also *bleed(-face) poster*.

bleed(-face) poster See previous.

bleed in the gutter To print an advertisement uninterrupted across the gutter of a spread in a periodical. To bridge a gutter. Also **gutter bleed**.

bleed margin The small, extra margin on the printed page necessary to ensure that a bleed covers the margin to the edge of the paper after the page is trimmed.

bleed page See *bleed*.

bleed poster See *bleed-face bulletin*.

bleed through 1. A problem resulting when the previous message used on an outdoor advertising structure can be seen through the current message. 2. In print advertising, the visibility of print or images from the reverse of the page carrying the advertisement.

blind An impression stamped without using ink so as to create a raised or sunken design, as on heavy paper or cardboard. See *blanking*.

blind ad A classified advertisement in which the advertiser is not identified.

blind embossing See *blanking*.

blind offer An offer placed inconspicuously in an advertisement; often used to measure reader attention. Also **buried offer**, **hidden offer**.

blind product test In marketing research, a test in which respondents are asked to evaluate products bearing no brand names or identification.

blind stamping See *blanking*.

blister pack A package consisting of a card faced with a convex plastic casing enclosing the product. Also *bubble card*, *skin pack*.

block A section of time in the daily schedule of a radio or television station.

block city A city on which the U.S. Bureau of the Census publishes block-by-block data.

blocked-out time Television or radio time that is not available for sale to advertisers.

blocking See *block programming*.

block letter In typography, a letter without serifs.

block out To eliminate areas from a photographic negative or print by masking or opaquing.

block programming The scheduling together of programs that appeal to the same audience, to improve audience flow. Also **blocking**, **mood programming**, **stacking**.

blow-in card A return postcard tucked into a magazine but not physically attached. See *bind-in card*.

blowup An enlargement of a photograph, illustration, graph, or other printed material.

blue See *blueline*.

blueline A proof of offset printing work, made on photosensitive paper and typically blue. Also **blue**. See *Vandyke*.

blueprint 1. An inexpensive photographic print that reproduces lines and solid shapes in white on a dark blue background. 2. To copy lines or figures on a blueprint.

blurb 1. A short description of a book, story, article, or other piece for promotional purposes. 2. See *publicity release*.

blurmeter An optical device used to obscure trademarks and other brand features of an advertisement in order to test the impact of the basic design.

BMI See *Broadcast Music*, Inc.

BNF See *Brand Names Foundation, Inc.*

board   1. A thick paper stock, such as cardboard or mat board, etc., used for mounting copy, drawing, and other art-related purposes. Also **artboard**. 2. (*sl.*) An outdoor advertising panel or bulletin.

body copy   The main text of a piece of printed matter , as opposed to a headline, sub-head, etc. Also **body text.**

body height   See next.

body line (BL)   The height of a line of type. Also **body height**.

body size   See *body type*.

body text   See *body copy*.

body type   Type for setting text; type used for body copy. Also **body size**. See *display type*.

B of A   See *Bureau of Advertising*.

bold   See next.

boldface (BF)   A typeface set extra heavy or darker than normal. Used to call attention to certain words without an increase in type size. Also **blackface, bold**.

boldline   A line set in boldface.

bond (paper)   A high-quality opaque paper with a high rag content, used for stationery, documents, envelopes, etc.

bonus circulation   Newspaper or magazine circulation in excess of an advertiser's expectations.

bonus goods   Goods given by a manufacturer to a retailer as a reward for a large purchase. See *buying allowance, free goods*.

bonus pack   A specially packaged product designed to provide purchasers with extra content at the usual price. See *twin pack*.

bonus spot   Advertising time or space given without charge, either to compensate for undelivered audience or as an inducement to buy additional spots. See *make good*.

bonus station   A television or radio station carrying a commercial network program free of extra charge in addition to the network stations whose time has been bought by the sponsor.

book   In periodical publishing and advertising, a magazine.

booking agent   See *agent*.

booking memo   See next.

booking sheet   An agreement between an advertising agency and a performer, sent to a union to check on membership. Also **booking memo**.

book insert   An advertising flyer inserted in new books by a publisher.

booklet   A small advertising brochure in book form. See *brochure, leaflet, pamphlet*.

book paper   Paper, other than newsprint, used for printing magazine pages. Often a lightly textured, bulky paper.

borax   Poorly designed and written advertising. See *buckeye*.

border   A rule, often ornate, used to outline advertising and set it apart from editorial or other matter.

borrowed interest   In advertising, the use of famous and/or attractive individuals, animals, etc., to call attention to products of less intrinsic interest.

bottle hanger   A paper advertisement designed to hang around the neck of a bottle.

boutique   An advertising agency specialized in one aspect of advertising. See *creative boutique*.

boxboard   A grade of heavy paper suitable for folding into boxes.

boxtop offer   An offer to a consumer of a gift, coupon refund, or premium in return for a boxtop or label from the package of a product.

BPA See *Business Publications Audit of Circulations, Inc.*

BPI See *brand potential index.*

brainstorm To meet in a small group to attack a specific problem, usually in a limited time frame. The goal is to come up with as many ideas and solutions to the problem as possible, regardless of the quality of those ideas.

brand 1. A graphic symbol, tradename, or combination of both that distinguishes a product or service of one seller from those of others. 2. A line of products or services distinguished by such means. See *brand name, trademark.*

brand association The connection, in the mind of a consumer, between a specific brand and its general product category. Used to measure the share of mind the brand enjoys. See *share of mind.*

brand attitude The opinion of consumers regarding a product.

brand awareness A consumer's knowledge of the existence of a brand. Also **brand consciousness**.

brand consciousness See *previous.*

brand development A measure of the concentration of a brand's consumption; typically, the units or dollars of a product consumed per thousand population.

brand development index (BDI) A measure of relative geographic concentration of a brand's sales, typically sales per thousand population of an area indexed to the national rate. See *brand potential index.*

brand differentiation The degree to which a brand has succeeded in establishing an image as unique, especially when its unique attributes are perceived as beneficial. Also *differentiation.*

brand extension A product-line addition or flanker item marketed under a single brand name. See *flanker.*

brand franchise A contractual arrangement between a manufacturer and a wholesaler or retail chain for exclusive distribution of a brand within a territory. See *brand loyalty.*

brand image The pattern of feelings, associations, and ideas held by the public generally in regard to a specific brand. Also **brand personality**.

brand loyalty The consistent purchase and use of a specific product by a consumer over a period of time.

brand manager An individual in charge of the marketing and advertising for a specific commercial product or service. Also **product manager**.

brand name A word or group of words, usually trademarked, that identify a product or service.

brand name advertising Advertising intended to persuade consumers that a particular brand is uniquely legitimate or reasonable.

Brand Names Foundation, Inc. (BNF) An organization of manufacturers and other groups using brand names, founded to popularize the purchase of products with brand names.

brand personality See *brand image.*

brand potential index (BPI) The ratio of brand development index to market development index for a brand in a geographic area, as indexed to its national share of market. See *brand development index, market development index.*

brand preference The degree to which potential customers consider a brand acceptable or unacceptable, especially relative to competitive brands.

brand rate A discount by broadcasters given to advertisers buying time for more than one product. See *contiguity rate.*

brand rating A measure of product name recognition by consumers.

Brand Rating Index (BRI) A rating service that provides annual marketing and media exposure patterns of adults for network television, magazines, radio, and newspapers.

brand recognition A measure of the consumer's familiarity with a brand.

brand share The comparison of sales between one brand and others in a product category, expressed as a percentage.

brand switching The changing from brand to brand by consumers. See *brand loyalty*.

BRC See *Electronic Media Rating Council*.

break A pause in a television or radio program to air commercials.

break copy The script material used during radio or television station breaks.

breakdown An analysis of a television or radio commercial script in terms of its requirements for casting, materials, time, cost, and other factors.

breakline A line of type that runs short of the width of a column, i.e., the last line of a paragraph.

break of the book The allocation of magazine pages to various sections.

break rating A radio or television rating of the time periods between programs.

BRI See *Brand Rating Index*.

bridge To run an advertisement across the gutter of a spread.

Broadcast Advertisers Reports, Inc. An organization that provides subscribers with information on television and radio commercials in selected markets.

Broadcast Advertising Producers Society of America (BAPSA) An organization of radio and television commercial producers.

broadcast calendar A calendar used in broadcasting for accounting purposes, containing months of four or five whole weeks, each month beginning on a Monday.

broadcast day The period between sunrise and 12 midnight local time.

Broadcast Music, Inc. (BMI) A society of music publishers that licenses performances of music copyrighted by members.

Broadcast Rating Council (BRC) See *Electronic Media Rating Council*.

broadcast standard The task of determining the acceptability of written script material for commercials in regard to laws, regulations, and self-regulatory standards.

broadsheet See next.

broadside 1. A newspaper-size advertisement, approximately 15 by 22 inches. Also **broadsheet**. 2. A large sheet printed on one side. 3. An advertisement printed on paper that when unfolded forms one large advertisement.

brochure A booklet, often elaborate, with four or a multiple of four pages.

brownline A printer's proof, identical to a blueprint, but printed in brown. Also **brownprint, Vandyke**. See *blueprint*.

brownprint see previous.

BTA See *best time(s) available*.

bubble card See *blister pack*.

buckeye Crude, tasteless advertising. See *borax*.

buffer (sample) In advertising research, sample that is hand drawn in situations when there is not enough computer-drawn sample because of a drop in the usability rate and/or consent rate and persons per household.

build-up A promotion intended to boost the popularity of a program, performer, or product.

bulk circulation   Quantity sales of a publication, as opposed to single-copy sales.

bulk discount   A quantity discount offered to advertisers.

bulk mail   A category of third-class mail used for sending large mailings to different addresses at a lower rate than standard third class. Also **bulk rate**.

bulk permit   A post office permit for senders of bulk mail.

bulk rate   See *bulk mail*.

bulldog   The early edition of a daily newspaper. See *bull pup*.

bullet   A heavy dot used to draw attention to an item of a list or to some other special feature, especially in sub-heads and body type.

bulletin   1. A short advertising announcement. 2. The larger of the two standard outdoor advertising structures. See *painted bulletin*.

bulletin spectacular   A semipermanent outdoor sign, often painted, as opposed to an outdoor board using printed poster paper.

bullpup   The first mail edition of a Sunday newspaper. See *bulldog*.

Bureau of Advertising (B of A)   A promotional agency of the American Newspaper Publishers Association.

Bureau of Broadcast Measurement (BBM)   A Canadian organization formed by broadcasters, advertisers, and advertising agencies to provide periodic broadcast audience survey data, both local and national.

buried ad   A print advertisement that is inconspicuous among other ads. See *bury*.

buried offer   See *blind offer*.

Burke test   A test that measures recall of advertising by those exposed to it the preceding day. Developed by Burke Marketing Research, Inc. See *day-after recall*.

burst   See *flight*.

bury   To obscure a print advertisement by inconspicuous positioning. See **buried ad**.

business-building test   A study to determine whether a proposed change in advertising or marketing will produce enough new business to justify the costs involved.

business magazine   See next.

business paper   A periodical devoted to a particular industry, trade, occupation, profession, etc. Also **business magazine**, **business publication**. See *trade press*.

business publication   See previous.

Business Publications Audit of Circulation, Inc. (BPA)   A national, independent, nonprofit corporation of advertisers, advertising agencies, and business publications. BPA audits and verifies the circulation claims of its publication members and issues, at least once a year, a report on each publication member.

business reply mail   Advertising mail that includes an envelope or postcard bearing postal indicia to allow the recipient to reply without paying postage.

busorama   Transit advertising on buses.

busy   Cluttered and excessively or chaotically detailed.

buy   A purchase of media time or space.

buy-back allowance   An allowance based on the quantity of merchandise purchased on a preceding deal.

buyer   See *media buyer*.

buying allowance   A temporary price reduction on merchandise offered to retailers by manufacturers or their representatives, often with specific cooperative terms of sale, such as that the retailer will temporarily lower the resale price to consumers.

Also **allowance, temporary allowance**. See *bonus goods, deal, free goods*.

buying committee See *merchandising committee*.

buying incentive An extra inducement for a buyer to purchase a product or service, often in the form of a discount, gift, or bonus goods.

buying loader A premium awarded to a retailer as a gift in exchange for the purchase of merchandise. See *dealer loader, display loader*.

buying service An advertising agency or consulting firm specializing in purchasing media time and space.

buy off A flat fee paid to talent for work on a commercial in lieu of pay based on the number of times the commercial is aired. See *residual*.

buyout A one-time fee to talent, writers, directors, etc.

buy rate A measure of pay-per-view households that purchase a program, expressed as a percentage.

buy sheet See *time sheet*.

B/W See *black and white*.

c See *first cover*.

© See *copyright*.

CA See *census agglomeration*, *commercial announcement*.

CAB See *Cable Advertising Bureau*.

Cable Advertising Bureau (CAB) A trade association of cable television systems and individuals who promote the use of cable for advertising purposes.

Cablecast A program aired on cable television.

cablecasting The programming carried by a cable television system. See *local origination*.

cable catalog A display of products on screen in catalog format. Viewers order through an 800 number. See *direct response advertising*.

cable lift The number of households subscribing to cable television and receiving certain premium channels.

cable penetration A measure of cable television households in a given area, expressed as a percentage.

cable subscriber A household paying a monthly fee to receive cable television.

cable (television) (CATV) 1. Television paid for by subscription and transmitted by cable into households. See *pay television*. 2. Television employing a single antenna to pick up broadcast signals, which are amplified and distributed to local individual sets via direct cable; useful in areas where reception is poor.

Cable Television Administration and Marketing Society (CTAM) A cable television association concerned with cable programming and marketing.

calendered paper A paper with a glossy, polished finish. See *antique paper*, *coated paper*.

call-back 1. In advertising research, a call by an interviewer to a respondent subsequent to a previous call, so as to reach a previously unavailable respondent, or as one of a series of interviews.

calligraphy 1. The art of lettering or writing elegantly by hand. 2. Hand lettering or hand writing.

call-in audience research A technique in which a sample audience calls a telephone number to hear a series of questions and then supply answers.

callout A word or words used to more clearly identify elements depicted in an illustration; often connected to the specific element in question by a straight line or arrow.

call report A written record of a meeting between an advertiser and an agency, prepared by an agency representative and circulated to all interested parties. Also **conference report, contact report**.

camera card A large card carrying titles, credits, and other graphics to be picked up by camera.

camera copy See *camera ready (copy)*.

camera effect See *camera optical*.

cameraless animation Animation by drawing or painting directly on film.

cameraless film Images, usually animated, created by drawing directly on the film stock.

camera lucida An optical device for projecting an image to a desired size or scale onto paper so that it can be copied. Also **lucey, lucy**.

camera mixing The selection of shots for transmission or recording. Also **camera switching**.

camera optical An optical made in the camera instead of by an optical printer. Also **camera effect**.

camera ready (copy) Copy that is finished and suitable for photographic reproduction.

camera shot See *shot*.

camera switching See *camera mixing*.

campaign 1. A program of coordinated advertisements and promotional activities intended to accomplish a specific marketing or sales objective. 2. A series of advertisements with a common selling theme.

Campbell Soup position First right-hand page following the main editorial section of a magazine; so called because the Campbell Soup Company has often specified this position for its advertisements.

Canadian Circulations Audit Board (CCAB) An organization of advertisers, advertising agencies, and publishers that audits circulation statements of controlled circulation periodicals in Canada.

Canadian Radio and Television Commission (CRTC) A government-appointed commission that regulates all aspects of television and radio broadcasting in Canada.

cancel To terminate an advertisement placement or contract after it is ordered or scheduled.

cancellation date The last date on which advertising may be cancelled for a publication, broadcast, etc. See *closing date*.

c and lc (c/lc, clc) The setting of words with an initial capital letter, followed by lowercase letters.

canned Transcribed or recorded for later use; "in the can."

cannibalize To draw sales away from one's own products and so diminishing profit, usually because of the introduction of new products, flankers, or line extensions.

canvass A round of visits to regular or potential customers in a particular territory for some specific purpose, such as market research.

capital (letter) An uppercase letter. See *lowercase*.

cap(s) See previous.

caption A legend describing a picture or a number of pictures grouped together. Also **title**.

car card An advertising sheet for display inside or outside a public transit vehicle. Generally 11 inches high, with 28, 42, and 56 inches the standard lengths. Also **baby billboard** (*sl.*).

card 1. A postcard. 2. A piece of pasteboard or bristol board. 3. A large advertising display.

cardboard engineer A designer of displays and packages.

card rate The standard rate charged for a quantity of space or time by a communications medium without regard to discounts; the charges as listed on a rate card. See *earned rate*, *gross rate*.

caret A proofreader's mark used to indicate where an insertion is to be made.

caricature A picture or description that exaggerates or distorts a person or object, usually for humorous purposes.

carrier presort Bulk mailings sorted by postal ZIP code; the sender receives a discount from the postal service.

carry-over audience See *inherited audience*.

carry-over effect The ability of advertising to affect buying habits even after a campaign is complete; a delayed response effect.

cartoon animation See *animation*.

cartouche 1. A scroll-like design. 2. A decorative panel or border outlining a graphic.

case A container of a stated number of products. See *display case*.

case allowance An allowance by a manufacturer to a retailer, proportional to the number of cases purchased, either continuously or in increments.

case-count method A form of acceptance of a wholesale delivery by a retailer on the evidence of the number of cases listed in an invoice rather than of a count of cases delivered.

case lot 1. A group of merchandise priced by the case rather than by the individual item. 2. A number of cases sold at one time for a flat price.

case pack The number of units of merchandise in a case.

cash-and-carry 1. Selling by a retailer for cash only with no delivery service. 2. Selling by a wholesaler to legitimate buyers who provide their own transportation.

cash buyer In direct marketing, a buyer who encloses payment with an order.

cash discount A discount on purchases of space or time in communications media to buyers as a reward for prompt payment.

cash plus An arrangement whereby a station pays for a syndicated program but gives the syndicator additional commercial time as part of the deal.

cash refund offer An offer by a manufacturer to refund money to a customer who mails in proof of purchase.

cast (off) 1. To calculate the printed space required by a certain quantity of manuscript copy in a specified size. Also **copy cast, copy fit, fit**. 2. To calculate the amount of manuscript copy required to fill a certain area when set in a specified type size.

cast coated paper A paper stock with a high-gloss coat.

cast commercial A television or radio commercial acted out by members of the program to which it belongs. See *star commercial*.

casting file A cross-indexed file containing information about talent. Usually kept by advertising agencies, directors, etc.

casual rate A one-time advertising rate. Used in Canada.

CAT See *computer aided typesetting*.

catalog 1. A book or booklet showing merchandise with descriptions and prices. Used especially in direct response marketing.

catalog buyer A person who buys products or services from a catalog.

catalogue See *catalog*.

category development index See *market development index*.

CATV See *cable television*.

caveat emptor A consumer warning for "as is" merchandise, restricted by laws regulating consumer protection and deceptive advertising. From the Latin for "let the buyer beware."

CC See *closed captioning, commercial continuity, controlled circulation*.

CCA   See *Controlled Circulation Audit*.

CCAB   See *Canadian Circulations Audit Board*.

CCMM   See *Council on Children, Media, and Merchandising*.

C county   See *county size*.

CCTV   See *closed circuit (television)*.

CD   See *creative director*.

CDT   Central Daylight Time. See *time zone*.

cease and desist order   An order to discontinue an unlawful practice, as one issued by the Federal Trade Commission regarding deceptive advertising.

cel   1. A sheet of cellulose acetate used for titles and graphics. Also **cell**. 2. A flexible, transparent sheet of acetate onto which animations are transferred and painted. When the cel is placed over the background, the animated characters appear to be within the setting.

cell   A single image in a film or unit on a story board. See *frame, (sample) cell*.

census   1. A survey canvassing all sampling units in a population. 2. A count of every member of a statistical population. See *survey*.

census agglomeration (CA)   An area with an urban center of at least 1,000 population, an adjacent built-up area with at least 1,000 population, and a density of at least 1,000 persons per square mile. Used in Canada.

Census Metropolitan Area (CMA)   A principal labor market area within a built-up area of 100,000 or more persons. Used in Canada.

census tract   An area with clearly identifiable boundaries and with a relatively homogeneous population segment of about 1,200 households.

center   To place an object, design element, headline, etc. so that it rests symmetrically on a center line or central point. See *center justified*.

centered dot   A bullet used as an ornament to highlight words, paragraphs, etc.

centerfold   A spread in the middle of a publication that unfolds to reveal two more pages.

center justified   The setting of type to allow equal white space on either side.

center of interest   The portion of a picture or advertisement to which the eye is drawn.

center spread   The two facing pages at the center of a periodical, desirable for an advertiser because the pages are contiguous with little or no interruption at the gutter.

centile   For a frequency distribution, one of 99 points creating 100 equal divisions.

central buying   The purchase of wholesale goods for individual store outlets from a central point, usually allowing discounts for quantity purchase and simplification of ordering.

centralized prepackaging   The packaging of items before delivery to stores.

cents-off   See *price pack*.

cents-off coupon   A coupon entitling the bearer to a discount on an item featured at time of purchase; may be distributed by retailer, clearing house, manufacturer, or through an advertisement.

certification mark   A mark applied to goods that attests to a certain quality or origin.

Certified Radio Marketing Consultant (CRMC)   A media sales representative accredited by the Radio Advertising Bureau, Inc.

chain   1. A group of retail outlets under common ownership. 2. A television or radio network. See *voluntary chain*.

chain break 1. A network affiliated station's interruption of network broadcasting for local station identification. See *station break*. 2. A commercial aired during this time.

chain store One of several retail stores under common ownership. See *chain*.

channel A broadcast frequency assigned to a television or radio station.

channel strip An extruded molding covering the front edge of a retail display shelf, used to exhibit price data or hold point-of-purchase advertising.

character A symbol—alphabetic, numeric, punctuation mark, etc.—used to represent information.

character count The total characters and spaces in a manuscript.

(character) pitch 1. The distance between successive characters. 2. The number of characters per inch of type.

character set The symbols on a standard typewriter.

characters per pica (CPP) The number of characters of a specified point size and typeface that will fit in one pica. See *pica*.

character style The features of a typeface that distinguish it from others.

charge sheet A list of newspaper advertising rates. See *rate card*.

chart the showing To select individual panels on streets for outdoor advertising to achieve maximum reach and frequency.

checkerboard A unit of magazine advertising; quarter-pages or spread half-pages placed in diagonal opposition.

checking 1. The process of verifying the printing, broadcasting, and showing of advertising. 2. In outdoor advertising, the inspection of each market to choose the outdoor advertising structures to be included in a contract or to verify that the posting meets contract specifications.

checking copy A copy of a periodical sent to an advertiser or advertising agency as proof that an advertisement ran as ordered.

cheshire label A name and address label reproduced on specially prepared paper to be mechanically affixed to a mailing piece.

china marker A grease pencil used to mark edit points on film and tape.

Chinese white A bluish-white paint used for retouching artwork and photographs.

chi square In communication research, a measure of statistical validity.

chop(mark) In printing, a symbol used to attest to the quality of the product.

chroma The saturation of a color without white.

chrome (*sl.*) Color film.

churn The turnover in cable television subscribers, resulting from disconnections and new customers.

churn rate A measure of changes in cable television subscriptions during a churn period.

circular An advertising flyer, leaflet, insert, etc., usually intended for wide distribution, that is mailed, inserted in packages, or distributed by hand.

circulation 1. The number of subscribers to a periodical as counted at some specific moment or as averaged over an extended period. See *readership*. 2. The estimated number of households or individuals in the audience of a given television or radio network or station at least once during some specified period of time. See *coverage*, *frequency*, *reach*. 3. The number of television households or individuals that tune to a broadcast signal or cable signal during a day or week. 4. The actual number of households or persons reached at least once during a specific period by a network or station. 5. The count of potential viewers to determine the value of an outdoor advertising location. See *traffic volume*.

circulation area The geographic area covered by a broadcast station, newspaper, flier, and so on. See *coverage*.

circulation guarantee The minimum number of copies of a periodical that are to be sent or delivered to subscribers.

circulation promotion The effort of maintaining or increasing circulation.

circulation research A study designed to elicit information concerning print media circulation.

city circulation The number of newspapers delivered or sold within a metropolitan area.

city-grade service Television transmission of the highest quality, usually found in the geographical area around the transmitter.

city zone An urban zone consisting of the central city of a local market along with nearby communities sharing the general character of the city.

claim 1. An assertion in an advertisement regarding a product's or service's performance in providing benefits to purchasers. 2. To make such an assertion.

classical Pertaining to serious musical forms in the European tradition (e.g., opera, symphony). See *format*.

classification data The information by which a territory, group, or medium can be characterized.

classified advertising Newspaper and magazine advertising subdivided according to the types of products and services offered or sought, such as help wanted, real estate, and used autos.

classified section The part of a newspaper or magazine set aside for classified advertising.

class magazine A periodical intended for a readership with a special range of common interests, which often reflect an above-average income.

class rate The cost of broadcast time for the different time periods. Sometimes designated as class AAAA, AAA, AA, A, B, C, and D, depending on the individual network or station. Class AAAA time carries the highest cost.

Clayton Act The 1914 statute that directed the Federal Trade Commission to prevent unfair methods of competition in commerce.

c/lc See *c and lc*.

clc See *c and lc*.

clean 1. To correct and update a mailing list. 2. Having no errors, as of a printer's proof.

clean copy Written material that needs little or no revision.

clean proof In typesetting, proof that is without errors.

clean rough A layout in which major elements of a printed page, poster, advertisement, etc., are sketched in considerable detail.

clear 1. To obtain official permission for use of a picture, quotation, etc., in an advertisement. 2. To reserve broadcasting time for an advertiser. 3. To verify the availability of a period of broadcasting time with network affiliates.

clearance 1. The act of clearing something, as the use of copyrighted matter in advertising or the availability of broadcast time. 2. The notification that something is cleared.

clear-channel station An AM radio station allowed 50,000 kilowatts, the maximum power allowed, and priority in the use of a frequency band. At sunset, other stations on this frequency sign off, since broadcasting range is extended after dark, and stations on the same frequency tend to interfere with one another. Also **powerhouse**. See *daytime station*.

client A business, organization, or individual who employs the services of an advertising agency; an account.

Clio An award to recognize excellence in radio and television advertising given at the American Television and Radio Commercials Festival.

clip 1. A short length of film cut from a complete motion picture or television production. 2. Loosely, a newspaper clipping. Also **cutting**.

clip art Commercially prepared artwork sold on sheets or in clip books ready to be photographed or cut out and used.

clipping bureau A commercial service that clips items of interest in various categories from numerous newspapers, magazines, and journals at the request of clients.

clip sheet A prepared page resembling a newspaper page that contains publicity material, news stories, fillers, photographs, and so forth, which may be used by a newspaper. It is distributed by a public relations office on behalf of a client.

clock-hour delay A postponement in the broadcasting of a television program originating in another time zone in order to air the program at the same clock time in both zones. Also **live-time delay**.

closed The state of a newspaper page that is ready for printing; no further changes are possible.

closed captioning (CC) A system of electronically encoded written subtitles in television broadcasts for the hearing impaired. A decoder is needed to view the captions.

closed circuit (television) A transmission system for sending video/audio signals to specific receivers, rather than for broadcasting. Monitors are connected to the studio by coaxial cable or microwave.

closed-end-diary A type of journal that lists specific time segments for each broadcast day to be covered by a survey. See *open-end diary*.

closed-end question See *fixed-alternative question*.

close-up (CU) A tightly framed camera shot showing details of a person or object.

closing date 1. The final date for contracting advertisements. Also **commercial deadline**. See *cancellation date*. 2. The final date for supplying typeset material to a periodical for advertisements.

closure A customer order placed as a result of direct mail advertising.

cloze procedure A method of testing the readability of an advertisement by leaving out words or letters to be filled in by the reader.

clubbing offer An offer of subscriptions to two or more magazines jointly at a reduced combined rate.

cluster 1. A sample of respondents in a survey drawn randomly from groups of respondents previously selected in a nonrandom manner. 2. A group of advertisements or commercials.

cluster analysis A method of statistical analysis that groups people or things by common characteristics of interest to the researcher.

clutter A large number of advertisements claiming the attention of the audience of a television or radio program, newspaper or magazine, etc. See *overcommercialization*.

CMA See *Census Metropolitan Area*.

CMSA See *Consolidated Metropolitan Statistical Area*.

coated paper A smoothly finished paper with a mineral-based, usually white coating used for aesthetic effect and for the reception of fine halftone printing. Also **coated stock, enameled paper**.

coated stock. See previous.

coat out See *paint out*.

coaxial cable An electrical transmission wire capable of carrying complex signal information, such as multiple telephone conversations or television transmissions.

COD See *collect on delivery*.

code dating The practice of coding packages of retail products to indicate the packing date, or termination of fresh sales life, or the name of its supplier, using symbols meaningless to the customer.

code number 1. A number meaningful in a special context, as to identify a commercial or to synchronize two lengths of film so that one follows the other without interrupting the action. 2. A number on a store-redeemable coupon used to identify the carrier publication after redemption.

coding 1. The classification of responses on a questionnaire, schedule, or diary to facilitate tabulation and summarization or to enable data processing. 2. An identifying device used on reply cards and coupons to identify the mailing list or other source from which the address was obtained. 3. A structure of letters and numbers used to classify characteristics of an address on a list.

coefficient of variation A statistical measure equal to the standard deviation divided by the arithmetic mean.

coincidental interview A research method in which respondents are telephoned and asked about their radio or television use at the time of the interview or just before the interview. Also **coincidental measurement, coincidental rating, coincidental survey**. See *recall interview*.

coined word A word, especially a trade name, not in the common vocabulary, which is created for a special purpose.

cold call A sales call made without a prior warning being given to the prospective customer.

collage An artwork made by piecing items together, often photographs, colored paper, and so on. See *montage*.

collate 1. To assemble individual elements of a mailing in sequence for inserting into a mailing envelope. 2. To make a complete set of pages from many copies of pages.

collateral The advertising and promotional material prepared for sales presentations, other than that presented through communications media.

collateral service An additional service, such as the brochure preparation, market research, promotion, etc., performed by an advertising agency for an additional fee.

collective mark A symbol used by an organization, association, union, etc., that serves as an identifying sign.

collect on delivery (COD) A distribution system in which a recipient is required to pay the purchase price of the item, and possibly postage or a handling fee as well, at the time of its delivery.

colophon A symbol used by a publisher and run on a title page; a publisher's trademark. See *logotype*.

color correction The adjustment of tonal qualities of photographs using gels, filters, lights, and computerized printing systems.

color fidelity The degree to which a color film, television picture, or photograph reproduces the colors of the actual scene.

color filter A filter that allows only one color of light to pass.

color guide A sketch prepared by an artist to assist the printer in preparing color plates from black-and-white copy. See *color overlay*.

colorimeter In printing, a device used to match colors visually.

color overlay In printing, a transparent guide superimposed on black-and-white camera copy for the addition of color.

color plate 1. An illustration printed in color. 2. A printing surface for such an illustration.

color radio A promotional term used to describe varied, lively radio programming.

color separation A set of negatives in the four primary printing colors—yellow, cyan (blue), magenta (red), and black—made using color filters for transformation into color printing plates. Also **process color**.

color transparency A color slide or other film viewed or projected by passing light through it.

column 1. An area of print running down a page of a periodical, composed of lines of equal width. 2. The typical or standard width of such an area of print, used as a measure of size for such a periodical. 3. A series of regular periodical articles by a journalist, usually under his or her byline.

column inch In periodical publishing, a unit of space one standard column wide and one inch deep; in a newspaper, 14 agate lines deep.

column inch rate The cost for a column inch in a newspaper or magazine advertisement.

column rule A vertical line printed between columns.

combination buy A purchase of media time or space at a combination rate.

combination commercial A television commercial that combines various techniques, such as live action, animation, or the display of still photographs or drawings. See *integrated commercial*.

combination feature A group of retail items promoted for sale together.

combination rate A rate, often discounted, for the purchase of advertising space or time in two or more periodicals, broadcast stations, etc., under a common ownership. Also **combo rate**.

combination run A reduced rate offered by printers who combine a number of smaller jobs on a large press and run them at the same time.

combo rate See *combination rate*.

comic strip A panel of consecutive drawings presenting humorous situations and adventures; usually found in newspapers.

commercial An advertisement on television or radio. See *commercial announcement, participating announcement, spot*.

commercial announcement (CA) An advertising message, such as a bonus spot or promo, for which any kind of charge is made. This does not include commercial continuity.

commercial art Artwork prepared for advertising purposes.

commercial audience The television or radio audience for a specific commercial; consists of those persons actually in the room with a set tuned in to the station when it is aired.

commercial break An interruption in a radio or television program for a commercial.

commercial code number A series of four letters followed by four numbers used to identify a television commercial film print's sponsor and content; assigned by the originating advertising agency in accordance with a standard industry system.

commercial continuity (CC) A radio or television program sponsor's advertising message.

commercial copy A sales message of an advertiser.

commercial credit The specific naming of a sponsor or a product on radio or television.

commercial deadline See *closing date*.

commercial delivery The actual exposure of a television or radio commercial as measured by the number of viewers or listeners.

commercial exposure potential The ratio or the number of sets actually tuned to a television or radio station at the time a commercial is delivered to the total number of sets able to receive the commercial.

commercial impression A unit for measuring gross message weight, representing the exposure to a radio or television commercial. See *exposure, gross rating points*.

commercial integration charge A fee paid to a television or radio station for including a commercial in its broadcast schedule. See *networking*.

commercial load The number of minutes of commercial matter in a broadcast hour.

commercial minute One minute of radio or television time.

commercial occasion See *occasion*.

commercial pool A set of available radio or television commercials that an advertiser has ready for airing. Also **pool**.

commercial protection The amount of time or space between commercials or advertisements for competing products or services. See *competitive separation*.

commercial sign A privately owned advertising structure used on roofs, walls, or other outdoor areas of business establishments or factories for purposes of identification or direction.

commercial straight A nonintegrated radio or television commercial, delivered during a break in a program or during a station break. See *integrated commercial*.

commercial time A standard maximum amount of time and number of interruptions set by the National Association of Broadcasters for nonprogram material (commercials, credits, billboards).

commercial unit A description of the length of a commercial occasion and the manner in which it will be used when multiple commercials are to appear within an occasion. See *piggyback unit*.

commissary store See industrial store.

commission A form of compensation to a salesperson, agent, etc., as a percentage of sales. See *agency commission*.

commissionable Pertaining to an advertising purchase that yields a commission to a recognized purchaser, usually an advertising agency.

Committee on Nationwide Television Audience Measurement (CONTAM) A ratings evaluation group established by the networks.

commodity advertising Generic advertising for a class of products as opposed to advertising for a specific brand, e.g., Wisconsin cheese, Florida orange juice.

communication mix The use of two or more of the mass media for advertising, services, information, and so on.

Communications Act of 1934 An act of Congress, as amended, that regulates radio and television broadcasting and other means of communication and established the Federal Communications Commissions.

communications director An executive in charge of external and internal corporate communications. See *advertising director*.

Communications Satellite Corporation See *Comsat*.

communications theory A body of experimental knowledge about sending and receiving messages through various channels, primarily based on the work of C. D. Shannon.

comp A complimentary subscription to a periodical. See *comprehensive layout*.

company store See *industrial store*.

comparable use rule The regulation that broadcast stations may not charge legally qualified political candidates more than what is charged other advertisers.

comparative advertising Advertising in which two or more competing products are compared; the advertiser is the manufacturer of the product that is found to be superior.

comparative proved name registration A measure of audience recall of an advertisement, as a proportion of a total number of respondents who have each seen the advertisement only once. Used by the research firm of Gallup and Robinson.

competitive-parity method A method for establishing a marketing budget by matching the anticipated expenditures or spending rates of competitors.

competitive plant An outdoor advertising operator offering services in the same market area as other operators.

competitive preference Consumers' choice of one brand of a given product over other brands, as a percentage of a specified group of consumers.

competitive separation A quantity of media space or time separating an advertisement or commercial, at the request of the advertiser, from directly competitive advertising. See *commercial protection*.

complete cancel See *paid cancel*.

complimentary Granted without the customary charge, usually as a sample, e.g., a free periodical subscription. Also **comp**.

comp list A periodical's list of its complimentary subscribers.

composing room A room at a newspaper, composition house, or printing plant where type is set.

composite 1. An actor's or model's resume, including multiple photographs in various settings and costumes and other vital data. 2. A motion picture, television film, or videotape bearing both images and sound. Also **marriage**.

composite daily print See *answer print*.

composite shot 1. An image showing two or more separate scenes simultaneously on different parts of a motion picture or television screen. Also **split image, split screen**. See *half lap*. 2. A camera shot in which one image is superimposed on another to create a special visual effect. Also **double exposure, double print**.

composition 1. The setting of type according to a predetermined layout in a form suitable for printing. 2. The layout of a page, advertisement, artwork, and so on. 3. The art of arranging persons or objects in a shot for a pleasing effect.

composition house A company that sets type and prepares reproduction proofs.

composition-set type Printing material for an advertisement that is prepared by a composition house on behalf of an advertiser or its agency to be sent camera ready for printing in a periodical. See *publication-set type*.

compositor 1. A person who sets type; a typesetter. 2. A company that performs typesetting services.

comprehensive layout (comp) A polished layout used for approval of an advertising piece before composition and printing costs are incurred. See *layout, rough.*

computer aided typesetting (CAT) The use of computers in composition, page make-up, justification, etc. Also **computer typesetting.**

computer-generated letter See next.

computer letter A personalized form letter generated electronically. Also **computer-generated letter, computer printed letter.** See *computer personalization.*

computer personalization The tailoring of a message to specific individuals by printing letters or other promotional pieces by computer, using names, addresses, special phrases, or other information based on data appearing in computer records.

computer printed letter See *computer letter.*

computer typesetting See *computer aided typesetting.*

Comsat An organization formed to receive the first federal license for use of communications satellites for profitable leasing operations. See *Intelsat.* Also **Communications Satellite Corporation.**

concentration ratio The share of market held collectively by the four leading firms in an industry. It serves as an indicator of the degree of competition in a market.

concept A briefly stated idea of a benefit that a product or service could provide to consumers. See *creative strategy* .

concept test A research tool designed to assess consumer reaction to a product or service concept in quantitative terms.

concurrent method A research technique that investigates events and activities as they occur.

condition To affect the attitudes and behavior of a person through psychological influences. In advertising research, the research situation itself may condition subjects' responses, thus making data gathered from them not reflective of their true attitudes.

conference report See *call report.*

confidence interval A range of values within which a true population value is expected to fall with a specified level of probability or assurance. It is a function of the variability of the sample plus a constant reflecting the desired degree of assurance.

confidence level The degree of assurance one uses in considering results obtained from statistical tests; such assurance is expressed in a probability (e.g., 95% confidence in the survey findings).

confirmation 1. A statement by a radio or television station or network that a time period is available for purchase. 2. The acceptance of an order by a station or network for broadcast time.

connotative mapping A research technique used to establish a diagram of consumers' perceptions of a product category and an individual brand's location on the map. Also **perceptual mapping.**

consecutive announcements Back-to-back commercials.

consecutive-weeks discount (CWD) A reduced rate for an advertiser who buys television or radio time for a continuous period, usually 26 to 52 weeks.

Consolidated Metropolitan Statistical Area (CMSA) A grouping of closely related Primary Metropolitan Statistical Areas, as defined by the U.S. Office of Management and Budget.

constant type See *standing type.*

consultant An individual, often an expert in a particular field, hired by a company to evaluate and suggest changes in order to improve a product, service, or some aspect of operations.

consumer 1. The ultimate user of a product or service; less accurately, a person who purchases the product or service. 2. The viewer, listener, reader, or other recipient of a radio or television program, periodical, etc.

consumer advertising The advertising directed at the public as a whole, rather than to a profession or industry.

consumer cooperative A nonprofit consumer group organized for the purchase and distribution of goods in order to reduce prices for its members.

consumer good A product designed to satisfy individual human needs or desires, such as food and clothing, as contrasted with goods sold for commercial or industrial use. See *industrial goods*.

consumerism The public movement, with its supporting laws, that favors protection of the consumer from improper marketing practices through examination of product performance, advertising and sales practices, etc.

consumer jury See *consumer panel*.

consumer list A set of names, usually with home addresses, that results from a common inquiry or buying activity, indicating a general or specific buying interest.

consumer magazine A magazine intended for the general public rather than for a trade or profession. See *professional magazine, trade press*.

consumer panel A sample of individuals or households from which data on media habits and product purchases is gathered on a long-term basis. Also **consumer jury**.

consumer product An item or commodity offered for sale to the general public rather than for commercial or industrial use; a product classified among consumer goods.

consumer profile The delineated traits—age, sex, income, buying habits, education, and so on—of a consumer.

consumer research An investigation of the behavior and motives of people as purchasers and consumers.

consumer survey An inquiry into public attitudes, buying habits, etc., especially one done among the actual or potential purchasers of a consumer product.

consumption The use of a product by a consumer, especially a use that so changes a product's form that its suitability for further use by the original consumer is reduced or eliminated.

contact executive See *account executive*.

contact man A sales and service representative of a wholesaler who makes periodic calls on retailers and advises them on management and merchandising.

contact producer 1. A producer representing a network, station, or advertising agency who assists or advises the program or commercial producer. 2. A producer who acts as liaison between an advertising agency and a station or network.

contact report See *call report*.

CONTAM See *Committee on Nationwide Television Audience Measurement*.

content analysis 1. The separation of qualitative or subjective responses to interview questions into manageable categories. 2. The systematic study of the content of mass media messages and the process of inferring effects of programs, messages, or even camera shots, angles, and so on.

contest A scheme in which a prize is awarded to an entrant judged to have qualified by virtue of superior skill. It is illegal in some states to require entrants to pay a fee or make a purchase to enter.

contiguity 1. Proximity without intervening elements, as of radio programs following one directly after the other. 2. A condition regarded as equivalent for billing purposes, created by an advertiser's purchase of a minimum amount of time either in one day (*vertical contiguity*) or in one week (*horizontal contiguity*).

contiguity rate A reduced rate for television or radio time offered to an advertiser who sponsors separate programs in adjacent time periods or whose sponsorship creates situations of vertical or horizontal contiguity. See *brand rate*, *contiguity*.

contingency An amount of money set aside for unexpected expenses.

continuing discount A previously earned radio or television advertising discount continued under a new contract.

continuity 1. Written script material. 2. The detailed plan of a radio or television program. 3. The presence of a single theme or idea throughout an advertising campaign. 4. The maintenance of uninterrupted media schedules.

continuity acceptance The approval of a commercial after a review for possible violations of law, regulations, or self-regulatory standards, and to ensure the absence of morally objectionable, illegal, or unsubstantiated claim material. Also **continuity clearance, program practices**. See *Standards and Practices*.

continuity book A folder that contains, in proper order, all of the commercials to be read over a radio or television station on a given day. Also **copy book**.

continuity clearance See *continuity acceptance*.

continuity department A broadcast station individual or department charged with

writing script material and often with continuity acceptance.

continuity strip An advertisement in comic strip format.

continuity writer A broadcast station, advertising agency, or network employee who writes copy.

continuous roll insert See *hi-fi insert*.

continuous season The scheduling of the start of new television programs throughout the year rather than just at the start of the fall season.

continuous tone Pertaining to printed photographs or the like that have continuous shading rather than shading rendered with halftone dots, hatching, etc.

contour A ring on a map that defines zones of television reception that are acceptable but inferior to that provided by city-grade service. A field intensity map shows two concentric contours, labeled A and B; B defines the outermost acceptable limit. See *coverage*.

contra A Canadian term for a barter of media space or time for something else of value, as one between two communications media or between a retailer and a local medium.

contract classified An advertisement run in the classified section of a newspaper or magazine on a continuing basis rather than on a one-time basis.

contract feature A sales item scheduled for a special merchandising effort, for which the distributor or retailer is compensated by the manufacturer of the item.

contract rate A discounted rate given to an advertiser upon the purchase of a specific number of ads or spots in a given period.

contract year The period from the first insertion of an advertisement in a periodical to the end of the 12-month period following.

contrast 1. The degree of difference between lightest and darkest tonal values, as in a photograph or television image. 2. The effect achieved through the placement of different ideas, objects, people, and so on, together for a comparison of composition.

control base 1. A characteristic common to a whole statistical sample that can serve as a basis for analysis. 2. A group or area that is not subjected to a test treatment but is measured in the same manner as the test group or area; differences between test and control samples are regarded as results of the test treatment. See next.

control group A sample selected for a research experiment to which the experimental factor is not applied.

controlled association See *association*.

controlled brand A product distributed exclusively by one wholesaler, retailer, or group of stores. See *franchised label*, *private label*.

controlled circulation The distribution at no charge of a publication to selected persons or households. Also **free circulation**, **qualified circulation**.

Controlled Circulation Audit (CCA) An organization that audits the circulation statements of controlled circulation publications. See **Audit Bureau of Circulations**.

controlled duplication The elimination of identical names and addresses from two or more computer lists to avoid sending multiple mailings to the same name or address.

controlled recognition technique A method of determining the reliability of a research interview respondent's claim to recognize an advertisement from previous exposure to it.

control room An area into which sound and/or picture signals are fed and from which a production is directed; usually adjacent to a radio or television studio.

control track A secondary film sound track placed alongside the main one, used to control the timing or the volume of the sound.

convenience good A consumer product intended to be purchased frequently in small quantities with a minimum of deliberation. See *impulse buy*.

convenience sample A nonscientific sample selected not on a probability basis but on the basis of interviewee availability. The results of a survey using a convenience sample are not statistically meaningful and may be misleading. See *probability sample*.

conventional wholesaling Wholesaling in which the wholesaler's markup is not revealed to the retailer. See *cost-plus wholesaling*.

conversation station A radio station using an all-talk format.

co-op See *cooperative advertising*.

cooperation rate See *response rate*.

cooperative advertising 1. The advertisements or commercials run by a local advertiser with copy supplied by a national advertiser; costs for media space or time are shared, and the names of both the local and national advertiser are mentioned. Also **co-op**. 2. In film, and agreement between an exhibitor and a distributor to share the expense of advertising and promotion.

cooperative affiliate A retailer belonging to an organization of retailers that collectively owns a wholesale operation.

cooperative association A group of independent retailers under a common name for combined purchasing and merchandising. See *voluntary chain*.

cooperative commercial A radio or television commercial aired on the basis of cooperative advertising.

cooperative mailing A packet of advertising or promotional material mailed to prospective buyers that contains material from two or more advertisers. Also **co-op mailing**.

cooperative merchandising agreement A contract between a wholesaler and a retailer that assigns merchandising costs and mutual obligations.

cooperative program A radio or television program planned for sponsorship by local advertisers. Also **co-op program**.

cooperative sales An advertising agreement wherein the media representative agrees to advertise the product in return for a fixed amount for each unit sold. See *per inquiry advertising*.

cooperative store A store owned by a consumer cooperative. Also **co-op, co-op store**.

cooperative wholesaler Also **co-op wholesaler**. See *retailer-owned wholesaler*.

co-op See *cooperative store*.

co-op mailing See *cooperative mailing*.

co-op program See *cooperative program*.

co-op store See *cooperative store*.

co-op wholesaler See *retailer-owned wholesaler*.

coordinated advertising Advertising and promotion through various media centered on a single theme or visual motif so that each type of advertisement supports the impact of the others. See *family resemblance*.

copack To obtain packaged goods for resale to wholesalers and retailers under one's own brand; done by manufacturers to reduce or eliminate investment in production facilities. See *house brand*, *private label*.

copy 1. The written portions of an advertisement, commercial, or promotional piece. 2. Textual and graphic material for reproduction. See *camera ready (copy)* 3. Loosely, advertisements. 4. A single, assembled unit of a periodical or document, or a single reproduction of a printed piece, tape, film, photographic print, etc.

copy approach The theme or major point of emphasis in a commercial or advertisement. Also **copy slant**.

copy area See *type area*.

copy block A body of type, often part of a printed ad with artwork.

copy book See *continuity book*.

copy camera A camera used to reproduce still photographs.

copy cast See *cast (off)*.

copy chief An individual who supervises the work of advertising copywriters. Also **copy group head, copy supervisor**.

copy-contact person An advertising agency executive who is responsible not only for maintaining liaison with and managing an account, but also for writing the copy for the account's advertising; generally in small agencies. See *account executive*.

copyfit See *cast* (off).

copy group head See *copy chief*.

copy heavy Pertaining to display ads that are too wordy.

copy negative A photographic negative made by photographing other photographic material.

copy platform A description of and rationale for an advertising campaign, usually based on an established creative strategy. It describes selling ideas and usually includes executional considerations. Also **copy policy**.

copy policy See previous.

copy print A photographic duplicate of artwork or an original photograph.

copy research The analysis and evaluation of an advertising message and its claims through pretesting and posttesting. See *copy test*.

copyright The exclusive legal right to publish, reproduce, or sell a literary, musical, or artistic work. Under the Copyright Act of 1976, copyrights are granted for the life of the author plus 50 years, with certain provisions for extensions. Works copyrighted usually carry the copyright protection symbol ©. See *patent*.

copyright notice The words and symbols used to indicate that material is copyrighted. The form of the notice requires that the copyrighted work contain (1) the letter C in a circle, the word "copyright," or the abbreviation "Copr." (2) the year of first publication of the work; and (3) the name of the owner of the copyright.

copy slant See *copy approach*.

copy supervisor See *copy chief*.

copy test A test of the effectiveness and appeal of an advertisement with purchasers, consumers, or an audience obtained for the test. See *copy research*.

copywriter A person employed to write advertising and/or promotional copy.

core market The primary market for a product.

corner bullet A small dot at each corner of an advertisement used to define the column width and linage depth of the advertisement for the printer. Also **corner dot**.

corner card An initial sentence or phrase on the outside of a mailing piece intended to intrigue recipients and persuade them to open the piece. See *teaser*.

corner dot See *corner bullet*.

corporate advertising Advertising that stresses the resources, skill, and/or character of a company to enhance its image, to establish a favorable market position, to redefine its mission, to pre-sell target markets, to influence the financial community, to establish a position on a specific issue, to build confidence in time of crisis, or to attract and hold quality employees. See next.

corporate campaign A series of advertisements or commercials intended to benefit the image of a business rather than to sell a specific product or service. See previous.

corporate chain A chain of stores under a common ownership; in general, each store receives stock and advertising from company headquarters, which also makes all major policy decisions.

corporate identity See *identity*.

corporate image See *image*.

corporate underwriter A national, regional, or local corporation that pays for the cost of producing or purchasing a noncommercial radio or television program.

Corporation for Public Broadcasting (CPB) A federally chartered organization created in 1967 to promote and help finance the development of public radio and television. See *Public Broadcasting Service*.

corrected print A photographic color print in which all hues and color values have been adjusted to create the proper balance.

correct increment method A technique for assigning media weight to a test market that attempts to apply the same ratio of test versus nontest advertising exposure levels as called for in the plans being tested versus actual plans. See *as-it-falls method*, *little America method*, *media translation*.

corrective advertising Advertising designed to correct an erroneous public impression created by earlier false advertising claims; required on occasion by the Federal Trade Commission.

corrective commercial   See previous.

correlation   The observed variation in statistics of one variable in accord with that of other variables. In **simple correlation**, only two variables are involved; in **multiple correlation**, one variable with two or more others. In **positive correlation**, all variables vary in the same direction, i.e., toward increase or decrease; in **negative correlation**, one variable varies in the opposite direction from the others; in **zero correlation**, all variation is independent. Correlation may or may not be due to a cause-effect relationship among the variables. See next.

correlation coefficient   A measure, from −1 to +1, of correlation. Plus 1 is perfect correlation; minus 1, perfect negative correlation; and 0, no correlation.

cosponsorship   The sponsorship of a radio or television program by more than one advertiser.

cost efficiency   The effectiveness of an advertising medium measured with reference to its actual or potential audience and its cost for advertising space or time; usually expressed in cost per thousand persons, homes, or other units reached or able to be reached.

cost per commercial minute   The average price for a minute of commercial time in a program, a media element, or a media schedule.

cost per gross rating point (CPGRP)   See *cost per point*.

cost per inquiry   The cost of reaching one person who responds to a mailing or advertisement.

cost per order   A measure of the effectiveness of mail-order advertising; the sales value of the mail orders received, divided by the cost of the advertising for the items ordered. See *cost per inquiry*, *cost per return*.

cost per point (CPP)   The cost of a rating point for a specific media schedule. May be determined by the cost per spot divided by the average rating, or the cost of the schedule divided by the gross rating points. Also **cost per gross rating point (CPGRP)**, **cost per rating point (CPRP)**.

cost per rating point (CPRP)   See previous.

cost per return   A measure of the effectiveness of a communications medium in promoting a sales offer that invites a direct response from the public (contest, coupon promotion, etc.); computed by dividing the advertising cost by the number of returns. See *cost per inquiry*, *cost per order*.

cost per thousand (CPM)   The advertising cost required to reach one thousand persons, homes, or other audience units. For periodicals, the advertising rate or actual advertisement cost is divided by the circulation (the estimated number of readers or ad-noters). For television and radio, the rate charged for commercial placement is divided by the average number of persons or homes tuned in.

cost plus   An advertising campaign, advertisement, or commercial that is produced for its production cost plus the advertising agency's expenses.

cost-plus wholesaling   Wholesaling in which the wholesaler's markup appears as a separate item on bills to the retailer. See *conventional wholesaling*.

cost ratio   An estimate of relative advertising readership efficiency. Readership is divided by the number of dollars spent on an advertisement, and the resulting figure is stated as a percentage of the average number of readers per dollar spent for all advertisements in the same issue. Used by the research firm of Starch & Associates.

counteradvertising Announcements made under the Fairness Doctrine by organizations or individuals opposed to an advertised product. See *corrective advertising*.

counter card A point-of-purchase sign containing the name of the product and usually its price.

counterprogramming The presentation of a television or radio program that is deliberately designed to appeal to the audience of a specific competing program on another station during the same time period.

country and western (C&W) A music category derived from the folk style of the southern United States of the Western cowboy, production of which is centered in Nashville, Tennessee. See *format*.

country edition An edition of a newspaper distributed nationally and dated the day of its distribution. See *predate*.

county size A set of designations—A, B, C, and D—created by A.C. Nielsen for the size of counties by population. A counties contain the 25 largest U.S. cities and consolidated urban areas. B counties either have more than 150,000 inhabitants or are part of a metropolitan area with more than 150,000 inhabitants. C counties either have more than 35,000 inhabitants or are in a metropolitan area with more than 35,000 inhabitants. D counties are counties that are not A, B, or C counties.

coupon 1. A certificate issued by a seller entitling a bearer to claim a stated discount on the purchase price of a designated item. 2. The portion of an advertisement intended to be filled in by a reader and returned to the advertiser to complete the action intended (e.g., to send a catalog, etc.).

Coupon Clearing House A service of A.C. Nielsen that processes store-redeemable coupons for clients under contract.

coupon clipper A person who responds to free or nominal-cost offers out of curiosity, with little or no serious interest or buying intent.

courtesy See next.

courtesy announcement 1. An announcement of a forthcoming television or radio series or broadcast made by a station or network at its own expense in order to stimulate audience interest. 2. An announcement made at the beginning or end of a preempted program that mentions the name of the sponsor of the program usually seen at that time. Also **courtesy**.

cover 1. The outer faces of a magazine. 2. Advertising space sold on magazine covers. See *first cover, fourth cover, position, second cover, third cover*.

coverage 1. The geographic extent to which a communications medium reaches. Also **coverage area, listening area, viewing area**. 2. The number of individuals or households, regardless of location, that buy or receive a specific periodical or are able to receive a given television or radio station or group of stations. See *circulation, contour, coverage map*. 3. The defined parameters of a market, usually a county or counties, and the percentage of this universe exposed to outdoor advertising structures. 4. The percentage of a universe under study that is represented in a sample panel.

coverage area See previous.

coverage map A geographic map showing the Grade A and Grade B contours of a broadcasting station. See *contour*.

cover rate The price charged for advertising on a periodical cover.

cover stock A heavy, strong paper used for the covers of booklets and the like, manufactured in a variety of basic weights, with a basic sheet size of 20 by 26 inches.

cowcatcher A commercial occurring at the beginning of and forming a part of a television or radio program. See *hitchhiker*.

CPB See *Corporation for Public Broadcasting*.

CPGRP See *cost per point*.

CPM See *cost per thousand, critical path method*.

CPP See *characters per pica*.

CRRP See *cost per point*.

CRAM See *Cumulative Radio Audience Method*.

crawl The vertical or horizontal movement of graphics mounted on a large drum or between two rollers. Also **crawling title, creeper, creeping title, running title, title crawl, title roll**. See *roller title*.

crawling title See previous.

crawl roll The drumlike mechanism on which film titles and credits are mounted so that their position can be continuously altered in printing on successive frames in order to create a crawl.

creative boutique An advertising organization differing from a full service agency in that its work is primarily confined to creative services, on a job-by-job or continuing basis with its clients. See *boutique*.

creative department The section of an advertising agency charged with developing advertisements, commercials, and campaigns.

creative direction See *creative strategy*.

creative director An advertising agency employee who conceives, designs, and coordinates creative work and supervises other creative personnel. See *account executive, associate creative director, executive creative director*.

creative strategy A statement of the communications goal and basic message, but not specific content, to be used in an advertisement or commercial, or an entire campaign. Strategy usually consists of a stated intent, target prospect description, the benefits to be promised, and the facts to be used to support these claims.

credit An allowance by a medium to compensate an advertiser for a loss in advertising service (e.g., cash refunds, extra service). See *make good*.

credit and delivery store A store allowing charge accounts and offering a delivery service. See *cash-and-carry*.

credit hold A withholding of further shipments until a previous shipment of magazines, merchandise, etc., is paid for.

credit line A statement of the name of the producer, artist, writer, photographer, or other person responsible for the artwork, story, etc., of a commercial or advertisement.

credits A list of the names of the production staff and cast at the beginning or end of a television program or motion picture. Also called credit title, creeping title.

credit title See previous.

creeping title See *crawl, credits*.

critical path method (CPM) A planning technique used to control extensive projects consisting of many independent but interlocking operations. CPM establishes which linear sequence of steps (i.e., the critical path) will determine the minimum time in which the project can be completed.

Cromalin™ 1. A dry positive working proofing system that produces a simulated press proof (usually 4-color). 2. An extremely thin polymer layered prepress proof made by the Cromalin system.

crop 1. To trim off an undesired part of a photograph or piece of art. 2. To mark a photograph or the like to indicate a portion to be deleted in final processing.

crop mark A mark, often a line, indicating the way in which artwork is to be cropped.

cross analysis In research, the use of one set of data established by a survey to illuminate another set of data from the same survey. Also **cross-sectional analysis**, **cross-tabulation analysis**.

cross channel affiliation The possession of a radio and a television station by the same individual or organization. Also **cross ownership**. See *cross media ownership*.

cross classification The further analysis of research data after an initial classification has taken place, in such a way that a member of any group in the first classification may be a member of any group in subsequent ones.

crosscutting See *intercutting*.

cross-fade To cause two kinds of sound, in television or radio, to change volume so that as one fades out the other fades in. See *dissolve, fade, segue*.

crosshatch A series of crossed lines used for line shading.

crosslight To light a photographic subject, motion picture, or television scene, etc., from one side.

cross media ownership The possession of two or more media outlets, such as a newspaper and a television station. See *cross channel affiliation*.

cross merchandising The display of related retail items in alternate order, as on opposite sides of a supermarket aisle; done so that a customer in search of one item may buy another on impulse.

cross ownership See *cross channel affiliation*.

cross plug 1. A television or radio commercial for an alternately scheduled sponsor that is not the main sponsor for the broadcast in question; arranged on a barter basis. Cross plugs give continuity of advertising for each of the sponsors. 2. A plug on differentmedia, such as a radio spot promoting a television program, a television program promoting a book, and so forth.

cross-sectional analysis See *cross analysis*.

cross-sectional design A survey design intended to compare or contrast experimentally defined groups on one or several variables of interest.

cross-tabulation analysis See *cross analysis*.

cross-validation See *validation*.

CRTC See *Canadian Radio and Television Commission*.

CST Central Standard Time. See *time zone*.

CTAM See *Cable Television Administration and Marketing Society*.

CU See *close-up*.

cue 1. A prearranged signal to a performer or other party active in a production to begin or end a certain action. Cues may be given by hand signal, cue cards, light, music, dialogue, the action of a performer, and so forth. 2. To prepare recorded material for playback. Also **cue up**.

cue board See next.

cue card A large card held near a camera, used to prompt a performer. Also **cue board, idiot card, prompter card**. See *cue*.

cue sheet An orderly list of all the cues in a performance; it may also provide notes on hand props to be used. See *cue card*.

cue up See *cue*.

cume See *cumulative audience*.

cume daypart combinations The unduplicated audience for combinations of dayparts.

cume persons The estimated number of different persons who listened to a station for a minimum of 5 minutes within a given daypart.

cume rating See *cumulative audience*.

cumulative audience (cume) The total nonduplicated audience for one or more of a series of telecasts, programs, messages, or time periods, expressed as a percentage of a given universe. A household or person counts once no matter how many times he or she may have viewed the telecast. Also **cumulative rating, cumulative reach**. See *circulation, gross audience, net reach, net unduplicated audience, reach*.

Cumulative Radio Audience Method (CRAM) An in-depth audience survey conducted by telephone by NBC in the 1960s. See *All Radio Methodology Study, Radio's All-Dimension Audience Research*.

cumulative rating See *cumulative audience*.

cumulative reach See *cumulative audience*.

cumulative time The total elapsed time since the beginning of a radio or television program. See *playing time, running time*.

cushion The extra material, sound, picture, or lines that can be inserted into or deleted from the end of a radio or television program so that it ends on time.

cut 1. An illustration embedded in text. 2. To edit in a manner that diminishes the length of a piece of copy, film, etc. 3. To record information, as a phonograph record, stencil, etc. 4. See *engraving*.

cut and hold A director's order for cameras to stop recording and performers to freeze.

cutaway A camera shot that focuses on something other than the main action; a reaction shot. Also **cutaway shot**.

cutaway shot See previous.

cutback See *flashback*.

cut in 1. A local commercial substituted for one being fed by a network. Also **local cut in**. 2. A camera shot inserted in a master shot. 3. An audio promo added near the end of a television program; usually while the credits are running. Also **cut in tag**. 4. See *sectional announcement*.

cut in tag See previous.

cutline A caption describing a printed illustration or a portion thereof.

cutoff See next.

cutoff rule A printed line separating two newspaper advertisements. Also **cutoff**.

cutout A device that extends past the surface of an outdoor bulletin to give a three-dimensional effect.

cut rate subscription A periodical subscription offered at a special low rate to stimulate circulation.

cutting See *clip*.

C&W See *country and western*.

CWD See *consecutive-weeks discount*.

cyc See *cyclorama*.

cycle A period, often a quarter (13 weeks), used as a unit of time in negotiations for purchase of commercial occasions in television and radio, or for the payment of commercial performers.

cycle discount A reduced charge for the purchase of television or radio time to run during an entire cycle, at a rate increasing according to the number of cycles purchased.

cyclic animation See *animation*.

cyclodrum A rotating drum with regularly spaced openings and a light source, used to create the effect of a passing train or automobile lights.

cyclorama (cyc) A curved backdrop used to give the effect of sky or distance in theater, film, or television.

DAGMAR An acronym for "Defining Advertising Goals for Measured Advertising Results"; the title of a book by Russell Colley, published by the Association of National Advertisers. The book recommends evaluation of advertising effectiveness by its attainment of communications goals (e.g., advertising awareness), rather than by concurrent sales results only.

dailies See *rushes*.

daily effective circulation (DEC) The audience that has an opportunity to see an outdoor advertising structure in a 24-hour period.

daily rate The charge for advertising space in a daily newspaper for all editions published Monday through Friday or Saturday.

daily report A statement of sales and expenses made daily by a salesperson in the field.

DAR See *day-after recall*.

dark week See *black week*.

data bank 1. A comprehensive file of information, updated regularly for various reasons such as the production of mailing lists. 2. A summary compilation of audience estimates for the various media, made by BBDO.

day-after recall (DAR) A measure of audience memory of an advertisement the day after it is exposed. See *Burke test*.

day-after survey An advertising research study made 15 to 24 hours after a test treatment, e.g., the broadcast of a test commercial.

day letter A daily bulletin sent to retailers by a chain or wholesaler.

daypart One of the time segments into which a broadcasting day is divided. Typical dayparts for television are **daytime**, sign-on to 5:00 p.m.; **early fringe**, 5:00 to 7:30 p.m.; **access**, 7:30 to 8:00 p.m.; **prime time**, 8:00 to 11:00 p.m. (Sundays, 7:00 to 11:00 p.m.; **late fringe**, 11:00 p.m. to sign-off; and **late night**, 1:00 a.m. to sign-off. Typical dayparts for radio are **morning drive** or **drive time**, sign-on to 10:00 a.m.; **housewife**, 10:00 a.m. to 3:00 p.m.; **afternoon drive** or **evening drive**, 3:00 to 7:00 p.m.; **night** or **teen**, 7:00 p.m. to sign-off; and **all night** or **overnight**, midnight to 6:00 a.m.

dayparting The changing of programming to fit the requirements of the various dayparts on radio and television.

daytime See *daypart*.

daytime drama See *soap opera*.

daytime operation See *daytime station*.

daytimer See next.

daytime station An AM radio station restricted to broadcasting between sunrise and sunset so that its signal, which nocturnal conditions would greatly strengthen, will not interfere with that of a clear-channel station. Also **daytime operation**, **daytimer**.

DB See *delayed broadcast*.

D county See *county size*.

deadline The latest time or date advertising material to be used may be received or approved.

deal A temporary offer to sell goods under terms varying from the customary terms in a manner that favors the buyer. See *buying allowance*.

dealer imprint The name, address, and sometimes telephone number of a local retailer added to a manufacturer-prepared advertisement, leaflet, brochure, catalog, poster, etc., usually printed or stamped in a space provided for the purpose. See *cooperative advertising, hooker*.

dealer listing A list of local retailers added to an advertisement used over a large geographic area. Such a list can be changed by city, state, or region when an advertisement is run nationally, depending on whether the publication produces such local editions.

dealer loader A premium given to retailers as an incentive to purchase a stated quantity of merchandise. Also **loader**. See *buying loader, display loader*.

dealer space The space on a brochure, flier, and so on, left blank for a dealer imprint.

dealer spot A radio or television commercial furnished by a manufacturer for use in local markets.

dealer super See *local tag*.

dealer tie-in A list of local dealers in an advertisement paid for entirely by a manufacturer.

dealer use The production of commercials by manufacturers or distributors and their use by retailers on local radio or television stations; station time is contracted for by the retailers. See *program use, wild spot*.

deal pack 1. A unit of merchandise packaged in a manner providing a special sales incentive. See *bonus pack, premium pack, price pack, twin pack*. 2. Merchandise sold on a deal basis.

DEC See *daily effective circulation*.

decentralize To give a measure of autonomy to divisional or store managers, in a retail chain, within the general regulations of the parent company.

deceptive advertising See *false advertising*.

decile One of ten equal parts into which the whole population of a statistical sample is divided, the parts being arranged in some meaningful order; every tenth centile in ascending or descending order.

decision tree The range of alternative courses of action, and the alternative consequences that may result from each, about which a decision or choice of alternative actions must be made.

deckle The untrimmed edge of a sheet of paper, sometimes retained for its decorative effect. Also **deckle edge**.

deckle edge See previous.

declining stage See *product life cycle*.

decode To give a personal interpretation to the elements of an advertisement with a greater or lesser amount of interest, comprehension, and belief, according to the advertisement's success. The concept is derived from communications research.

decoy A unique or fictitious name inserted in a mailing list to check for possible usage by unauthorized individuals. Also **dummy name**.

defamation The act of harming the reputation of another through libel or slander.

defensive spending Designating expenditures for marketing activities to protect an established business from competitive inroads. See *offensive spending*.

deferred discount See *patronage dividend*.

defocusing See *out-of-focus dissolve*.

delayed broadcast The transmission of a network program at some time after the nationally scheduled time.

deluxe urban bulletin A painted outdoor advertising sign that is 13 feet, 4 inches high by 46 feet, 10 inches wide.

demand The amount of desire on the part of the buying public for a type of product or service, or for such a product or service from one company.

demassification The move by the mass media from attempting to reach the greatest possible audience to appealing to smaller, often upscale, audiences. See *fragmentation*.

demo See *demonstration*.

demographic Pertaining to the study of population group data in terms of external characteristics, e.g., age, income, occupation, education level, race, and national origin. See *psychographic*.

demographic adjustment factor A factor used in computing Nielsen Station Index ratings to compensate for the difference in persons per television household between the in-tab sample and the universe.

demographic breakout A section of a publication aimed at a specific, demographically defined audience.

demographic characteristics The various social and economic characteristics of a group of households or individuals, such as age, sex, education, occupation, and income.

demographic edition See next.

demographic publication A periodical aimed at a specific market—geographic, age, sex, occupation, ethnic group, and so forth. Also **demographic edition**. See *demographic breakout*.

demographics (demos) The classification of audience characteristics based on social and economic conditions. Among the classifying characteristics in general use are age, sex, education, income, race, and working status of household members.

demographic weight See *weight*.

demographic weighting A statistical procedure designed to reduce the effects of differences between the demographic characteristics of a sample and the characteristics, either known or estimated, of the universe the sample is intended to represent.

demonstration (demo) 1. A disc, audiotape, film, videotape, or other medium containing commercials, programs, air checks, and so on, used by production studios, directors, performers, advertising agencies, and others for audition purposes. Also **demo tape**. See *demo reel*. 2. An active display showing a product or service in use or being consumed.

demo reel A sample reel of commercials or the like, used by production studios, advertising agencies, directors, writers, etc., as a means of exhibiting their work. Also **sample reel**.

demos See *demographics*.

demo tape See *demonstration*.

departmental display A unified retail display of all related items from one manufacturer.

dependent variable In statistics, a variable to be predicted whose value is a function of other variables or constants in an experimental design. See *independent variable*.

depth The number of inches or agate lines in a newspaper or magazine column.

depth interview An interview in which a respondent is questioned intensively to obtain full information about product knowledge, attitudes, etc.

depth of exposure The extent to which the size or duration of an advertisement or the frequency of its repetition heightens the consciousness of it on the part of the audience.

design 1. A visual plan depicting the appearance of a symbol, trademark, object, or setting intended to communicate desired qualities. 2. The arrangement of the visual elements of a magazine, brochure, catalog, etc. 3. The art of preparing such depictions and arrangements. 4. The pattern of procedures used in a research project. See *experimental design*. 5. To prepare visual or research plans.

designated community The community listed in Title 47 of the *Code of Federal Regulations*, paragraph 76.51, as the primary community of a major television market.

Designated Market Area (DMA) A market definition used by A.C. Nielsen for a group of adjacent counties in which the major share of audience is obtained by television stations within these counties; each U.S. county is part of only one such area. See *Area of Dominant Influence*.

design house See *art service*.

detailer A salesperson whose work is primarily the promotion of goodwill among professionals, especially doctors, etc., who may influence the purchase of products or services represented by the detailer.

detail man See next.

detail rep A manufacturer's or broker's representative who calls on retailers to check sales and the condition of stock and to render sales assistance. Also **detail man**, **field man**, **field rep**, **retail man**, **retail rep**.

develop 1. To bring forth photographic images on exposed film or paper by the use of a chemical solution. 2. To encourage the growth of sales of a product or product class. See *brand development*, *market development*.

deviation The numerical distance of a score, rating, number, and so on, from a central point such as a mean or median.

DGA See *Directors Guild of America*.

diary A written record used in consumer research, in which respondents keep a log of periodicals read, television programs viewed, or products purchased.

diary reinterview An interview conducted with a household that has already cooperated in a diary measurement. Diary reinterviews are valuable because they allow the researcher to prescreen respondents by information previously collected in the original diary measurement. Diary reinterviews generally have extremely high cooperation rates.

die cut 1. Paper or cardboard that has been cut to the shape desired by a die. 2. The cut so made.

die stamping The embossing of paper by means of a die to create a raised or recessed design or image on the sheet.

differential See *rate differential*.

differential survey treatment (DST) A method of encouraging black and Hispanic households to complete and return media diaries. Target respondents in predesignated areas are mailed diaries and receive increased premiums. Three follow-up calls are made to all respondent homes.

differentiation See *brand differentiation*.

digest A periodical providing a summary of a variety of subjects, including condensations of longer works that may have appeared in other publications.

digest-sized page A unit of magazine advertising space measuring 5 by 7 inches, included in a larger magazine; so called from the page size of *Reader's Digest*.

diorama 1. A specially lighted advertising display, usually three-dimensional and often animated. 2. A model or miniature set, shot in such a way as to give the illusion of being an actual scene.

direct advertising Printed advertising materials that are distributed by hand or mail to prospective buyers; includes direct mail advertising.

direct buyer A person who is permitted to buy directly from a manufacturer, usually a retailer with a number of stores and a warehouse.

directional microphone A microphone sensitive to sounds within a limited arc; useful for screening out potentially distracting background noise.

directive interview An interview in which respondents' answers are restricted to those offered in a questionnaire. See *nondirective interview*, *structured interview*.

direct mail See next.

direct mail advertising Advertising or promotional material sent to prospective buyers through the mail or by some other direct delivery service. Also **direct mail**.

Direct Mail Advertising Association (DMAA) An organization of national and local users of direct mail advertising, formed to further member interests and promote this advertising medium.

direct mail agency A company that sells magazine subscriptions through the mail; usually accomplished through massive promotions and prizes.

direct mail campaign A promotional or sales campaign using the mail for the delivery of the message and designed to maximize the number of responses in the shortest possible period.

Direct Mail/Marketing Association (DM/MA) The former name of the Direct Marketing Association.

direct marketing (DM) The selling of goods or services directly to a consumer.

Direct Marketing Association (DMA) An international trade association of suppliers, advertisers, and other professionals of direct marketing. Formerly the Direct Mail/Marketing Association.

direct media The communications outlets that are used for one-on-one selling, such as telephone and mail. See *indirect media*.

director The individual in charge of all artistic aspects of a radio or television program or commercial, including acting, sets, lighting, camera composition, audio, and so forth. Others may be in charge of various aspects—for example, a lighting director—but the director is responsible for all actions and decisions. See *producer*.

director of research See *research director*.

Directors Guild of America (DGA) A professional organization of film and television directors.

directory advertising Advertising that appears in a specialized commercial or industrial directory, such as the commercial telephone pages.

direct recording See *lip synchronization*.

direct response advertising Advertising that requires a simple reply from the prospective customer to the advertiser, such as mail order, direct mail, telemarketing, and cable television home shopping channels.

direct response card A business reply postcard, often part of a booklet or deck of cards, to be returned to a business by the recipient to order product or request information.

direct sales Sales made without the service of a broker or third party (e.g., a magazine subscription ordered directly from the publisher instead of a subscription agent).

direct store delivery A shipment of merchandise from a manufacturer directly to a retailer. Also **store door delivery**. See *drop shipment*.

direct subscriber A subscriber who orders periodicals directly from the publisher rather than through an agency. See *indirect subscriber*.

disc jockey (DJ)   A radio entertainer whose program consists mainly of popular records, interspersed with commentary, live and recorded commercials, and other announcements. Also **disk jockey, jock**.

discount   A reduction from a stated price or rate of payment, made for a variety of reasons. An advertiser may receive a discount for purchasing a large quantity of space or time in a communications medium. An advertising agency may receive much of its revenue in the form of discounts from media on billings to advertisers.

discounter   See next.

discount house   A retail outlet offering a variety of durable or non-food packaged goods at a relatively low markup, usually featuring a minimum level of credit, delivery, and guarantee services. Also **discounter, discount store**. See *mass merchandiser*.

discount store   See previous.

discrete data   Noncontinuous data that is characterized by gaps in the scale. For example, children and other audience members come in discrete quantities; no family has 2.7 children.

discrete demographics   The uncombined or nonoverlapping sex/age groupings used for listening estimates (e.g., women age 18 to 24, 25 to 34, 35 to 44), as opposed to target group demographics (e.g., men age 18 or older, 18 to 34, 18 to 49, 25 to 49). Also **uncombined listening estimates**.

discretionary time   The time left to an individual after sleeping, eating, working; time left for mass media consumption.

discriminant functional analysis   A multivariate statistical technique that maximizes group differences relative to the error or variability found within such groups. Groups are defined through experimental

design, and each is evaluated on a number of dimensions by separate, independent groups assigned randomly to each such concept. Some combination of these dimensions forms in a manner tending to maximally differentiate these groups.

disk jockey   See *disc jockey*.

dispersion   The degree or pattern of distribution of statistical measurements of frequency or other observed factors.

dispersion pattern   1. The audience flow at the end of a television or radio program. 2. The placement of advertising messages, in terms of coverage and frequency, to attain an objective.

display   1. A physically contiguous arrangement of goods or advertising, possibly with decorative material and props, intended to call attention to and prompt the sale of the product or service being displayed. 2. To create such an arrangement.

display advertising   1. Print advertising designed to attract attention by the use of large type, borders, white space, illustrations, and so forth. 2. Advertising mounted in a display. See *classified advertising*.

display allowance   A price reduction granted to retailers in return for the opportunity to display merchandise, usually off-shelf.

display bin   An open bin, usually of heavy paper or cardboard, for the display of small items piled inside; usually a dump bin.

display card   A printed or hand-lettered advertisement attached to a store display. See *shelf talker*.

display case   A container for merchandise that becomes a display when opened. See *case*.

display classified advertising   Classified advertising that uses display type, illustrations, borders, and other special features, and that occupies more space for its text than the regular advertising in a classified section.

display loader A dealer loader premium that is built into a display; it is received by the dealer when the display is taken down.

display period The exposure time for an outdoor advertising message. Posters are normally contracted for monthly exposure; bulletins, rotating or permanent, usually display the same copy for 4 months.

display size A size of type; for newspapers, 14 points or larger. See *body type, display type*.

display type A large, boldface type used for headlines and sub-heads, rather than text. See *body type*.

dissolve A technique for beginning or ending a film or television shot by putting the camera gradually out of or into focus. See *lap dissolve*.

distortion 1. The false recollection of an experience; e.g., of an advertising message, so as to make the message fit readily into a personal frame of reference. 2. An intentional change in the width of a newspaper advertisement to accommodate individual newspaper column widths; an alternative to cropping or completely resizing an advertisement.

distribution 1. The extent to which dealers carry a retail item; measured either by the percentage of dealers who carry the item (**store count basis**), or by the percentage of the total volume of business done by those who carry the item (**all commodity volume basis**). 2. The means by which a manufactured product reaches the customer, including storage, transportation, sales, etc., and the way these are organized.

distribution allowance A discount made by a manufacturer to a wholesaler or store chain to cover the cost of distributing a product, especially for the first time.

distributor 1. A supplier of stock to retailers or wholesalers from a central warehouse. Also **jobber**. 2. A retail or wholesale sales merchant.

distributor's brand A brand owned by a wholesaler or chain rather than by a manufacturer or single retailer.

district A geographic sales territory covered by one salesperson or broker. Also **section**.

DJ See *disc jockey*.

DMA See *Direct Marketing Association, Designated Market Area*.

DMAA See *Direct Mail Advertising Association*.

DM/MA See *Direct Mail/Marketing Association*.

documentation 1. The requirement by the Federal Trade Commission that advertisers substantiate the claims made in advertisements and commercials. 2. The printed materials furnished by a seller, such as manuals and schematics, that explain how to operate and maintain equipment.

dog and pony show A presentation made by an advertising agency, prospective employee, etc., to demonstrate the qualifications required to excel at a given assignment. See *presentation*.

dollar volume discount A price reduction to a purchaser who buys a certain number of dollars' worth of merchandise, usually increasing with the amount purchased.

domsat A domestic satellite whose transponders are for lease to commercial customers in addition to military and government use.

donor acknowledgment An announcement made on a noncommercial broadcasting station specifically mentioning the person or company that donated money or goods.

donut A recorded radio or television commercial distributed to local stations and having a blank central section to be filled with a local advertiser's message. Also **sandwich, wraparound**.

door opener An inexpensive gift from a salesperson offered as an inducement to gain a prospect's attention.

door-to-door sales A distribution system employing salespeople to make retail sales calls on individual consumers at their homes.

double coating An unusually heavy paper coating; the term is used regardless of the number of coating operations.

double-decker An outdoor advertising display in two separate tiers.

double duty envelope An envelope so formed that when portions are torn away a self-addressed return envelope remains.

double exposure 1. A television film shown over two different stations in the same week. 2. See *composite shot*.

double image See *ghost*.

double-page spread See **double spread**.

double postcard A postcard in the form of a folded double-sized sheet, one leaf addressed to the recipient, the other addressed to be returned to the sender, privately printed and often sent bulk rate. See next.

double postal card A postcard similar in form to a double postcard, but issued by the U.S. Postal Service.

double print 1. A combination on a printing plate of line and halftone, created by the photographic exposure of two different negatives in register in the same area, type overprinting the photographic area. 2. A sheet printed from such a plate. See *overprint*. See *composite shot*.

double pyramid A form of newspaper layout in which a center section of editorial matter is flanked by columns of advertising. See *pyramid makeup*.

double spotting The broadcasting of two commercials consecutively. Stations and networks also use triple spotting.

double spread Two facing pages in a periodical that are made up as a unit. Also **double-page spread, double truck**. See *center spread*.

double system The recording of images and sound on separate occasions for later combination and use in film or television.

double truck 1. An advertisement running across a pair of facing pages in a periodical. 2. See *double spread*.

down-and-under 1. The decrease of volume of music or sound effects in television or radio to a level permitting dialogue to be heard. 2. A direction to a musician or sound effects person.

downscale Pertaining to the lower end of a range in a demographic parameter, in terms of education, income, etc. See *upscale*.

downstage The direction toward the cameras or audience. See *upstage*.

down-the-street sell The portion of a drive period following headquarters sales office calls, when salespeople make sales and service calls on store managers and independent store owners.

downtrend A gradual decrease in ratings, sales, subscribers, and so on, over a period of time.

dress 1. The properties and the like intended to add realism to a scene in television, theater, or motion pictures, but not required specifically by the action. Also **dressing**. 2. To ready a scene for a performance. See *dress rehearsal*.

dressing See previous.

dress rehearsal The final rehearsal of a play or television program before it is performed; done without stopping and as if the play or program were being presented to an audience. See *dry run*, *run-through*.

drive-in Pertaining to a customer sales or service facility equipped to accommodate customers in their cars. Also **drive-up**.

drive period A limited time scheduled by a manufacturer or wholesaler sales organization for offering deal and promotional terms to retail sales prospects and consumers. Also **promotion drive period, promotion period, promotional period**.

drive time See *daypart*.

drive-up See *drive-in*.

drop in A local commercial inserted in a nationally sponsored network television program. See *cut in*.

drop in ad An advertisement for one product contained within the space allocated to another advertisement; often used by advertisers to promote public service events.

drop shipment 1. A direct delivery of merchandise to a retailer from a manufacturer, billed through a wholesaler or chain headquarters. See *direct store delivery*. 2. Orders sent from a manufacturer to a consumer that are billed through a retail seller.

drumbeater See *press agent*.

dry offset A form of printing in which the areas to be inked are raised by etching around them, in contrast to the ordinary planographic form of offset printing. Also **letterset**.

dry rehearsal See next.

dry run A complete rehearsal but without costumes, props, or cameras. Also **dry rehearsal**. See *run-through*.

DST See *differential survey treatment*.

dual channel market A market area in which at least two television stations, local or nonlocal, are readily received.

dual rate A radio or television station that has two rate cards; usually national and local.

dub 1. To blend sound into the previously recorded sound track of a film, audiotape, or videotape. Also **dub in**. 2. A tape-recorded or filmed duplicate; especially a tape copy intended for release to media.

dub in See previous.

due bill 1. A statement of television or radio barter time acquired. 2. An agreement for the barter of services from an advertiser, as a hotel, in exchange for space or time in a communications medium.

dummy 1. A layout or diagram of a newspaper or magazine page showing the location of each item. 2. A simulation of a finished printed piece, such as a booklet or brochure, prepared prior to printing and indicating the characteristics of its design and production.

dummy name See *decoy*.

dump bin A display bin in which merchandise is dumped rather than stacked.

dump table A display table on which items are dumped rather than stacked.

dupe An informal term for *duplicate*, as of a photographic negative, film, recording tape, or printing plate.

duplex paper Paper with a different tint on each side.

duplex technique A telephone audience-interviewing method in which the activities of a potential audience at the time of the interview and over the previous 15 minutes are examined.

duplicate A tape recording produced by dubbing; a replica. See *dub*, *dupe*.

duplicate audience The viewers common to two or more programs or commercials.

duplicated audience The audience produced by duplication of media.

duplicate plate   A printing plate made from an original, as for multiple distribution to newspapers or magazines.

duplication   1. The receipt by a household or individual of the advertising messages of two or more different media. 2. The exposure of a household or individual to the same commercial or program more than once. 3. The amount of exposure of the known audience of a medium of the same type carrying the same advertising, or to more than one appearance of the same advertising in the same medium, such as successive issues of the same magazine. See *duplicated audience*.

duplication elimination   A controlled mailing system that provides that no matter how many times a name and address appears on a list and no matter how many lists contain that name and address, it will be accepted for mailing only one time by that mailer.

duplicator   A machine for printing multiple paper copies of typing, drawings, etc., from a master or stencil.

durable good   An imperishable product that need not be consumed in bulk to obtain its primary benefits.

dutch door   A magazine space unit of two-part, full-page gatefolds folding to a common center; stacked or single half-page gatefolds.

early fringe See *daypart*.

earned rate The actual rate for advertising space or time charged to an advertiser, taking into account all discounts for volume and frequency. See *card rate*.

easy listening (EZ) A form of music consisting of instrumentals and/or vocals that ranges from background music to light popular songs. See *format*.

echo chamber A resonant acoustic chamber used to give sounds an echolike effect in television, radio, or motion picture production.

ECU See *extreme close-up*.

ED See *every day*.

edit 1. To alter the content or organization of a piece of copy, tape, manuscript, film, etc. 2. To splice or record a replacement commercial into a television film or videotape in place of a commercial originally recorded. 3. To supervise the publication of a periodical.

editing house A company that specializes in postproduction work in videotape and film.

editing machine 1. A vertical or horizontal viewing and synchronizing device for editing film. See *Moviola*. 2. A machine for editing videotape.

editing script The script used to select the scenes and edit points for a television commercial.

edition 1. One of a series of sequential or geographic revisions of a single issue of a periodical. 2. One of a series of revisions in form or content of a book volume or set. 3. One of several printings of a newspaper during a day, such as **bull dog, bull pup, extra**, etc.

editorial 1. A statement of a point of view on public issues, expressed by an advertiser in some form of advocacy advertising, or by the management of a periodical or broadcast station. 2. The interjection of opinions into news stories by editors, reporters, and television and radio news anchorpersons. 3. Pertaining to editorial matter.

editorial alteration (EA) In proofreading, a correction or change made by a publisher other than one made at an author's request or one to correct a printer's error. See *author's alteration, printer's error*.

editorial authority 1. A credibility advantage established by a media vehicle's public reputation for accuracy and objectivity in its editorial matter. 2. A goal of advertising, sought either by placement of advertisements in media vehicles judged to be of high authority to prospective customers, or by designing advertisements to imitate the appearance of editorial matter in the media in which they appear.

editorial calendar A plan that contains the editorial content of a magazine or other publication for the coming year (or other period). Used by advertisers in selecting issues where the editorial environment might better support their advertising message.

editorial classification The system of major sections or departments used to organize a periodical, especially a newspaper.

editorial content See *editorial matter*.

editorial environment 1. The standard editorial content, tone, and philosophy of a medium; seen as potentially supportive or destructive of the effectiveness of advertising using the medium. 2. Special feature material, taking up a major portion of a single issue of a periodical, which is relevant to the advertiser's message.

editorial matter 1. The reading material prepared by the staff of a periodical or accepted from contributors, as opposed to advertising, which is run for a fee. Also **editorial, editorial content**. 2. The programs on television and radio, exclusive of commercial matter.

EDT Eastern Daylight Time. See *time zone*.

educational radio See *noncommercial broadcasting*.

educational television See *noncommercial broadcasting*.

effect A technique or device used to create a visual or auditory illusion. See **optical, sound effects, special effects**.

effective Pertaining to advertising that accomplishes its objectives, as demonstrated in the marketplace or as inferred from its performance in pretest measures.

effective circulation The estimated number of passersby who might reasonably be considered to have seen an outdoor advertisement. Calculated as half of pedestrian, truck, and automotive traffic and a quarter of public transit riders by the Traffic Audit Bureau.

effective distribution The all commodity distribution after deducting out-of-stock distribution from total distribution. Also **net effective distribution**.

effectiveness See *impact*.

effective sample base (ESB) An estimate of the size of a simple random sample that would provide the same standard error as the actual sampling plan and methodology on which a survey result is based. Also **effective sample size, equivalent simple random sample size**.

effective sample size See previous.

effects animation The creation of the illusion of noncharacter movements, such as rain, smoke, lightning, or water.

effects machine A device used to create special effects such as snow, fog, and thunder. See next.

effects projector A scenic projector, often involving multiple slides and/or motion. See previous.

effects track The sound track that carries the special effects to be mixed later with the music and dialogue tracks for a television or radio commercial.

efficiency The advertising audience size in comparison with the cost of placing the advertising; usually expressed as a cost per thousand exposed audience units (households, readers, viewers, listeners, prospects, target audience members, etc.). For newspapers, a milline rate may be used.

Effie An award presented by the advertising industry for excellence in advertising.

elasticity The degree of responsiveness of consumer demand to changes in price or marketing support for a product, service, or category.

electric spectacular A large outdoor advertisement in which the words and designs are formed by lights.

electronic editing A postproduction procedure involving computer selection and reassembly of a tape without mechanical editing.

electronic media The broadcast mass media: radio, television, cable television, and so on. See *print media*.

Electronic Media Rating Council (EMRC)
An organization of advertising agencies, broadcasters, and others that accredits rating companies to maintain research standards. Formerly Broadcast Rating Service (BRC).

electronic monitoring See *Mediawatch.*

element 1. A single shot in a television commercial. 2. The smallest detail distinguishable in a television scanning line; in color television, a dot.

elementary sampling unit See next.

elementary unit The basic unit about which a statistical survey is intended to gather information. In broadcast surveys, the elementary unit is often either a household or an individual. Also **elementary sampling unit**.

elements package The negative film elements necessary to produce a master finished commercial, from which film prints may be derived after processing.

elevation A drawing that shows the vertical configuration of a stage or set.

elite A common type size; 12 characters per inch. See *pica.*

Elliot machine A device for printing mailing addresses on envelopes using flexible stenciled cards as printing masters.

em In typesetting, a unit of horizontal measurement equal to the point size of the type being set. A 12-point type em is 12 points wide. Indentations are measured in ems, as are dashes. See *en.*

embellished painted bulletin See *semi-spectacular.*

embellishment 1. A shaped piece extending a visual image beyond its customary frame, as in an outdoor bulletin. Also **extension**. 2. A letter, fixture, package, mechanical device, etc., that is attached to the face of an outdoor advertising structure to provide a three-dimensional effect.

emboss To raise portions of the surface of paper, metal, or other material in a relief pattern by means of a die.

emcee See *master of ceremonies.*

em dash A dash the length of an em.

em indention A paragraph indention specified to be one em, two ems, and so on.

Emmy The annual awards given by the National Academy of Television Arts and Sciences in recognition of outstanding work in many categories of television production.

em quad In typesetting, a blank space the length of an em. Also **em space, mutton quad**.

EMRC See *Electronic Media Rating Council.*

em space See *em quad.*

en In typesetting, a unit of horizontal measurement equal to one-half the size of an em. Also **nut**.

enameled paper See *coated paper.*

enamel proof See *reproduction proof.*

en dash A dash the length of an en.

endorsement A statement by a well-known individual in a commercial or advertisement that encourages people to buy the product or service.

end rate The actual rate the advertiser pays for commercial time or space after all discounts have been applied.

engraving 1. A metal plate used to reproduce a design or drawing. Also **cut**. See *halftone.* 2. A print made from an engraving. See *intaglio.*

enlarged type A style of type that is expanded to approximately twice its normal width without raising its corresponding height. Also **wide type**.

en quad In typesetting, a blank space the length of an en. Also **en space, nut quad**. See *em quad.*

en space See previous.

envelope stuffer A printed advertising piece enclosed with a bill or other matter in a mailing envelope.

EOD See *every other day*.

EOW See *every other week*.

EOWTF See *every other week till forbid*.

equivalent live time program A radio or television program recorded so as to be broadcast at the same clock time in more than one time zone. See *clock-hour delay*.

equivalent simple random sample size See *effective sample base*.

error The extent of statistical variability not accounted for in a controlled experiment after a prediction has been made.

ESB See *effective sample base*.

esquisse A rough layout sketch; a thumbnail.

EST Eastern Standard Time. See *time zone*.

establishing shot The opening shot of a film or television program or scene that provides the viewer with the interrelationships of the subsequent close-ups.

estimate 1. A notice of anticipated costs, often sent from agency to client as a request for approval of the campaign budget. 2. To produce such a notice.

estimated rating A predicted rating for a television show or radio program to be broadcast at a certain time on a certain station.

estimator An advertising agency employee who prepares media cost estimates, usually for media buys.

ethical 1. Conforming to industry standards of fairness and honesty. 2. Pertaining to advertising of ethical medicines, as opposed to proprietary pharmaceuticals.

ethical medicine A drug sold only with a doctor's prescription.

ethnic media The communications media designed to reach specific racial or nationality groups.

ethnic press The newspapers designed to reach specific racial or nationality groups.

ethnic radio A broadcast station format designed for one or more minority groups.

ETV Educational television. See *noncommercial broadcasting*.

evening drive See *daypart*.

evergreen See *standard*.

every day (ED) An instruction for scheduling or ordering newspaper advertising space.

every other day (EOD) A term used in scheduling or ordering newspaper advertising.

every other week (EOW) A term used in ordering or scheduling newspaper advertising.

every other week till forbid (EOWTF) A term used in ordering or scheduling newspaper advertising. See *till forbid*.

exchange ad An arrangement between publishers of newspapers or periodicals to give free space on an equal basis to the other. See *barter*.

exchange commercial The final commercial presented on a program by the program's alternate sponsor.

exclusive affiliation A radio or television station that binds itself to carrying the programs from only one national network.

exclusive coverage area See *exclusive market area*.

exclusive cume listening The estimated number of cume persons in a metropolitan area who listen to only one station in a given daypart.

exclusive distribution The distribution of a product within a certain territory by a distributor with the sole license to do so. See *open distribution*.

exclusive market area A group of counties or other areas whose radio or television audiences are predominantly drawn to stations in a designated market area; used for spot broadcast audience measurement. Each measurement service employs a proprietary, synonymous term to describe such areas: A.C. Nielsen, **Designated Market Area**; Arbitron, **Area of Dominant Influence**; Pulse, **Radio Area of Dominant Influence**. Also **exclusive coverage area**.

exclusivity The absence of competing advertising within a given communications medium accomplished when an advertiser makes major space or time purchases. Also **program exclusivity**.

execute To prepare an advertisement to meet a stated creative strategy.

executive creative director An advertising agency employee responsible for managing the operations and personnel of a creative department. See *creative director*.

ex height See *x height*.

exhibitor A company or organization that sets up and staffs a display booth at a trade or industrial show or convention.

expansion plan A plan for expanding distribution, advertising, and sales of a product or service from a narrow geographic base to a broader or national base, usually in a series of stages.

experimental design A plan for measuring the effect of test variables or treatments in a manner that minimizes the influence of other variables.

experimental error The variation in response from subjects that have been treated uniformly by the experimenter; used as a check on variations in response

by similar subjects when treated in a non-uniform way.

exploitation The use of advertising or promotional matter to advertise a motion picture or television program.

exposure 1. The number of people able to perceive an advertisement or a commercial. 2. In surveys of print media, the act of opening a publication to a space containing an advertisement.

exposure factor A BBDO estimate of the proportion of viewers who will have the opportunity to see a television commercial.

extended cover A pamphlet or brochure cover that extends beyond the trim of the pages. Also **overhang, overlap**.

extended product See *product*.

extended service A method of adjusting a loss of outdoor advertising service by exposing the advertiser's message to the public beyond the period specified in the contract. See *extra service*.

extender See *shelf extender*.

extension 1. An additional period granted by a periodical to an advertiser after a closing date for receipt of printing materials. 2. See *embellishment*. 3. A seller's agreement to prolong the time available to a prospect for consideration of an option to purchase radio or television time.

exterior Pertaining to sets, shots, and the like intended to simulate the outdoors, or which actually take place outdoors.

external house organ See *house organ*.

extra 1. An actor who speaks no lines whatsoever as an individual, but who may be heard—singly or in concert—as part of a group or crowd. Also **extra player**. 2. A newspaper edition run in addition to regular editions; a rare occurrence now.

extra close-up See *extreme close-up*.

extract See *flashback*.

extra player   See *extra*.

extrapolate   To estimate unknown stat- istical data by projections from known data, as for forecasts of future trends. See *interpolate*.

extra service   A method of adjusting the loss of outdoor advertising service by post- ing additional panels beyond the number specified in the contract. In the case of a bulletin, a mutually acceptable substitute location may be offered. See *extended service*.

extreme close-up (ECU) (XCU)   The closest possible shot of an object or person. Also **extra close-up**.

extreme long shot   The longest possible shot of an object, person, or scene. Out- doors, usually a panoramic view; indoors, the complete set. See previous.

eye camera   In advertising copy testing, a camera used to record the eye movements of research subjects to measure the relative amounts of visual stimulation.

eyepatch   A distinctive visual or symbolic device used to identify a specific series of advertisements. Derived from the prop used in the classic Hathaway shirt advert- isements.

EZ   Easy listening. See *format*.

f See *f stop*.

face The specific design of a complete alphabet of type, with its numerals, punctuation marks, and other accompanying characters; usually repeated with minor variations in a range of type sizes. See *font*. 2. To be on the page opposite. 3. The surface of an outdoor advertising structure on which the advertising message is posted or painted.

face up To arrange retail merchandise on a shelf or in a display in an orderly manner. See next.

facing 1. A single outdoor billboard, or a number of billboards, so arranged as to permit a visually coordinated display; termed "single," "double," etc., according to the number of adjacent billboards separated by no more than 25 feet. 2. The direction in which an outdoor billboard faces (e.g., a north facing). 3. A single exposure of a retail item on a store shelf; the appearance of the shelf is measured in terms of the number of facings per item.

facing editorial See next.

facing text A preferred position for printed advertising in a newspaper or magazine. Also **facing editorial**. See *Campbell Soup position*.

facsimile 1. An exact, or nearly exact, reproduction of flat visual material (writing, graphics, print, etc.). 2. A form of transmission by telephone line of documents and fixed images. Also **fax**.

facsimile broadcasting The use of radio waves to transmit signals used to reproduce visual material.

fact An item of information having objective reality, as opposed to opinion.

factor 1. A number used for multiplication or division. 2. A more or less constant influence on a class of events.

factor analysis One of a variety of techniques used in statistics to study the degree of association between, and corresponding significance or meaningfulness of variables involved in, phenomena under study.

fade To change the volume of reproduced or transmitted sound so that it becomes inaudible (**fade out**) or audible and louder (**fade in**). See *cross-fade*.

fade to black A gradual obliteration of a television or film image by means of a steadily decreased camera aperture, until only black remains. Also **go to black**.

fading An intermittent or continuous reduction in the strength of a broadcast signal at a receiver.

fading area A geographic area within normal broadcasting range in which fading of signals from a television or radio station is common.

fair trade A principle according to which retailers agree to sell a commodity at no less than the price agreed upon between the manufacturer and the other retailers in the area; until outlawed as anticompetitive in 1975, such practices were often enforced by a state law (fair trade law).

fake color process The reproduction of a black-and-white illustration or photograph in full color by introducing yellow, red, and blue printing plates in proper tonal values to approximate true color overall.

false advertising An advertisement or commercial that is misleading in a material respect. Also **fraudulent advertising, misleading advertisement**.

family resemblance A common look among the advertisements of a campaign, created by common format, theme, style of illustration and/or type, etc.

FAP See *field-activated promotion*.

farm out To subcontract work such as printing, artwork, writing, and photography. See *freelance*.

farm publication A periodical edited to interest farmers and their families.

fast evening persons report A weekly report from *Nielsen Television Index* that provides estimates of audience composition data for prime-time network television programs.

fast weekly household audience report (FWH) A weekly report from *Nielsen Television Index* that provides estimates of household audiences for all sponsored network television programs.

favored-nations clause An agreement by a medium with an advertiser that no comparable purchase shall be made by another advertiser on more advantageous terms without an adjustment in the original terms of purchase.

favoring shot A camera shot that gives a pictorial advantage to one performer over another.

fax See *facsimile*.

FCC See *Federal Communications Commission*.

FCC coverage area A television or radio coverage area within which a stated percentage of all receivers can be expected to receive the signal of a given station satisfactorily; as defined by the Federal Communications Commission.

FDA See *Food and Drug Administration*.

feature 1. A retail item being given special sales promotion, especially notice of a price reduction. 2. An important characteristic of a product or service. 3. To give a retail item special sales promotion.

Federal Communications Commission (FCC) A U.S. government agency that licenses television and radio broadcasting stations, assigns transmitting frequencies, and supervises station activities.

Federal Trade Commission (FTC) A U.S. government administrative agency created in 1915 to assist in maintaining a free-enterprise, competitive economic system.

Federal Trademark Act The 1946 statute that grants to manufacturers the exclusive right to use names and symbols associated with their products or services. Also **Lanham Act**. See *trademark*.

fee A payment for services made to an advertising agency by an advertiser, either as an agreed-upon alternative to commission compensation, or in situations where commission is not provided by the agency's supplier.

feed 1. To transmit a television or radio program from one station to another for rebroadcast. 2. A program so transmitted.

feedback The response of a listener or viewer to the stimulation received from an advertisement or other communication.

fidelity The faithfulness of reproduction of a sound or image, as in audio, film, or television, to an original.

field 1. The geographic area in which consumers are involved with products or services in real life; hence such terms as *field research*. 2. The area of a television or motion picture set or scene appearing in view at any given moment.

field-activated promotion (FAP) A sales promotion initiated by a sales representative and a retailer or store manager, rather than in accordance with a marketer's drive period schedule or by a chain's headquarters.

field intensity map A map showing the areas of relative signal strength of a television or radio station. See *contour*.

field interviewer An interviewer who functions as an independent contractor under a research company's supervision and direction to contact, recruit, and follow up with sample households.

field man See *detail rep*.

field pickup See *remote*.

field production See *remote*.

field rep See *detail rep*.

field strength The power of a television or radio signal within its coverage area.

field test See *pretest*.

fifteen and two A 15 percent commission on the card rate and a 2 percent discount for prompt payment; the typical discounts offered by communications media to adverising agencies.

fifty-fifty plan A plan by which the cost of cooperative advertising is shared equally by a manufacturer and a wholesaler or retailer.

filler A short item placed at the bottom of a newspaper column to fill empty space; can be used for public relations releases.

fill-in 1. A special order from a retailer, made to maintain stock, to correct an error in ordering, or to obtain items whose delivery could not be made at the time of the original order. 2. A name, address, salutation, or other words added to a pre-printed letter.

film archive See *film library*.

film clip A short section of film footage for insertion into a live television taping or into a longer film. Also *film sequence*.

film commercial A commercial for television on film, as opposed to live or on tape.

film library 1. A reference library of films. 2. A collection of stock shots. Also **film archive**.

film loop A short length of motion picture film spliced head to tail and used as a continuing background or for special effects. See *loop*.

film sequence See *film clip*.

filmstrip An audio-visual 35mm film with a different picture in each frame. It is not intended to run as a motion picture, but it may be used as a sales or presentation tool.

film studio 1. A studio in which motion picture films are recorded. 2. A firm that specializes in arranging the production of movies or commercials.

film-to-tape transfer A process by which images originally recorded on photographic film are recorded on videotape.

film transfer A film copy of a television production. See *kinescope*.

filter 1. A transparent or semitransparent camera lens fitting used for special effect (e.g., to reduce glare, diffuse light, add hue, simulate night, etc.). See *color filter*. 2. A device for distorting sound for special effect (e.g., to simulate telephone conversations). Also **filter microphone**.

filter microphone See previous.

filter question A question used in a survey to determine whether to continue an interview. If the survey is concerned with television, for example, and the respondent does not own a television set, the interview is terminated.

final consumer See *ultimate consumer*.

fine cut A finished television or motion picture work print, fully edited and ready for reproduction and distribution after final approval. See *answer print*, *rough cut*.

fine screen A halftone with a high number of lines per inch.

finish The textural quality of a sheet of paper.

finished art See *original*.

firm order An advertiser's positive order for media space or time.

firm order date A date after which an order for advertising space or time cannot be cancelled.

first class The postal service category of sealed written matter. See *fourth class*, *second class*, *third class*.

first cover The front outside cover of a magazine; in trade magazines sometimes available for advertising. Also **C**, **front cover, outside front cover**.

first proof The first copy of an advertisement pulled for checking purposes.

first refusal The right of an incumbent to renew sponsorship of a television or radio program before it is offered to others. Also **renewal right, right of first refusal**.

first revise A first proof after corrections have been made.

fiscal year A period of roughly twelve months in length designated by an organization as its basic annual financial planning unit.

fishbowl An observation booth in a television or radio studio available for use by advertisers and advertising agency personnel.

fit See *cast (off)*.

fixed-alternative question A question for which the possible answers have been listed on a questionnaire. Also **closed-end question, structured question**. See *open-end question*.

fixed position 1. A space in a periodical occupied by one advertiser for two or more consecutive issues. 2. A space in a periodical specified by an advertiser. 3. A specific period of station broadcasting time reserved for an advertiser and sold at a premium rate. See *position, run-of-book, run-of-schedule*.

fixed rate A premium rate paid for a broadcast commercial for which the specific time on the schedule is guaranteed.

flack 1. A slang term for a press agent. 2. A release sent out by a press agent.

flag 1. The front-page title of a newspaper. Also **flag line, nameplate, title line**. See *logotype, masthead*. 2. A tear in paper used on an outdoor advertising structure that causes the paper to hang loose and flap. See *flagging*. 3. A package design element intended to dramatize and convey special information.

flagging The peeling of outdoor posters at corners and edges.

flag line See *flag*.

flagship 1. The principal station of a television or radio network. 2. The best-selling brand or item in a manufacturer's product line.

flanker A new product marketed under an existing brand name, intended for use in a different (but usually related) product category than the "parent" brand's original product or product line. Also **flanker item**.

flanker item See previous.

flap A sheet of paper attached to the back top of a piece of artwork or a mechanical and folded over the front for protection.

flash A very brief scene, sequence, or announcement in television or radio.

flash approach An outdoor advertising space position value factor. Specifically, the term is applied to a panel that is visible for less than 40 feet to pedestrian traffic, less than 100 feet to vehicular traffic traveling faster than 35 miles per hour, or less than

7.5 feet to traffic moving slower than 35 miles per hour.

flashback   1. A scene in which past action is inserted to show previous character or plot development. 2. A return to a previously shown scene. Also **cutback, extract, retrospect**.

flash card   A card shown to interviewees in a survey that lists various possible responses, such as income brackets and age breakdowns.

flash   A commercial announcement of 30 seconds or less. See *spot*.

flash forward   A scene in which future action is inserted. See *flashback*.

flat advertising rate   See *flat rate*.

flat animation   Animation done in two dimensions, without any attempt to add depth.

flat display   A two-dimensional display.

flat fee   See *flat rate*.

flat rate   A stated price, as for advertising space or time, that is not subject to discounting of any kind. Also **flat advertising rate, flat fee**.

flat response   The frequency response of a component or system that does not vary significantly throughout its range.

Flesch formula   An index of readability based on the length of words and sentences. See *cloze procedure, Gunning formula*.

flex-form advertisement   A printed advertisement not contained by the usual (rectangular) shape.

flexichrome   A black-and-white photograph that has been hand-colored to approximate natural colors when reproduced.

flier   A printed piece, usually a single sheet, used as an advertising handbill or mailing piece. Also **flyer**.

flight   1. A period of advertising activity scheduled between periods of inactivity. Also **burst**. See *hiatus*. 2. To alternate active and inactive or hiatus periods of advertising schedules.

flighting   Scheduling of a broadcast commercial to run for a specific time period, usually a minimum of three weeks instead of continuously. See *flight, hiatus*.

flight saturation   The maximum concentration of spot television or radio advertising within a short period, to a point at which any further advertising would presumably have diminishing or negative effects.

flip cards   A set of title cards or other graphics mounted in sequence to be changed by a quick hand motion.

flip chart   A tablet sheet bearing one of a sequence of messages, for use in a presentation.

flipper   See *barn door*.

flip stand   An easel for holding graphics that are to be flipped during a broadcast.

float   1. To print an advertisement in a space larger than that for which the ad was intended. 2. To center a design or copy in the available space. 3. An amount of money received from client billing but not yet paid to the supplier of the merchandise or services billed.

floating time   See *run of schedule*.

floor   1. The sales display area of a store. 2. The performance area of a stage, television studio, or radio studio.

floor director   See next.

floor manager   The member of the television production crew assigned to direct the activities of the talent and the crew physically present in the studio by relaying commands from the director in the control room. Also **floor director**.

floor plan A scale drawing of the physical details of a studio or stage, used to show the location of sets, lights, props, and so on. Also **plot plan**.

floor pyramid A merchandise display of several levels, approximately to eye height.

floor stand A standing mount for the display of retail merchandise.

floor stock protection A manufacturer's agreement to protect a distributor's inventory of the manufacturer's goods against a price decline for a specified time. In the event of such declines, the manufacturer is to issue a rebate to the distributor.

flop To reverse artwork, etc., from right to left or vice versa on film so that a mirror image of the original advertisement results. Also **flop over**.

flop over See previous.

flow chart A scheduling calendar for the production and/or implementation of an advertising campaign.

flub See *beard*.

fluff See *beard*.

flush Describing type that is set with margins even on the left edge (**flush left**) or right edge (**flush right**) or on both edges. See *justification, ragged*.

flush and hang A style of typesetting in which the first line is flush with the left margin and subsequent lines are indented. Also **flush and indent, hanging indent, hanging indentation, hanging indention**.

flush and indent See previous.

flush cover A cover of a booklet or the like, trimmed even with its pages.

flush left and right See *justification*.

fly 1. To suspend scenery, lights, etc., above the visible performance area. 2. The space above a stage.

flyer See *flier*.

fly sheet 1. A form used by a salesperson to record the authorization of a display order. 2. A single-page advertising circular. See *flier*.

FM Frequency modulation. 1. A system of modulation in which the instantaneous radio frequency varies in proportion to the instantaneous amplitude of the modulating signal, and the instantaneous radio frequency is independent of the frequency of the modulating signal. 2. Radio stations licensed to employ frequency modulation as a means of signal delivery. See *AM*.

FM broadcast band The band of frequencies from 88 to 108 megahertz.

FOB See *free on board*.

focus 1. The point where rays of light that have passed through a lens meet to form an image. 2. The state of definition of an image recorded by a camera. 3. The sharpest form of such a state (e.g., in focus). 4. That portion of a drawing or illustration that draws first attention. 5. To bring into focus, as in aiming and adjusting a camera lens.

focus group A research technique that employs small consumer group discussions, led by trained moderators, to obtain insight into consumer behavior and perceptions of television and radio programs, commercials, products, and so forth.

focus of sale The basic claim or claims employed by a brand in its advertising creative strategy, together with supportive material designed to ensure the believability of such claims.

folder An advertising or promotional piece, usually folded several times.

folio 1. A large case or folder made to hold artwork, loose papers, etc. 2. Loosely, any book with very large pages. 3. A number identifying the successive pages of a book.

following and next to reading matter
Immediately after and alongside part of the main editorial section of a periodical; used in ordering advertising space. See *Campbell Soup position*.

follow style   An instruction to a typesetter to set in accordance with previously established style.

follow-up   1. A mailing to a potential customer who has expressed interest in a product or service. 2. A sales visit to such a potential customer. Also **follow-up call**. 3. The actions subsequent to the introduction of a new product or advertising campaign.

follow-up call   See previous.

font   The complete selection of a specific face and size of type characters.

Food and Drug Administration (FDA)   A U.S. government administrative agency created to regulate the content, labeling, recommended use, and advertising claims for a variety of food and drug products, as specified in the Food, Drug, and Cosmetic Act of 1938.

Food and Drug Index   See *Food Index*.

food day   See *best food day*.

Food, Drug, and Cosmetic Act   A federal statute prohibiting the misbranding, falsification, or adulteration of any of certain articles of interstate commerce; enforced by the Food and Drug Administration.

Food Index   A service syndicated by the A.C. Nielsen Company that reports consumer purchases in contract-specified product categories using bimonthly sample audits of food, drug, and mass merchandiser outlets.

food service   The sale of food purchased and used by institutions on a continuing basis.

food store   See *grocery*.

foot   1. A unit of measure of film length; one foot is approximately equal to 16 frames of 35mm film or 40 frames of 16mm film.

footage   The length of a piece of film or tape, usually expressed as the amount of film or tape recorded or projected. 2. A method of measuring film length and screen time.

forced combination   A combination of media, particularly newspapers, whose advertising space or time must be purchased in equal quantities by an advertiser in any one of them.

forced distribution   1. The distribution of a product by retailers as a consequence of anticipated or actual customer demand created by advertising or promotion. 2. The automatic placement of products in panels of cooperating stores in test markets.

foreign advertising   1. Newspaper advertising purchased by an advertiser whose business is principally outside the locality. 2. Advertising placed outside the retailer's own country.

form   1. Pages of type or other matter that is ready for printing or duplicating. 2. See *format*. 3. The physical properties of a product, e.g., powder, liquid, cream, aerosol, etc.

format   1. The general pattern of a television program of series. 2. The type of programming carried by a radio station; e.g., **all news, all talk, classical, country and western, easy listening, middle-of-the-road, nostalgia radio, rock, top 40**. 3. The general design and/or organization scheme of a brochure, catalog, periodical page, advertisement, piece of graphic art, or book. See *layout*. 4. A standardized intro and/or outro to a radio or television program. 5. The shape, size, and general style of a book, magazine, brochure, or other publication.

former buyer A person who has bought one or more times from a company but has made no purchase in the last 12 months.

forms-close date The final date for getting advertising copy, cuts, etc., to a publication or printer.

formula 1. A stock plot or dramatic action plan that is used repeatedly in television programs, motion pictures, books, and so on. Also **formula writing**. 2. One of various radio station programming formats. Also **The Formula**: music, news, sports, and weather.

formula writing See previous.

Fototype™ Printed characters, available in various fonts, for assembly into camera ready display copy.

Four A's See *American Association of Advertising Agencies*.

four color (4/c) Pertaining to halftone printing in yellow, red, blue, and black, in combination, to give a complete range of hues and tonal values to match the artwork. See *full color*.

fourth class The postal service category of printed matter, books, magazines, and so on. See *first class*, *second class*. *third class*.

fourth cover See *back cover*.

fourth network The Public Broadcasting Service (PBS), Fox, the DuMont Television Network, and Turner Broadcasting have each been referred to at various times as the fourth network, following ABC, CBS, and NBC.

Fox Broadcasting Company A late-1980s entry into the television scene as the fourth commercial television network.

fractionalization The division of radio and television audiences by the presence of multiple sources of programming. See *fragmentation*.

fractional page A periodical advertising space occupying less than a full page.

fractional showing The exposure of outdoor advertising panels in a quantity of less than one-fourth of that deemed adequate for full coverage.

fragmentation 1. The increasing number of audience subdivisions that, together, constitute the total television receiver usage. Fragmentation can result from growth in the number of program alternatives, such as broadcast, pay cable, and basic cable; from an increase in the number of specific interests to which those alternatives appeal; or from other uses of the television receiver, such as VCR recording and playback and video disc playback. 2. The use of a great variety of types of media for a single advertising campaign, with no single medium used predominantly or heavily.

frame 1. A single image of a motion picture or television film. See *field*. 2. See *cell*. 3. A basic reference source in research for finding names for a population sample, as a directory, set of tax records, etc. 4. To adjust a projected image so that a full frame appears.

frame frequency The number of times a complete television picture is scanned per second. In the United States, the standard is 30 frames per second; in Europe, 25 frames per second.

frames per second The number of frames of film exposed in a camera or run through a projector in one second. Normally, 24 frames per second.

franchise 1. A contract between a supplier of products or services and an individual or organization granting the right to market the supplier's goods, usually in a prescribed territory or location; may pertain to a distributor or retailer carrying the supplier's line among other lines, or to operators of retail outlets who pay the supplier for use of its brand name, products, services, methods, or other support. 2. An agreement granting an advertiser the right to retain the sponsorship of a television or radio program, with no obligation to do so.

franchised label A brand (i.e., a logotype and trademark) granted to a local distributor through a franchise for exclusive use in that territory. See *controlled brand.*

franchise position A position in a periodical reserved to an advertiser through a franchise.

fraternal magazine A magazine published for members of a fraternal order or society.

fraud order An order from the Postmaster General to halt mail used for fraudulent or other unlawful purposes.

fraudulent advertising See *false advertising.*

fraudulent billing The issuing to an advertiser, advertising agency, station representative, manufacturer, distributor, jobber, or any other party, of a bill, invoice, affidavit, or other document that contains false information concerning the amount actually charged by the licensee for the broadcast advertising for which such document is issued, or which misrepresents the quantity of advertising actually broadcast (number or length of advertising messages) or the time of day or date at which it was broadcast.

free advertising 1. The use of trade names instead of generic names in news copy. 2. A publicity release aired or printed as news. Also **free puff**.

free association 1. An interview technique in which respondents are encouraged to state the first word or phrase that comes to mind in an uninhibited response to a word or phrase stated by the interviewer. 2. See *association.*

free circulation See *controlled circulation.*

Freedom of Information Act A 1966 statute, expanded in 1974, that requires all federal executive and administrative agencies to furnish information to the public when it is requested, unless that information is in one of nine protected categories.

free form A radio station characterized by a lack of format.

free goods 1. Merchandise conferred without charge or obligation. 2. Formerly, a synonym for bonus goods; use discouraged by the Federal Trade Commission. See *bonus goods, buying allowance.*

freelance To work independently, being paid by the job, rather than as a salaried employee.

free on board (FOB) Carrying no charge for loading or delivering goods.

free publication 1. A publication distributed without cost, especially to a selected list of readers. See *controlled circulation.* 2. A periodical that does not meet the Audit Bureau of Circulations requirement of 70 percent paid circulation during a 6-month period.

free puff See *free advertising.*

free rider A retailer who takes advantage of mass media advertising without sharing in the costs of the advertising.

freestanding insert A preprinted advertisement in single-page or multiple-page form, inserted loose into newspapers, particularly Sunday editions. Also **freestanding stuffer**.

freestanding stuffer See previous.

free television A designation by broadcasters to distinguish commercial television from cable television or subscription television.

freeze frame An effect of suspended time and action in television or motion pictures, produced by repetition of a single still frame. Also **stop action**, **stop frame**.

French fold A fold used for four-page leaflets made from sheets printed on one side only, in which pages 1 and 4 are printed on one half of the sheet upside-down, and pages 2 and 3 on the other half rightside-up; a transverse fold is followed by a vertical one.

French rule A type rule thicker in the middle than at the ends.

frequency 1. The average number of periods, out of a set of specified periods, in which households or individuals are in the audience of a given television or radio network, station, or program. See *reach*. 2. The average number of times households or persons viewed a given program, station, or advertisement during a specific period. This number is derived by dividing the gross rating points (GRP) by the total non-duplicated audience (cume). See *cumulative audience, reach*. 3. The number of times the average individual or family has the opportunity to be exposed to an outdoor advertising message during a defined period. Frequency and reach in the outdoor medium usually refer to the calendar month as the basic reference, because this period coincides with standard contract and exposure practices. See *repetition*. 4. The number of times a person orders goods by mail within a specific period of time. 5. The average number of times the unduplicated viewers will be exposed to a schedule of commercials or spots. 6. The number of times in the course of a year or some other specified period that an advertiser runs an advertisement in a given periodical in order to earn a special discounted rate. See *frequency discount*.

frequency discount A discount to an advertiser for running a certain number of advertisements within a specified period. Also **quantity discount, time discount**.

frequency distribution A tabulation that shows the number, or the proportion, of times that given values or characteristics occur in a set of statistical observations.

frequency modulation See *FM*.

fresh air The unprinted, white space on a newspaper or magazine page. See *white space*.

fringe area An area too far from a broadcasting station to receive a satisfactory signal at all times.

fringe time 1. See *daypart*. 2. A period of time on radio and television with fewer viewers than during prime time.

front cover See *first cover*.

front end 1. The checkout area of a supermarket. 2. The advertising area under the front windows of a bus or the like. 3. The activities necessary or the measurement of direct marketing activities leading to an order or a contribution.

frontis See next.

frontispiece 1. The first page in a magazine containing editorial matter, often the table of contents and the masthead. 2. An illustration facing the title page of a book. Also **frontis**.

front lighting Lighting from the general direction of the viewer.

frontload 1. To schedule the use of the main part of an advertising budget for the first part of an advertising campaign to ensure that all of the budget is used for its originally designated purpose. 2. To schedule new radio or television programs or episodes at the beginning of a time period to attract a new audience.

front of book The section of a magazine preceding the main editorial section. See **back of the book (matter)**.

FS See *full shot*.

f stop A standardized measure of the aperture of a camera's diaphragm; along with film speed and shutter speed, a key variable in calculating the proper exposure of photographic film. Also **f**.

FTC See *Federal Trade Commission*.

full color See *four color*.

fulfillment house A commercial organization that assists publishers with circulation and advertisers with dispensing promotional and other requested materials.

full line A line of type that fills the available space completely without justification. Also **full measure**.

full measure See *full line*.

full network All of the radio or television stations affiliated with a network.

full network station A network radio or television station carrying at least 85 percent of network prime-time programs.

full position A preferred position for newspaper and magazine advertising, with editorial on both sides or at the top of the page; more expensive than run-of-paper.

full program sponsorship The sponsorship of a television or radio program by one advertiser only.

full run 1. The insertion of an advertisement in every edition of a daily newspaper during one day. 2. See *full showing*.

full service agency An advertising agency offering its clients a full range of staff service, including marketing planning and management, creative, media, research, accounting, and often such services as merchandising and advertising-related legal counsel.

full shot (FS) A long shot that shows the entire body or object or group of persons or objects.

full showing 1. A transit advertising contract that requires a card to be placed on every bus, streetcar, and so on, in a given area. Also **full run**. 2. An outdoor posting of the number of boards conventionally regarded as adequate in a given geographic area. See *intensity*.

full-time station A station authorized for unlimited time operation.

functional discount See *trade discount*.

FWH See *fast weekly household audience report*.

FX See *optical, sound effects, special effects*.

FYI For your information. Material received for information only, and not for publication.

gaffer An electrician on a television or motion picture production.

gaffoon A radio or television sound-effects person (informal).

gag 1. A laugh-producing joke, situation, or device. 2. The forcible restraint of free speech.

gag writer A radio or television writer who develops one-liners or scripts containing humorous lines and situations.

gain 1. An increase of sound volume. 2. The electronic control that varies sound level.

galley 1. A tray for holding metal type. 2. A proof or print made from type set in metal or film before makeup into pages or final positioning. Also **galley proof, slip proof**.

galley proof See *galley*.

Gallup and Robinson A research firm that conducts print and broadcast media advertising effectiveness surveys.

Gallup Poll A public opinion poll. See *American Institute of Public Opinion*.

galvanic skin response (GSR) A physiological reaction to psychological stimuli (e.g., fear or arousal), whose intensity is measurable by the degree of skin conductivity created by varying perspiration rates; used to determine respondents' reactions to advertising. Also **psychogalvanic skin response**. See *arousal method, psychogalvanometer*.

galvanometer See *psychogalvanometer*.

gatefold A special multi-part insert or cover of a magazine that must be unfolded for viewing.

gathering 1. The assembling of individual printed pieces of a collateral print job prior to inserting in envelopes. See *collate*. 2. The process of assembling book signatures for binding.

Gaussian curve See *normal distribution curve*.

gaze motion The movement of a viewer's or reader's eyes. See *eye camera*.

gel A translucent color filter for a spotlight. Also **gelatin**.

gelatin See previous.

general advertising See *national advertising*.

general editorial magazine See next.

general interest magazine A magazine that contains information with a broad appeal for a wide range of readers. Also **general editorial magazine, general magazine**.

general magazine See previous.

general rate See *national rate*.

generation 1. A stage in the duplication of a film or recording, the first being the original that succeeding generations reproduce. 2. A new development that derives from an earlier concept (e.g., second-generation, third-generation).

generic Pertaining to a product or service category as a whole. See *brand*.

generic advertising A commercial or advertisement that is specific about the benefits of a type of product or service but that does not mention the brand or the local outlets where it may be obtained.

generic product   See *product*.

generic promo   A radio or television promo that encourages the audience to stay tuned to the station, without specifically promoting a particular series, episode, personality, and so on.

geodemographics   The demographics of individuals or groups who reside in the same geographic area. See *psychographic*.

geographic edition   An edition of a publication designed for a particular geographic area; generally available not only to national advertisers but also to regional advertisers who wish to purchase the circulation of that particular edition.

geographics   A method of subdividing a mailing list based on geographic or political subdivisions (postal ZIP codes, sectional centers, cities, counties, states, or regions).

geographic split run   A periodical advertising split run determined by geographic areas of distribution.

gestalt theory   A theory in psychology that asserts that each thing in a group of associated things must be considered in its relation to the whole group rather than merely as an independent object, because a subject will respond to the group as a whole as well as to its components. See *principle of closure*.

ghost   A secondary, weaker image on a television screen imitating the principal image and usually caused by a reflected as well as a direct transmission of the signal. Also **double image**.

ghosted view   See *phantom section*.

ghost writer   A person who is contracted to write so that someone else, usually a celebrity, may take credit for the work.

gimmick   1. A device, idea, or trick used to attract attention to a product, promotion,

etc. 2. The characteristic of a television or radio program that sets it apart from similar programs.

gingerbread   Artwork characterized by showy, overdone decoration.

giveaway   1. An item offered free for promotional purposes. See *premium*. 2. A radio or television program that offers prizes to contestants.

GNH   See *gross night hour*.

going year   A period of 12 consecutive months of advertising budgeting for a product or service. See *sustaining advertising*.

Golden Age of Radio   Generally, the period from 1926 to 1948, from the advent of the networks to the decline of network radio.

golden hours   See next.

golden time   The working time for which workers are compensated at special overtime rates, generally as indicated by union contracts. Also **golden hours**.

Gold Screen Award   The award given by the Television Bureau of Advertising for "outstanding performance in the art of total communication to promote an industry through advertising."

go to black   See *fade to black*.

Grade A   The coverage or service of a television station within which satisfactory service is received at least 90 percent of the time by at least 70 percent of receivers.

Grade B   The coverage or service of a television station within which satisfactory service is received at least 90 percent of the time by at least 50 percent of receivers.

graphic   A visual device of an informative, symbolic, or decorative nature.

graphic arts   The arts that express ideas through line, color, characters, and other means, e.g., printing, engraving, painting, drawing, and so on.

graphic design The design of printed material.

graphic display terminal 1. A computer terminal that enables the user to display works in graphic form. 2. A computer terminal that enables the user to view a typeset page.

graphics 1. Illustrative material as opposed to text. 2. The artwork, pictures, charts, credits, etc., used in television and film production.

graphics generator A device used to prepare graphics electronically.

graphics studio See *art service*.

gray scale 1. An achromatic slide, test pattern, or other standard test card having 10 steps of gray ranging from white to black. 2. A scale used to judge tonal values in color separation negatives for balance and uniformity of tone.

Greek An advertising artwork legend of meaningless shapes or garbled letters, intended to show the location and size of type to be added later, or to test public response to the design alone of a package, advertisement, and so forth.

grid card An advertising rate card in matrix form.

grip A person employed to provide manual assistance on a television or motion picture production; a general handyman. Also **key grip**.

grocery 1. A retail store primarily designed to provide household food, beverages, and basic laundry and cleaning products. Also **food store**. See *supermarket*. 2. A food product sold by a grocery.

gross The amount charged for advertising time or space exclusive of discounts.

gross audience The total number of households or individuals in a television audience that view for two or more periods in a schedule of spots or programs without regard to duplication. See *cumulative audience, net audience, net unduplicated audience*.

gross billing 1. The cost of print or broadcast advertising before discounts. 2. The total amount of advertisers' funds handled annually by an advertising agency.

gross circulation In outdoor advertising, the total number of persons passing an advertisement during a given period, without regard to the direction these persons may be going. See *net circulation*.

gross cost 1. The cost for services by an advertising agency, including the agency commission. 2. See *gross rate*.

gross impression The sum of all exposures to an advertiser's advertising in a given media schedule.

gross less An informal expression for the actual cost of an advertisement after a discount from the gross rate.

gross margin See *margin*.

gross message weight The total gross rating points received by an advertisement or advertising effort over a stated period.

gross night hour (GNH) The card rate for sponsorship of one hour of television or radio station prime time; used as a basis for determining other commercial rates.

gross rate The published rate for advertising space or time charged by a communications medium without regard to agency or seller's commissions. Also **card rate, gross cost**.

gross rating point (GRP) A unit of measurement of television, radio, or outdoor advertising audience size, equal to 1 percent of the total potential audience universe. Exposure to commercials is measured without regard to multiple exposure of the same advertising to individuals. Also, the product of reach times frequency.

ground bulletin A standard outdoor bulletin built on the ground, as opposed to one on a building.

group advertising Advertising by a group of independent retailers, often members of a voluntary chain.

group discount A discount offered to advertisers who buy time on two or more group-owned radio or television stations.

group interview An informal interview conducted for research purposes with three or more subjects.

growth stage See *product life cycle*.

GRP See *gross rating point*.

GSR See *galvanic skin response*.

guarantee 1. A commitment from a medium to assure an advertiser of an agreed-on rate or audience level. 2. A manufacturer's commitment to retail purchasers that a product or service will perform as specified, or be replaced, repaired at no cost, or have its purchase price refunded. 3. The minimum amount of money required by union contract to be paid to an employee regardless of the actual time worked.

guaranteed sale A distribution of goods to a retailer with the proviso that the retailer may receive full credit on goods not sold within a certain period if returned in their original cases.

guild Generally, a union of performing artists, such as the Screen Actors Guild, American Federation of Radio and Television Artists, Directors Guild of America, and so on. May also be a nonunion association of persons interested in and associated with a particular profession.

Gunning formula A technique for assessing readability based on average sentence length, verb force, proportion of familiar and abstract words, and percentage of personal references and long words. See *cloze procedure, Flesch formula*.

gutter The margins in a book or other publication formed by a pair of facing pages at their bound or folded juncture.

gutter bleed See *bleed in the gutter*.

gutter position An advertising position beside the gutter on a page of a periodical.

HABA See *health and beauty aids*.

hack A hired writer; usually not of top quality and willing to accept any assignment for money. Also **word jobber**, **word slinger**, **wordsmith**. See *freelance*.

hairline An extremely thin line or type rule.

hair space A very thin space used to justify and space type.

halation A blurred, glowing effect caused by diffused light.

half-inch A size of videotape used in home video cassette recorders and also in industrial and broadcast television.

half lap A television or film shot in which two images appear simultaneously on the screen, one on each half. Also **side-by-side shot**. See *composite shot*.

half-page spread An arrangement for an advertisement or editorial matter consisting of the upper or lower half of each of two facing pages in a periodical.

half run See *half showing*.

half service See next.

half showing 1. A transit advertising contract that requires a car card to be placed on every other bus, streetcar, and so on, in a given area. 2. An outdoor showing with a 50-intensity. Also **half run**, **half service**. See *full showing*, *intensity*, *quarter showing*.

halftone 1. A technique for reproducing images by photographing them through a screen, which transforms the image into small dots of varying sizes. See *benday*. 2.

A printing plate used to make a halftone. 3. A photograph printed by the halftone process.

halftone blowup An enlargement from a halftone negative that also enlarges the halftone dots, giving a coarse or grainy effect.

halftone negative A photographic negative exposed through a halftone screen, used in preparing a halftone print or printing plate.

halftones The intermediate shades of gray between highlights and shadows.

halftone screen A screen through which a photograph is taken to make a halftone negative. It is made of two pieces of glass with finely ruled parallel lines, horizontal and vertical, which break up the continuous tones of the image into dots of varying sizes, larger ones representing the denser values. Also **line screen**, **screen**.

halo effect A subjective reaction to an individual feature of an advertisement or product, conditioned by attitudes regarding the company as a whole. See *corporate advertising*.

hammer See *barker*.

H&BA See *health and beauty aids*.

handbill A printed advertising sheet intended for distribution by hand to persons encountered on the street or to homes, offices, etc. Sometimes left under the windshield wipers of cars. Also **throwaway**. See *flier*.

handbook A reference book for a particular subject.

hand lettering Lettering done with a pen or brush, as opposed to electronic or mechanical type.

handling allowance A price reduction from a manufacturer to a distributor or retailer for dealing with merchandise requiring special attention, e.g., coupon redemption.

handling charge A charge made to a manufacturer by a distributor in lieu of a handling allowance.

hand model An individual whose hands are the only visible part of the body that appear in a commercial.

hands-on Pertaining to practical or actual experience, as opposed to theoretical knowledge.

hanging indent See *flush and hang*.

hanging indentation See *flush and hang*.

hanging indention See *flush and hang*.

hard edge 1. An unwanted visible edge around a vignetted illustration that is supposed to tone in gradually with the surrounding page; a technical flaw. 2. A style of artwork characterized by large sections of sharply defined colors with clearly marked boundaries.

hard good A manufactured durable good of metal or plastic, such as hardware or household appliances.

hard sell A radio or television commercial delivered in a rapid, forceful, and vigorous manner, usually requesting listeners or viewers to buy right away. Also **slug commercial**. See *soft sell*.

hatch To mark an area of a drawing with closely spaced lines to indicate modeling or shading or to indicate a material seen in cross-section.

Hawthorne effect A bias introduced into research when the subjects know that they are part of an experiment.

head 1. A title or other display material at the top of a page, chapter, article, etc. 2. See *header, heading, headline*.

header A title or document identification printed at the top of a page.

headhunter An independent personnel agent used to scout, locate, recruit, and, occasionally, select management employment prospects.

heading 1. The largest display matter of an advertisement, setting the theme of the copy. Also **headline**. 2. A title or other matter standing at the head of an article, chapter, and so forth.

headletter The type used for headlines.

headline 1. A heading establishing the tone of an advertisement. 2. The head of a newspaper article, giving its major subject. 3. The head of a newspaper front page, giving the most important story. 4. See *heading*.

head of household A person responsible for the management of a household or family; includes single women and single or married men (usually the primary source of household income).

head-on location An outdoor board or bulletin that faces oncoming traffic.

head-on shot A shot of a performer moving directly toward the camera.

headquarters call A sales call on the central buying office of a chain of retail stores.

headroom 1. The distance between the head of an actor or the top of some other framed subject or object and the top of the television or film picture. 2. The unexploited potential for additional consumption of a category or brand of product or service. Also **sales potential**. See *brand potential index, market potential*.

head sheet See next.

head shot A photograph of a performer's head or head and shoulders used for publicity or employment purposes. Also **head sheet**, **mug shot**. See *composite*.

health and beauty aids (HABA) (H&BA) The whole category of hair and body care items, nonprescription remedies, cosmetics, etc., especially when sold in a single section of a grocery or supermarket.

heartland See *primary marketing area*.

heavy-half users 1. The users of a product or service that account for half or more of its total consumption, but number less than half of the total user population. 2. The half of the user population that consumes more than half of the product or service. See *heavy users*.

heavy-up To increase advertising activity briefly or temporarily. See *flight*.

heavy users The users of a brand or category of product or service whose rate of consumption is significantly above average; as a rule of thumb, that one-third of users who consume two-thirds of the product or service. See *heavy-half users*.

helps 1. The advertising and promotional matter supplied to a dealer by a manufacturer. 2. Help wanted ads.

HH See *households*.

hiatus 1. A temporary cessation of advertising schedules, as between flights. Also **out period**. 2. A temporary interruption of a sponsored program, typically during the 8 to 13 weeks of the summer season.

hidden camera A format for television commercials involving a concealed camera to record subjects either relating their experiences with the product advertised to an interviewer or using the product.

hidden offer See *blind offer*.

hi-fi See *hi-fi insert*, *preprint*.

hi-fi color See *hi-fi insert*.

hi-fi insert A full-page, high-quality, four-color advertisement that is preprinted on a coated stock and furnished to a newspaper in roll form for insertion during its press run. As the roll is fed into the press, editorial copy or other advertising is printed on the reverse side, and, in some cases, a column of type is imprinted on the hi-fi insert itself. Also **continuous roll insert**, **preprint**.

high-angle shot A camera shot from an angle higher than eye level. Also **high shot**.

high-key lighting Lighting of a photographic subject, motion picture, or television scene, etc., in which the key light is strongly emphasized so that a brilliant high-contrast effect results. Also **high lighting**.

high lighting See *high-key lighting*.

high pressure Pertaining to a commercial or performer that is overly intense and dynamic. See *soft sell*.

high shot See *high-angle shot*.

high spot bulletin A large outdoor advertising structure located at a strategic place to permit opportunities for high exposure levels. High spot bulletins are often larger than other bulletins sold in the market.

high-ticket Pertaining to a high markup or expensive retail cost on consumer merchandise.

hitchhiker A television or radio commercial following a show and advertising a second product by the sponsor of the show. See *cowcatcher*.

holding fee A residual payment to talent for previous work in a commercial or program that maintains the advertiser's or sponsor's right to use the property later for the same payment.

holding power The ability of a television or radio show to retain its audience; measured as a percentage of the total number of those hearing any part of the program, versus the average audience.

holdover audience   See *inherited audience.*

home   See *household.*

home ADI market   An Arbitron-designated market in which a station's home county is located. See next.

home county   A county in which a broadcast station is licensed to operate, and, by extension, a newspaper is operated. See previous.

home number   A unique four-digit number assigned to each household within a county being sampled.

home service book   A magazine whose editorial content centers on various aspects of domestic living. Also **shelter magazine**.

homes per dollar   See *households per dollar.*

homes per rating point (HPRP)   See *gross rating point.*

homes reached   See *households reached.*

home station   A radio or television station originating signals within a geographic survey area. See *outside station.*

homes using television   See *households using television.*

homogeneity   The degree to which an audience, population, sample, and so on, is similar as to demographic characteristics, attitudes, opinions, etc.

hook   1. A device in a printed advertisement intended to stimulate an immediate response or inquiry. 2. A premium offered to purchasers of a product or service. 3. An offer made on a television or radio program intended to stimulate audience response and thus measure audience size.

hooker   1. A local tie-in announcement. 2. A particularly attractive feature of a package deal. 3. See *dealer imprint, teaser.*

horizontal buy   See *horizontal saturation.*

horizontal contiguity   See *contiguity.*

horizontal cume   A cumulative audience rating for radio or television programs in the same time period on successive days. See *vertical cume.*

horizontal discount   A reduced price to an advertiser who buys radio or television time over an extended period, usually a year. See *vertical discount.*

horizontal half-page   The upper or lower half of a periodical page, especially as purchased for an advertisement. See *vertical half-page.*

horizontal marketing system   A cooperative marketing venture between organizations involved in similar but usually noncompetitive businesses. Also *symbiotic marketing.* See *vertical marketing system.*

horizontal publication   A trade publication for persons holding similar positions in different types of businesses. See *vertical publication.*

horizontal rotation   The rotation of commercial messages on a broadcast station during the same time period on different days of the week or month.

horizontal saturation   The use of the same time slot on successive days on the same station or stations by an advertising campaign. Also **horizontal buy**. See *reach, vertical saturation.*

horizontal selling   Selling to all legitimate buyers regardless of their area of industry. See *vertical selling.*

hot   Excessively bright, as referring to studio lighting or a televised image.

hot microphone   A live microphone.

house ad   1. An advertisement promoting the publication in which it appears or another publication by the same publisher.

2. An advertisement promoting the agency that prepared it.

house agency An advertising agency owned or controlled by an advertiser. Also **in-house agency**.

house brand A product owned and sold by a single retailer or retail chain.

household (HH) A group of individuals, related or unrelated, occupying a dwelling that is considered a housing unit by the Bureau of the Census. Also **home**. See *housing unit*.

household audience The tabulation of the number of households of which at least one member was reached by some medium during a specified period.

household diary A written record of daily behavior, e.g., television viewing, for all members of a household, rather than for one individual. See *individual diary*.

household meter An electronic device that identifies and records the station tuned to and the on/off status of each television receiver in a household.

household ranking A list of television program audiences from largest to smallest, based on the number of households reached during an average minute of the program.

households per dollar The ratio of the estimated number of households in a television or radio audience at the time a commercial is broadcast to the cost of that commercial in dollars. Also **homes per dollar**. See *cost per thousand*.

households reached The estimated number of households in the audience of a television or radio network, station, or program during a specified period, regardless of their location. Also **homes reached**.

households using radio (HUR) The actual number of households in radio audiences at a given time. See *households-using-radio rating*, *sets-in-use rating*.

households-using-radio rating A rating for radio in general rather than for a specific network, station, or program; the estimated percentage of households in the audience for all stations in the area at a given time. See *households using radio*, *sets-in-use rating*.

households using television (HUT) The percentage of all television viewing households in the survey area with one or more receivers in use during a specific period. The sum of the average ratings for a given period will sometimes be higher than the households using television number because of households viewing multiple receivers. See *persons viewing television*.

households-using-television rating A rating for television in general rather than for a specific network, station, or program; the estimated percentage of households in the audience for all area stations at a given time. See *households using television*, *sets-in-use rating*.

Household Tracking Report (HTR) A statement from *Nielsen Television Index* that provides a 13- to 24-month track record of individual network program ratings. Also **program rating summary report**.

house list A list of names owned by a company as a result of compilation, inquiry or buyer action, or acquisition, as opposed to a mailing list rented from an agent.

house magazine A publication edited and published within a company or organization, usually, but not always, designed for internal distribution. See next.

house organ A periodical published by a company, with editorial content devoted to company activities. An **internal house organ** is edited primarily for company personnel, and an **external house organ** is intended for company customers, shareholders, and others outside the company. Also **internal publication**. See previous.

house public relations   The public relations activities developed by, and for the benefit of, an advertising agency; a Canadian term particularly.

housewife   See *daypart*.

housing unit   A group of rooms, or a single room, that is occupied (or intended for occupancy) as separate living quarters, as defined by the U.S. Bureau of the Census. Housing units do not include institutions, barracks, dormitories, or other group quarters.

HPRP   Homes per rating point. See *gross rating point*.

HTR   See *Household Tracking Report*.

huckster   An obsolete, derogatory term for an advertising account executive.

HUR   See *households using radio*.

HUT   See *households using television*.

hype   1. The stock-in-trade of a press agent; overly enthusiastic promotion. 2. See *hypoing*. 3. To use hype.

hyphenated market   A broadcast market that contains two or more communities, such as Minneapolis–St. Paul, Dallas–Fort Worth.

hyping   See *hypoing*.

hypo   1. To add vitality to a program. 2. See *hype*, *hypoing*.

hypoing   1. An activity calculated to distort or inflate audience measurements during a survey period (e.g., contests, unusual advertising, special programming, etc.). 2. An attempt by a medium to increase its listeners, viewers, or readers by calling attention to scheduled audience measurements, including survey announcements by broadcast stations. Also **hype**, **hyping**.

IAMS See *Instantaneous Audience Measurement Service*.

IARI letter grade A score in letter form, A being the highest and E the lowest, assigned to periodical advertisements as a measure of their recollection among all advertisements in the same issue, advertisements of comparable size, and advertisements for the same general class of products. Introduced by the Industrial Advertising Research Institute.

IBC See *inside back cover*.

iconography The art of representing symbolically through pictures or images.

ID Identification. See *identification commercial, station identification*.

identification The tendency of an individual to identify herself or himself with persons or things with whom she or he closely associates or desires to emulate.

identification announcement See *station identification*.

identification commercial A 10-second radio or television commercial. Also **identification spot**.

identification line A line of type that names the subject of a photograph or illustration.

identification spot See *identification commercial*.

identity 1. The planned visual elements—name, logo, or symbol—in varied applications that are used to distinguish one corporation from all others; a visual statement of who and what a company is. 2. Loosely, the manner in which corporate

owners, employees, and various segments of the general public conceive of a company. Also **corporate identity**. See *corporate advertising, image*.

ideogram A graphic symbol or picture used to represent or convey a particular idea or meaning.

idiot card See *cue card*.

IFC See *inside front cover*.

IIC See *International Institute of Communications*.

illuminated Pertaining to an outdoor advertising structure with electrical equipment installed for illumination of the message at night.

illustration A drawing, painting, photograph, and so forth, designed to clarify or decorate a book, magazine, brochure, advertisement, etc.

illustrator One who uses nonphotographic means, such as paint, pencil, or ink, to create pictures for use in print and television advertisements, brochures, magazines, books, etc.

image The combined impact on an observer of all the planned (and unplanned) visual and verbal components generated by the corporation or by outside influences; all the elements that influence how a corporation is perceived by its various target publics or by even a single customer. Also **corporate image**. See *identity*.

image advertising See *corporate advertising, image*.

image resolution A measure of the number of dots per square inch produced on a dot matrix or other printer.

imagery transfer The hoped-for transfer of an audience's awareness of a program or personality to the commercial product being advertised.

impact 1. The effect of a communications medium on its audience. 2. The effect of advertising on a medium's audience, measured either by the extent and degree of its awareness attainment or by the sales it produces. Also **effectiveness**.

impact scheduling The scheduling of two television or radio commercials for one brand within a short period so as to expose the same audience to the same message twice.

impression A person's or household's exposure to an advertisement. See *gross rating point*.

impression study A study of the kinds of impression made on the public by advertisements in periodicals; conducted by the research firm of Starch & Associates.

imprint 1. To reprint a piece of printed matter in order to add special copy. 2. The special copy thus added, e.g., the name and address of a local retailer. 3. A strip on an outdoor advertising poster with the name, address, and phone number of the local dealer handling the product advertised.

impulse buy A consumer purchase motivated by chance rather than planned. The sight of a product on display in a retail outlet visited for other purposes can motivate such a purchase. Also *impulse purchase*.

impulse purchase See previous.

in-ad coupon A coupon contained in a printed advertisement.

INAE See *International Newspaper Advertising Executives*.

in-and-out promotion A very brief retail feature for an item, intended only to encourage the sale of other items.

incentive 1. The payment in goods, services, or money given to survey participants to secure their cooperation. 2. An enticement made by a medium to secure an advertiser's business. 3. See *sales incentive*.

inch See *agate line, column inch*.

inches per second (IPS) The measure of tape speed.

incidence The percentage of an identifiable demographic group within a given geographic area.

incidental music See next.

incidental sound The effects or music that enhance the atmosphere during a scene. Also **incidental music**. See *transition*.

incoming Pertaining to an outdoor advertising structure that exposes the message to traffic approaching a central business district, major shopping center, retail location of the advertiser, and so on.

incremental analysis A method for predicting the relation of varying advertising budgets to the resulting gains or losses of audience.

incremental spending The increased advertising or promotion expenditures for a product or service, as motivated by investment plans, defensive needs, the desire to dispose of excess profits, etc. See *investment spending*.

incumbent A current sponsor, advertising agency, and so on.

indent To set type so that a line begins inside an established margin, as at the beginning of a paragraph.

indentation See next.

indention The beginning of a line or lines of type inside the margin; a recess in a border. Also **indentation**.

independent 1. A business organization not affiliated with, or owned by, a larger organization. 2. A television or radio station carrying fewer than 10 hours a week of network programs. Also **indie, indy**.

independent network A program-originating U.S. commercial broadcast network not associated with "the big three": NBC, CBS, and ABC.

independent store 1. A retail store under individual management. 2. A single store or a branch store of a retail chain with no more than three outlets, as defined by A.C. Nielsen in its retail indices.

independent television market The home market for one or more independent television stations.

independent variable A variable subjected to controlled change in order to observe associated changes in dependent variables.

index 1. A alphabetical directory of contents in a publication. 2. A subject reference publication, as *Nielsen Station Index*.

index counter An audiotape or videotape transport counter that indicates the approximate location of a specific point on a tape.

indicia An envelope marking accepted by the U.S. Postal Service in lieu of stamps on bulk mailings.

indie See *independent*.

indirect interview An unstructured interview that uses open-ended questions to elicit responses.

indirect media The communications outlets that reach large groups of people and are not involved in one-on-one selling to individuals: radio, television, newspapers, and so on. See *direct media*.

indirect questionnaire A questionnaire in which the true questions are disguised, their answers being inferred from the responses given to other questions

indirect subscriber A person who orders magazines or other periodicals through an agency. See *direct subscriber*.

individual diary A written record of daily behavior; e.g., television or radio activity, for a particular individual rather than for all members of a household. Also **personal diary**. See *household diary*.

individual location An outdoor advertising location used for a single billboard.

individuals reached The estimated number of people in the audience of a television or radio network, station, or program during a specified period, regardless of where located. Also **persons reached**.

individuals-using-radio rating A rating for radio in general, rather than for a specific network, station, or program; the estimated percentage of individuals in the audience for all radio stations in the area at any specified time. Also **persons-using-radio rating**.

individuals-using-television rating A rating for television in general, rather than for a specific network, station, or program; the estimated percentage of individuals in the audience for all television stations in the area at any specified time.

industrial advertising The advertising of industrial goods and services.

industrial film See *industrial motion picture*.

industrial good An item or commodity used for production or for supplying services within industry, rather than for direct use by consumers. Also **producer goods**. See *consumer goods*.

industrial motion picture A film made to promote the image of an organization or the use of its products or services, to offer training in the use of its products or services, or to provide education or instruction. Also **industrial film**.

industrial product A manufactured industrial item or commodity.

industrial store A retail store for use by the employees of a company, usually owned and operated by the company. Also **commissary store, company store**.

indy See *independent*.

inflow The portion of the audience that changes channels at the beginning of a television program. See *outflow*.

infomercial See *product programming*.

inherited audience The members of an audience who viewed or listened to the immediately preceding program on the same station. Also **carry-over audience, hold-over audience**.

in-home Pertaining to exposure to media advertising in the home.

in-house agency See *house agency*.

initial The first letter in a block of copy; sometimes enlarged beyond normal font size or otherwise distinctively treated.

initially designated household A household selected as part of a sample for survey purposes.

initial sale A purchase of a product or service by a buyer who has not previously purchased the product or service, but who is a prospect for future purchases.

inky See *baby spotlight*.

inky-dinky See *baby spotlight*.

inline A category of display type having an unprinted inner part, showing white against black. See *outline*.

in-pack coupon A store-redeemable coupon enclosed in a product's package for potential use by the product's buyer; may be redeemed on a subsequent purchase of the same product, or on a different product. See *on-pack coupon*.

in-pack event A sales promotion featuring use of an in-pack premium or coupon.

in-pack premium A premium item enclosed in a product's package; usually offered with the product at no extra charge.

in point 1. The film or television frame selected by an editor as the beginning of a shot. See *out point*. 2. The starting point of a scene.

inquiry A request from a potential customer, generally made in response to an advertisement, for literature or other information about a product or service; useful in determining advertising effectiveness, the audience characteristics for different media, etc. A catalog request is normally considered a specific type of inquiry.

inquiry response mailing A bulk mailing that seeks an inquiry rather than one that solicits an order.

inquiry test A test of advertising based on responses such as inquiries or coupon returns.

insert 1. A separately printed section of a periodical that may or may not contain advertising, generally on a single, specific topic, which is bound with or tucked into the regular pages. An insert may be printed either by the periodical or by an advertiser. It is usually printed on special stock and may have color work superior to that of the rest of the magazine. Also **insert section**. 2. A preprinted advertisement bound into a magazine.

insert camera A television camera used for graphics.

insert card See *bind-in card, blow-in card*.

insertion A single advertisement in a periodical or commercial on radio or television.

insertion order An authorization from an advertiser or advertising agency to a periodical to print an advertisement of a specified size on a specified date. Location on

89

the page or in the publication may also be specified.

insert section See *insert*.

inset A piece of artwork or a photograph that is made to appear as part of another piece of artwork or photograph.

inside back cover (IBC) A preferred position for advertising in a magazine. Also **third cover**.

inside front cover (IFC) A preferred position for advertising in a magazine. Also **second cover**.

inside panel A set of outdoor advertising panels erected as a group, facing the same direction, except for the one closest to traffic. The code is A for all the panels except for the one closest to the street, which is coded AE.

inside spread A set of two facing pages in a newspaper or magazine. See *center spread*.

Instantaneous Audience Measurement Service (IAMS) A CBS device for feeding a high-frequency audio signal to radio receivers equipped to return the signal to a central point.

instantaneous audience rating The size of a television or radio audience as of a given instant, expressed as a percentage of some specified base. See *total audience rating*.

instantaneous-reference recording A recording made from a live radio program for sponsor reference; an air check.

instant lettering Letters, numbers, symbols, and so on, with an adhesive backing for making signs, cards, graphics, etc.

Institute of Outdoor Advertising (IOA) An organization formed in 1974 by suppliers of outdoor advertising space and affiliates to further promote advertisers' and advertising agencies' understanding and use of the outdoor advertising medium.

institutional advertising Advertising designed to promote goodwill for a company or organization rather than to promote a specific product or service. See *corporate advertising*.

institutions advertising Advertising for institutions or establishments, e.g., hospitals, schools, hotels, etc.

in sync Pertaining to a state of perfect synchronization between video action and audio.

in-tab In-tabulation. See *in-tab sample*.

in-tab goal The Arbitron usable in-tab diary sample objective for television households in the ADI. The size of the in-tab goal is relative to the number of television households in the ADI.

in-tab sample The number of usable returned diaries or meter households actually tabulated in producing a market report. In-tab consists of television households that returned one or more usable diaries, plus a selected percentage of planned-no-viewing households. This percentage will vary from county to county and from survey to survey.

in-tab sample size See *sample size*.

intaglio 1. A printing method in which the design is engraved or incised into a metal plate. See *letterpress*, *lithography*, *surface printing*. 2. A print made by this method.

integrate To insert a sequence, such as a commercial, into a television program.

integrated commercial 1. A commercial in which more than a single product or service is advertised. 2. A commercial delivered by the talent on a radio or television program so that no perceptible interruption of the action takes place. See *combination commercial*.

integrated format A television or radio program format giving two or more sponsoring advertisers exposure according to the proportion of time purchased by each.

Intelsat An organization established in 1964 to operate a worldwide communications satellite system. Comsat is the U.S. member of Intelsat. Also **International Telecommunications Satellite Organization**.

intensity The amount and kind of outdoor advertising space purchased, with specific reference to a certain mixture of illuminated and unilluminated poster panels, in certain quantities, that are regarded as affording full coverage under local conditions. Full coverage is described as 100-intensity, with less than full coverage given a proportionally lower figure. See *full showing, saturation showing*.

interaction In statistics, an effect due to a combination of factors or predictor variables on a dependent or criterion variable, in an analysis involving a linear model. Interaction is evident when the influence of two or more factors or predictor variables in combination is different from their separate influence.

interconnect 1. The connection between a cable television system and its program suppliers, such as satellite distribution, microwave, antennas, and so on, or between two or more television systems. 2. Several cable systems joined together in a specific area for purposes of selling advertising.

intercutting The back-and-forth presentation of two or more independent scenes so that the separate actions appear to be taking place simultaneously. Also **crosscutting**.

interference The static or other factors that interfere with television or radio reception.

interim statement A sworn, unaudited circulation statement by a periodical publisher, made quarterly or on special occasions.

interior monologue A monologue heard by a motion picture or television audience but supposed to be taking place only in an actor's thoughts.

interlock A television commercial in its earliest edited form, consisting of audio and visual elements on synchronized but separate tracks (e.g., film and tape); used during postproduction to decide on what editing and refinement should be incorporated in the final, integrated print.

intermediary See *middleman*.

intern A student who works for experience in an advertising agency or media organization, usually without pay.

internal house organ See *house organ*.

internal movement The pattern of changes in product purchasing in a certain market or group of markets.

internal publication See *house organ*.

International Broadcasting Awards The awards given by the Hollywood Radio and Television Society for commercials that "stimulate artistic, creative, and technical excellence" in broadcast advertising on an international basis.

international design See *Swiss design*.

International Institute of Communications (IIC) An international forum for the study of the social, economic, political, and cultural legal issues in mass communications.

International Newspaper Advertising Executives Association (INAE) An organization of advertising executives of daily newspapers, founded in 1911; formerly Newspaper Advertising Executives Association.

International Radio and Television Society (IRTS) An organization founded in 1952 of persons in management, sales, and executive production in radio, television, and related industries.

International Telecommunications Satellite Organization See *Intelsat*.

internegative A negative copy of a camera original color reversal film; normally used to make release prints.

interpolate 1. To substitute estimated values for missing or erroneous data. See *extrapolate*. 2. To alter by inserting new or foreign matter, as by inserting words into a text.

interpositive A fine-grain color positive print made from a color negative; normally used to make color dupe negatives.

interspacing See *letterspacing*.

interstate commerce The commerce beyond boundaries of single states, thus subject to federal law. See *intrastate commerce*.

interurbia A metropolitan area containing two or more cities.

intervening variable A nonobservable or nonidentifiable factor in the effect a message has on a receiver.

interviewing bias A survey error that occurs when an interviewer either fails to ask questions according to instructions or inadvertently influences the person being interviewed. See *nonsampling error*.

in the can Pertaining to a completed program or commercial on tape or film ready for use. Also **on the shelf**.

in the field Pertaining to a film or tape that is shot on location, as opposed to one shot in a studio.

in-the-market traffic The traffic that originates in the market in which an outdoor advertising plant operates. See *out-of-market traffic*.

in tight Pertaining to a camera close-up.

intra-list duplication The duplication of names and addresses within a given mailing list.

intrastate commerce The commerce within the boundaries of a state, thus subject only to state law. See *interstate commerce*.

intro The opening copy, lines, music, sound effects, picture, and so on, that set the scene for what is to follow. See *outro*.

introduction 1. The initial stage of an advertising campaign. 2. An opening tag for a taped or filmed commercial. 3. See *previous*.

introductory offer A special offer made to stimulate interest in a new or improved consumer product.

introductory stage See *product life cycle*.

introductory year The first year of a new brand or a new advertising campaign, dated usually from the time of its presentation to the public.

inventory 1. The total space or time that a communications medium has available for sale to advertisers. 2. The amount and kind of merchandise on hand, whether owned by a manufacturer, distributor, or retailer.

investment spending An increased advertising or promotion expenditure for a product or service, typically funded by temporary reductions in the profit rate in the expectation of future increases in sales and profits. See *business-building test*, *incremental spending*, *payout*.

invoice An itemized list identifying goods shipped, along with such other information as quantity, price, and size; may also serve as a bill or receipt.

involuntary attention The attention paid to advertising without deliberation or conscious effort, especially when such attention is provoked contrary to an individual's intent.

IOA See *Institute of Outdoor Advertising*.

Iris award The award given by the National Association of Television Program

Executives for local television programs and commercials.

IRTS See *International Radio and Television Society*.

island See next.

island display A retail store display accessible on all sides. Also **island**.

island position 1. A periodical advertisement position completely surrounded by editorial matter. 2. The position of a television or radio commercial with program content directly before and after it.

isolated Pertaining to a television or radio commercial with no other commercial immediately before or after it.

issue The set of copies of a periodical published on a given date, bearing uniform editorial and advertising content.

issue life The period during which a given issue of a periodical is assumed to be read by the average reader, typically 5 weeks for a weekly and 3 months for a monthly.

ital See *italic*.

italic A typeface that slants to the right while retaining the other characteristics of its roman counterpart; used for emphasis. Often plural—*italics*.

iteration The arrival at a mathematical solution through repeated trial; used when application of a formula is not possible.

itinerant display A traveling display; Canadian term.

jacket The outside pages of a booklet or pamphlet.

jargon The technical or characteristic terminology used by persons a given industry.

jazz An unconventional, free-form page layout style.

jig A guide or template used in hand lettering, layout, design, and so on.

jingle 1. The music and verse combined in a commercial; often sung, and usually characterized by a compelling rhyme scheme. 2. A commercial musical signature.

jingle house A company that makes music tracks for commercials.

jingle package A series of radio station identification spots set to music; a musical logo.

jingle track The score of a melody written especially for a commercial.

jobber 1. A person who buys in quantity from various sources for resale to retail stores. See *distributor, service wholesaler.* 2. A job printer.

job printer A printer who undertakes miscellaneous printing jobs such as circulars, forms, and cards. Also **job shop**.

job shop See previous.

job ticket A document, usually an envelope with a printed form on its face, used by advertising agencies to transmit instructions regarding a production or printing job, and to serve as a record of execution. Also **work order**.

jock See *disc jockey.*

joint promotion A commercial in which more than one advertiser features or highlights more than one product or service.

joint venture A cooperative business enterprise involving two independently owned business firms, established on the basis of licensing, joint ownership, or contract; in international marketing, usually involves foreign and resident national firms.

journal A general term for any periodical publication.

journalese The jargon of journalism.

journalism The business of publishing newspapers and magazines.

jumble display A loosely arranged display of uniformly priced but heterogeneous objects offered for sale in a retail store.

jump cut A cut between shots in a film or television production, executed in a manner adding an improper discontinuity to continuous action.

jumpover A two-page spread other than a double truck.

jump the gutter To make titles, illustrations, or other matter continue from one page to a facing page.

junior page See *junior unit.*

junior panel 1. A 6-sheet outdoor poster, as opposed to the larger 24-sheet and 30-sheet posters. 2. A transit advertising display unit of smaller than standard poster size.

junior spread See *pony spread.*

junior unit   A magazine advertisement produced in a single size consisting of a full page in some publications, but a partial page in others, with editorial matter on top or bottom and one side. Also **junior page, pony unit**. See *digest-sized page*.

junk mail   A derogatory term for mail containing solicitations to buy goods or services.

justification   The spacing of lines of type so that each line is the same length. Also **flush left and right**. See *ragged*.

k See *key*.

kc Kilocycle. See *kilohertz*.

keep standing 1. To hold type or printing forms used in a completed job on file until further instructions from the customer. 2. An order to a typesetter or printer.

keeptake A camera shot that is considered good enough for possible inclusion in the completed motion picture. See *outtake*.

kerning 1. The reduction of space between certain pairs of type characters to improve their appearance. 2. The compression of a type line for justification purposes. See *letterspacing*.

key (k) 1. The relative lightness or darkness of tonal value in a painting or photograph. 2. A black printing plate. 3. A positioning guide used in letterpress printing, lithography, and so on. 4. See *keyline*. 5. A coded word or symbol in an advertisement, such as a box number, used to determine the mailing list source of a response. See *key code*. 6. To insert such a code word or symbol into an advertisement.

key account 1. A major client of an advertising agency. 2. A major retailer, from the viewpoint of a manufacturer or a distributor.

key code A group of letters or numbers, colors, or other markings used to measure the specific effectiveness of media, mailing lists, advertisements, and offers. Also **key**.

keyed advertisement A print or mail advertisement containing an identifying mark, number, code, and so on, so that the specific advertisement eliciting the response

might be identified. Also **keyed insertion**. See **key, key code**.

keyed insertion See previous.

key grip See *grip*.

key light The major lighting source for a scene in television, film, or photography, that establishes character, atmosphere, and mood; especially a spotlight directed to a small but critical portion of the scene.

keyline An arrangement of all typographic and visual elements of an advertisement, brochure, mailer, etc., showing precisely the size and position of each element; normally with reproduction-type proofs in position, as well as photostats of illustrations showing size and positioning. Also **key, mechanical, pasteup, type mechanical**.

key station The station of a broadcasting network that originates its major programs.

kHz See *kilohertz*.

kickback An unethical and sometimes illegal rebate on advertising rates or talent fees.

kidvid (*sl.*) A television program intended to appeal exclusively to children.

kill To cut, cut off, delete, eliminate, or otherwise end (e.g., a scene, an advertising campaign, standing type held by a printer, etc.). See *keep standing*.

kill copy A copy of a periodical marked to show material (advertising, etc.) not to be run in the next issue.

kilocycle (KC) An obsolete term. See *kilohertz*.

kilohertz (kHz) One thousand cycles per second.

kine See *kinescope, kinescope recording.*

kinescope (kine) 1. The picture tube in a television receiver or monitor. 2. A motion picture made from an image on a picture tube. See next.

kinescope recording (kine) A recording made by a film camera from a television picture tube. Also **telerecording, television recording**. See previous.

knee shot A camera shot that covers a performer from the knees up.

knockout A square or rectangular hole used to outline photographs or artwork.

Kodachrome™ 1. A multilayer film for color transparencies. 2. A transparency made with this film.

Kodacolor™ A color film for making full-color negative transparencies and photo-print positives.

Kodalith™ A film used in phototypesetting.

kraft board A cardboard made with unbleached sulphite wood pulp.

Krylon™ A clear spray used as a fixative or protective coating on artwork, type proofs, etc.

LAA See *League of Advertising Agencies*.

label 1. A design borne by a banner fixed to a unit container of a product. 2. The banner itself. 3. A product name or other descriptor printed, keyed, or superimposed over an object. 4. A slip of paper on a mass mailing envelope with the name and address of a mail order customer. 5. The identification printed on a tape reel, cartridge, cassette, disc, and so on.

laboratory method The study of respondent reactions to advertising under artificial, controlled conditions.

Lanham Act See *Federal Trademark Act*.

lap dissolve A dissolve at the end of a television or motion picture shot that leaves the focused image of the new shot in its place.

large close-up (LCU) See *extreme close-up*.

last telecast (LT) (LTC) The last date on which a commercial or program is scheduled for television broadcast.

late fringe See *daypart*.

late night See *daypart*.

law of closure See *principle of closure*.

layout 1. A diagram or sketch intended to show the planned contents and visual appearance—including headlines, text, illustrations, logo, etc.—of an advertisement, printed page, poster, and so forth. Also **spread**. See *comprehensive, rough, storyboard*.

layout designer A person responsible for the visual arrangement of the various graphic and typographic elements of an advertisement; someone who creates a layout.

layout paper A translucent paper used to sketch different versions of an illustration or rough layout until a satisfactory design is produced.

LC See *lowercase*.

LCU Large close-up. See *extreme close-up*.

leader 1. A line of periods, bullets, etc., used to connect widely separated columns of type. 2. A length of blank motion picture film or magnetic tape, used for holding the end of the film or tape in a takeup reel. 3. The section of tape preceding a television program that provides setup signals and sequence information.

lead-in 1. A television or radio program that precedes another. 2. An introduction to a commercial, program, or scene. 3. An introductory segment that is used in more than one episode of a prime-time dramatic and/or high-budget television series.

lead-in audience The audience from a previous television or radio program that continues to watch or listen to the following program.

leading 1. The amount of space between lines of type, created by the use of lead strips or some other means. 2. The spacing of lines of type in excess of the minimum. See *solid*.

Leading National Advertisers–Publishers' Information Bureau (LNA-PIB) A service that publishes monthly reports on advertising space and revenues of national and regional magazines, as well as the space and estimated spending of advertisers using these magazines.

leading question An interview question that may bias the response by the way the question is worded.

lead-out 1. A television or radio program that follows another, with regard to its effect on audience flow. See *lead-in, program following*. 2. An outro to a commercial, program, etc.

lead time The period between product, program, or advertising design and the completion or marketing of it.

leaflet A printed sheet, usually consisting of two to six folded pages. See *brochure, pamphlet*.

League of Advertising Agencies (LAA) An association of advertising agencies.

learning curve 1. In research, a graphic depiction of the rate at which respondents produce a response that is rewarded. 2. In marketing, a graphic depiction of the rate at which product unit costs decline as the manufacturer gains marketing experience.

lease-back A business technique in which the seller of something, e.g., a building, rents it from its new owner with certain options.

lease broker An outdoor advertising plant employee who negotiates the right to erect signs. Also **lease man**.

leased inventory A credit technique used to obtain the first inventory of a new retail store. The wholesaler lends the merchandise and collects payment, with interest, from the retailer's daily cash receipts. This allows the retailer to begin business without investing in merchandise.

lease man See *lease broker*.

leave-behind See next.

leave piece A flier or brochure left with a prospect by a salesperson at the conclusion of a sales call. Also **leave-behind**.

leftover matter The typeset copy not used in an issue of a periodical; usually set in case it is needed to fill empty space. Also **overmatter, overset matter**.

leg The part of a network fed from a single station.

legend 1. A short piece of writing or lettering meant to be read as an individual entity. 2. A piece of descriptive writing used as a picture caption or the explanation of symbols on a map or chart. See *callout, caption*.

legibility The relative ease of reading or deciphering type or handwriting. See *readability*.

letter gadget An object attached to or enclosed with an advertising mailing piece to arouse interest in an advertising message.

letterhead Stationery printed or engraved with the name of a business firm, organization, or individual used for formal correspondence.

lettering The formation of letters or words by hand to produce a headline, title, or legend.

letter of adherence A letter furnished to a union or guild by a producer, advertising agency, or studio certifying that it will abide by the terms and conditions set forth in union or guild codes of fair practice and other agreements.

letter of intent A letter stating a commitment to enter a business relationship, such as to purchase media space or time.

letterpress A printing technique in which the ink is carried by raised surfaces; as opposed to intaglio, where recessed surfaces carry the ink, and planography, where the printing surfaces are flush with the non-printing surface.

letterpress supplement A newspaper supplement printed on newsprint or similar stock by letterpress rather than by the more common rotogravure process.

letter quality Pertaining to a document typed on a typewriter or set in type, as compared to dot matrix quality.

letterset See *dry offset*.

lettershop A business that handles the mechanical details of mailings (e.g., addressing, imprinting, collating, printing, binding, proofreading, and some degree of creative direct mail services).

letterspacing The insertion of spaces between the letters of a word in type composition for the purpose of justification. Also **interspacing**. See *kerning*.

lf See *light face*.

libel Harming a person's character, usually through written material; however, broadcast defamation, with or without a script, is considered to be libel because of the media's widespread influence. See *defamation*.

library footage See *stock footage*.

library material See *stock footage*.

library music See *stock music*.

library shot See *stock shot*.

life The ability of an advertisement or promotion to elicit intended action as indicated by the continuation of such reaction upon repeated exposures of the advertisement. See *wearout*.

life style The pattern of spending used by individuals or families to express their values and means.

lift A section of recorded or filmed material from an earlier radio or television commercial reused in a new commercial, either to save money or maintain uniform execution of a key sequence.

light box A boxlike device faced with translucent white material on one side and containing an electric light source; used to view photographic transparencies.

light face (lf) A typeface with strokes that are thinner than those of regular or medium weight type.

Likert scale An attitude measurement scale in which respondents state their agreement or disagreement with statements in a range of possible positions.

limbo A television or motion picture scene shot without a visible or distinguishable background.

limited animation See *animation*.

limited distribution 1. The distribution of a product to one or more specific geographic areas rather than nationwide. 2. A less than complete distribution of a product in the stores of an area.

limited response question A survey question to which there are only a few possible replies, such as yes/no, multiple choice, and so on.

limited-time station A television or radio station whose frequency band overlaps with another station and is therefore restricted in broadcasting to certain hours when the other station is off the air. See *part-time station*.

linage A total amount of periodical advertising space; the number of lines run.

line 1. See *agate line*. 2. See *cutline*. 3. A row of characters. 4. See *credit line*. 5. A sentence or phrase in a commercial or print advertisement that reflects the advertiser's key message. See *slogan*. 6. See *product line*. 7. The words spoken by a performer without interruption. 8. See *line art*. 9. Pertaining to artwork or plates rendered with lines, solid areas, or hatching, etc.; not requiring halftone reproduction.

linear programming A BBDO mathematical model used in media planning that enables the media planner to specify reach, frequency, and seasonal and demographic goals for an advertising campaign.

line art A drawing that appears as black or white rather than in continuous tones. Also **line copy**. See *halftone*.

line copy See *line art*.

line cut A photoengraving of a line drawing, usually on zinc or copper. Also *line engraving*.

line drawing A sketch, drawing, or illustration done in lines only without shading or tonal values; see *line art*. Also *line illustration*.

line engraving See *line cut*.

line extension A new product marketed under an existing brand name, intended for use in the same category as the parent brand's original product or product line, while being designed to attract new users to the brand from products competitive to the original product; e.g., "dry" and "oily" new shampoo products using the brand name of an existing shampoo are line extensions. See *brand extension, flanker*.

line gauge A printer's measuring ruler, marked in pica increments and inches. Also *measuring stick, pica rule, pica stick, type gauge*.

line graph See *graph*.

line height The height of one line of type expressed as a fraction of the number of lines per inch.

line illustration See *line drawing*.

line length The length of a printed line, measured in picas and points. Also **line measure, measure**.

line measure See previous.

line negative A photographic negative of a line drawing, made without a halftone screen.

line of travel In outdoor advertising, the center of a lane of traffic moving in one direction.

line rate The charge per line for newspaper space.

lines The written material spoken by a performer.

line screen See *halftone screen*.

line spacing 1. A measure of the vertical spacing between lines of type, measured in points and half points. 2. The addition of space between lines of type.

lineup 1. The stations that carry a particular network program. 2. The network television programs that will be broadcast during an upcoming season.

lip sync The mouthing of words by a performer to a recorded song or dialogue; the recorded voice may be the performer's own voice or that of another performer. See next.

lip synchronization 1. The direct recording of sound during the filming of a television program or motion picture; so called because the actual voices of the actors are recorded. Also **direct recording**. See *lip sync*. 2. The matched timing of video and audio signals in a television production or motion picture, involving on-camera spoken lines.

list 1. The retail price of an item. 2. See *mailing list*.

list ad A printed advertisement for more than one item of a kind, such as a list of books for sale.

list broker 1. An agent who sells lists of sales prospects. 2. See *mailing list broker*.

list buyer See *mailing list buyer*.

list cleaning The process of removing entries from a list because they are no longer correct or required. See *mailing list cleaning*.

list compiler See *mailing list compiler*.

listed sample The names, addresses, and telephone numbers of selected potential diary keepers derived from telephone directories and provided to Arbitron by Metromail, Inc.

listener A person in the audience of a radio station. See *viewer*.

listener diary A daily record of television or radio programs seen or heard, kept by a respondent in an audience rating survey.

listening area See *coverage*.

listening level 1. Generally, the size of a radio station's audience. 2. Generally, the length of time an individual listens to a radio station.

list exchange See *mailing list exchange*.

list house An organization acting as a list broker.

list maintenance See *mailing list maintenance*.

list price The retail price of an item before any discount or sale pricing. Also *list*.

list rental See *mailing list rental*.

list respondent An individual who is selected for a research study from a mailing list.

list salting See *salting*.

list sample See mailing list sample.

list segmentation See mailing list selection.

list selection See mailing list selection.

list sequence See mailing list sequence.

list sort See *mailing list sort*.

list test See *mailing list test*.

list usage See *mailing list rental*.

litho See *lithograph*, *lithography*.

lithograph A reproduction made by lithographic means. Also **litho**.

lithography A printing method in which an image is applied to a stone or metal plate, then washed with an acid solution. Ink is then applied to the surface, adhering to the image portion only. Also **litho**. See *letterpress*, *photo offset lithography*, *planography*.

litho sheet A lithographed poster sheet.

little America method A technique for translating the media delivery of national advertising media plans into the media of one or more local areas by attempting to match local deliveries to those that would be obtained nationally. Also **little U.S. method**. See *as-it-falls method*, *correct increment method*, *media translation*.

little U.S. method See previous.

live 1. Pertaining to a radio or television program broadcast as it is happening; not taped or filmed. 2. Pertaining to a device or component that is turned on. 3. Pertaining to material that is not edited. 4. Pertaining to plates, cuts, or type matter that is in use or is set and ready for use. Also **alive**, **live matter**, **live type**.

live action 1. Not recorded. 2. Human action as opposed to animation.

live animation See *animation*.

live copy Written material as read by an announcer, as opposed to recorded copy.

live fade A diminution of transmitted sound created in the television or radio studio rather than in the control room.

live matter 1. See *live*. 2. The copy and illustrations in a full or partial bleed magazine advertisement that are kept within a fixed field to avoid being trimmed off in the publication's binding process.

live tag A local announcement following a recorded commercial that gives price, store address, and so on.

live time The time during which a television or radio station transmitter is fed a live performance from another station.

live-time delay See *clock-hour delay*.

live title A title shot in television made directly by a studio camera from the set rather than being introduced on a slide or film.

live type See *live*.

LNA–PIB See *Leading National Advertisers –Publishers' Information Bureau*.

load 1. To increase an order from a retailer by offering a premium or some other incentive. See *dealer loader*. 2. To insert a tape, cartridge, cassette, and so forth, into a recorder or player.

loader See *dealer loader*.

load factor The estimated average number of passengers per automobile, used to estimate exposure to outdoor advertising. The Traffic Audit Bureau national load factor is 1.75.

loading deal A deal in which a retailer receives a premium or some other incentive for a quantity purchase of a particular product. See *dealer loader*.

local advertising 1. Advertising for a local merchant or business as opposed to regional or national advertising. 2. Advertising placed at rates available to local merchants. See *retail advertising*.

local-channel station A television or radio station licensed to transmit to its own locality only.

local cut in See *cut in*.

locally edited supplement A Sunday newspaper supplement owned and edited by the newspaper itself; sometimes associated with other such supplements for the purpose of obtaining national advertising.

local media The communications media whose audiences are drawn primarily from the same locality as the media. These media customarily have a preferential rate for local advertisers.

local origination The programming produced by a broadcast station or cable television system. See *cablecasting*.

local participating program A program available to more than one advertiser and not sponsored by any advertiser.

local program A program originated or produced by a broadcast station, or for the production of which the station is primarily responsible, and that employs live talent more than half the time.

local qualitative radio (LQR) A Pulse rating service that breaks down the audience by occupation, income, education, and other demographic characteristics.

local rate The advertising rate charged by a local communications medium to a local advertiser; usually lower than the national rate. See *national rate*, *regional rate*.

local sales The sale of radio or television station time to retail merchants and businesses. See *national sales*.

local station A television or radio station serving a single market area, typically low-powered and broadcasting on a frequency that may be shared by other stations 100 miles or more distant.

local tag An identification of a local dealer added to a recorded television or radio commercial announcement. Also **dealer super**.

local talent The use of talent from the community that a station serves.

location 1. A place other than a motion picture studio or lot used for filming. 2.

The site of a radio or television remote broadcast.

location list A list describing the location of all outdoor advertising panels sold and delivered.

lock out See *standard close*.

Loewy panel A type of outdoor advertising poster panel designed by Raymond Loewy for the Outdoor Advertising Association of America. Distinguished by light grey or white molding of metal or plastic.

log 1. A book or other record kept to note and preserve the details of a prolonged and recurring event, as the broadcasting day of a television or radio station. 2. To insert information into a log.

logo See next.

logotype A brand name, publication title, or the like, presented in a special lettering style or typeface and used in the manner of a trademark. Also **ad cut**, **logo**. See *colophon, flag, mark, trademark*.

longitudinal study A study that traces continuity and change over a period of years.

long play See next.

long playing record (LP) A disc with a playing time over 5 minutes. Usually a 10-inch or 12-inch, 33-1/3 RPM disc recorded with approximately 150 to 300 grooves per inch.

long shot (LS) A camera shot of a distant subject. See *close-up*.

loop A length of film or tape spliced to its own end in a continuous band for continuous sound or picture.

looping A process used in dubbing dialogue, music, sound effects, and so on, to film or tape. A continuous picture loop is displayed to allow the performers to lip sync accurately with the picture. See *dub*.

loose 1. Pertaining to a layout or artwork that is sketchy in appearance, giving a general impression but not details. 2. See *loose shot*.

loose framing See next.

loose shot A type of camera framing that leaves sufficient room for performer movement. Also **loose**, **loose framing**.

loss leader A retail item advertised at an invitingly low price to attract customers for the purchase of other, more profitable merchandise.

lottery The allotting by chance of proceeds or parts thereof, derived from the sale of tickets or chances, to one or more chance takers or ticket purchasers. Prize, chance, and consideration must all be present before the drawing may be considered a lottery. See *contest, sweepstakes*.

lowercase (LC) Pertaining to the small letters of an alphabet of type or lettering, as opposed to capital letters. See *uppercase*.

lowest common denominator A reference to television programming that is designed to attract the largest possible audience; a program with a juvenile plot and characters.

LP See *long playing record*.

LQR See *local qualitative radio*.

LS See *long shot*.

LT See *last telecast*.

LTC See *last telecast*.

lucey See *camera lucida*.

lucy See *camera lucida*.

luminous Pertaining to any paint or the like used for lettering or tinting outdoor boards, posters, and so forth in such a way that they appear vividly under street lighting, blacklight, etc.

M Roman numeral for 1,000, as in cost per thousand (CPM), as used in marketing, media, and printing terms.

MAB See *Magazine Advertising Bureau*.

machine composition The setting of type by mechanical means, as opposed to setting type by hand.

mackle A blurred or double impression made in printing.

Madison Avenue 1. The highly publicized street in New York City that has become a synonym for the home of the advertising agencies, although few major agencies are still on Madison Avenue. 2. Loosely, the advertising agency business.

Madisonese The jargon of advertising.

magazine 1. A periodical that contains stories, articles, special features, advertising, and so on. It may be specialized or designed for the general reader. It usually includes a great deal of color work and bears a superior production quality to newspapers.

Magazine Advertising Bureau (MAB) An organization that promotes magazines as an advertising medium. See *Magazine Publishers Association*.

magazine concept 1. A format for a television or radio program; several feature segments on various topics are broadcast within a program, similar to the format used in magazines. 2. The idea of a radio or television program having commercials by two or more advertisers rather than using program sponsorship. Also **magazine format**.

magazine format See previous.

magazine group An organization that publishes more than one magazine.

magazine plan A plan by which advertising aimed at a certain geographical zone can be placed in magazines for distribution only in that zone.

Magazine Publishers Association (MPA) An organization of magazine publishers whose purposes are to promote magazines both as a means of improving readers' lives and as an advertising medium and to supply its members with information and services. The Magazine Advertising Bureau is its sales arm.

magazine supplement A preprinted tabloid or magazine-size supplement distributed in newspapers, usually in Saturday or Sunday editions.

magic bullet The theory that exposure to the mass media has an effect on audiences through a significant feature of the message.

magnetic track A sound track recorded on a magnetic strip on the border of a motion picture film. Also **mag track**. See *optical track*.

mag track See previous.

mail-ballot map A map prepared through returns from a mail survey questionnaire.

mail dates The dates on which a mailing list user has the obligation—by prior agreement with the list owner—to mail a specific list. No other date is acceptable without express approval of the list owner.

mailer   1. A direct mail advertiser. 2. A printed direct mail advertising piece. See *self-mailer*. 3. A promotional brochure, media kit, etc., sent by radio and television stations to advertisers, advertising agencies, station representatives, and so on. 4. A folding carton, wrapper, or tube used to protect materials in the mail.

mailing   A large number of brochures, circulars, letters, fliers, and so on, mailed at one time to potential buyers.

mailing list   The names and addresses of individuals or companies having in common a specific interest, characteristic, or activity; used for direct mail solicitation. Also **list**.

mailing list broker   A specialist who makes the necessary arrangements for one company to make use of the lists of another company. A broker's services may include research, selection, recommendation, and subsequent evaluation. Also **list broker**.

mailing list buyer   One who orders mailing lists for a one-time or frequent use. Also **list buyer**.

mailing list cleaning   The process of correcting or removing a name or address from a mailing list because it is no longer correct or required. Also used in the identification and elimination of house list duplication.

mailing list compiler   One who develops lists of names and addresses from directories, newspapers, public records, sales slips, trade-show registrations, and other sources for identifying groups of people or companies with something in common. Also **list compiler**.

mailing list exchange   A barter arrangement between two companies for the use of mailing lists. The arrangement may be list for list, list for space, or list for comparable value other than money. Also **list exchange**.

mailing list guarantee   An assurance to a mailing list buyer that a certain percentage

of the names and addresses on the mailing list will be current and deliverable.

mailing list maintenance   A manual, mechanical, or electronic system for keeping name and address records (with or without other data) up-to-date at all times.

mailing list profile   The demographic characteristics of a mailing list.

mailing list rental   An arrangement in which a list owner furnishes a list to a mailer for a one-time use only, unless otherwise specified in advance. Also **list usage, mailing list usage, rental**.

mailing list salting   See *salting*.

mailing list sample   A group of names selected from a list to evaluate the responsiveness of that list.

mailing list segmentation   See next.

mailing list selection   The characteristics used to define smaller groups within a list. Also **mailing list segmentation**.

mailing list sequence   The order in which names and addresses appear in a list, such as postal zip code sequence, alphabetical, or chronological.

mailing list sort   The process of putting a list in a specific sequence from another sequence or from no sequence. Also **list sort**.

mailing list test   A part of a list, selected to try to determine the effectiveness of the entire list. Also **list test, test mailing**. See *mailing list sample*.

mailing list usage   See *mailing list rental*.

mailing machine   A machine that attaches labels to mailing pieces and otherwise prepares such pieces for deposit in the postal system.

mailing package   A direct mail combination consisting of an envelope, letter, promotional material, and a return postcard or envelope.

mail-in premium A premium obtained by mailing in a suitable response to the manufacturer or distributor, with or without money.

mail merge A computer program that automatically combines database information with a word processor document. Used extensively in mass mailings.

mail order An order for goods or services that is received through the mail.

Mail Order Action Line (MOAL) A service of the Direct Mail/Marketing Association that assists consumers in resolving problems with mail order purchases.

mail order advertising Advertising soliciting an order for purchase through the mail. See *direct mail advertising*.

mail order buyer A person who orders and pays for a product or service through the mail. Those who use the telephone to order from direct response advertising may be included in this category although, technically, they are not mail order buyers.

mail order house A retail company selling primarily through mail orders.

mail preference service (MPS) A service of the Direct Marketing Association whereby consumers can request to have their names removed from or added to mailing lists.

mail questionnaire A method of data collection that consists of sending a questionnaire to a respondent by mail, requesting that the respondent answer a series of questions and return the completed questionnaire by mail.

mail response list A mailing list compiled of persons who have previously purchased goods or services through the mail.

mail survey map A map of radio or television station coverage prepared with the help of solicited or unsolicited mail to the station.

main head The principal display head of a body of printed matter such as an advertisement.

majuscule A capital or uppercase letter. See *minuscule*.

make good 1. To present a commercial announcement after its scheduled time because of an error. 2. To rerun a commercial announcement because of technical difficulties the first time it was run. 3. To reprint a newspaper or magazine advertisement because of an error in running it the first time. See *bonus spot*.

makeready The process of preparing a press for printing, especially in four-color work.

makeup The arrangement of typographic and illustrative elements on a printed piece, as an advertisement or a complete magazine.

makeup restriction A restriction on an advertising layout imposed by a periodical publisher to ensure that no unsalable advertising space is created by oddly proportioned advertisements.

malice In defamation, a statement made with knowledge that it is false, or with a reckless disregard for the truth.

management 1. The combined application of prediction and control to the affairs of an organization or an operational process. 2. Loosely, the "art" of accomplishing objectives by working with subordinates. 3. The leading executives of an organization responsible for decisions of the greatest importance to the organization. Also **senior management, top management**. 4. The employees of an organization responsible for guiding its operations to the fulfillment of its objectives. See *middle management*.

management consultant An independent counselor employed by corporate management to suggest ways in which the organization's operations, plans, or personnel may be improved.

management supervisor A senior advertising agency employee responsible for managing designated accounts, and for liaison with client management. See *account supervisor*.

mandatory See next.

mandatory copy The copy legally required for inclusion on a package label, in a television commercial, or in a print advertisement. Also **mandatory**.

mandatory message The legally required information broadcast as part of a commercial message or a program, such as the products, prizes, and promotional fees paid by companies.

M and E track Music and effects track. The film tracks used for dubbing music and effects in television and motion pictures. Dialogue is recorded separately.

manufacturer's agent See *manufacturer's representative*.

manufacturer's brand A brand sold by a manufacturer rather than by a wholesaler or distributor.

manufacturer's courtesy store A retail store operated by a manufacturer for the public, for the purpose of disposing of seconds, remainders, and overruns.

manufacturer's representative A sales representative of a manufacturer, who may be either a salaried employee or a broker acting for several manufacturers on commission. Also **manufacturer's agent**.

manuscript (ms.) 1. A handwritten or typewritten copy. 2. A draft copy of the text of a book or play, as sent by its author, an agent, or an editor to a publisher, producer, or typesetter.

margin 1. The white space between the print or artwork and the edges of a page or layout. 2. The difference between cost and selling price of a product; computed either as a cash figure or as a percentage of the selling price. Also **gross margin**, **markup**.

mark A device or expression that can be registered under the Trademark Act of 1946. See *certification mark*, *collective mark*, *service mark*, *trademark*.

markdown A reduction in price to promote increased sales.

market 1. A population, group, industry, geographic area, etc., regarded as a source of current or potential demand for a product or service. Also **marketplace**. 2. A place where goods are bought and sold (e.g., supermarket). 3. The extent of demand for a product or service. 4. To offer a product or service for sale.

market-by-market allocation (MBM) See *area-by-area allocation*.

market clustering The tying together of similar products, such as books, records, and tapes, to decrease the total cost of advertising and distribution.

market development 1. Loosely, a product's, service's, or category's rate of usage in markets and market segments to which it is available. 2. The number of units or dollar value of all brands of a product or service category that have been sold per thousand population in an area in a stated period. Also **category development**. See *brand development*.

market development index (MDI) The ratio between a local market development rate and the national rate; used as an indicator of category or brand sales potential. Also **category development index**, **market index**. See *brand development index*.

marketer An individual or organization that offers a product or service for sale.

market index See *market development index*.

marketing The business activities that affect the distribution and sales of goods and services from producer to consumer; including product or service development, pricing, packaging, advertising, merchandising, and distribution.

Marketing Communications Executives International (MCEI) An association of advertising and public relations people in all facets of the industry.

marketing concept See *marketing plan*.

marketing director An employee of a manufacturer or mass service organization responsible for review and approval of marketing plans; may include responsibility for sales management.

marketing mix The levels and interplay of the constituent elements of a product's or service's marketing efforts, including product features, pricing, packaging, advertising, merchandisng, distribution, and marketing budget, especially as decisions relating to these elements affect sales results.

marketing plan 1. A strategy devised for marketing a product or service. Also **marketing concept**. 2. A comprehensive document containing background and supportive details for a marketer's objectives and strategies. Also **plan**.

marketing research The systematic gathering, recording, analyzing, and use of data used to promote the marketing of goods and services.

marketing research director See *research director*.

market mapping study A market research study that depicts key groupings of consumers or their product or service attitudes graphically. Also **perceptual mapping study**. See *market structure study*.

market pattern The pattern of concentration of purchases of a product in a general or specific market. A pattern of extensive purchasing by the market as a whole (**thick market pattern**) or of meager purchasing by the market as a whole (**thin market pattern**) often appears.

market penetration The degree of usage of a product, service, or category among current users.

marketplace See *market*.

market position The reputation, or lack thereof, of a company or brand as seen by members of the community. See *image*.

market potential The sales volume for a product or service that may be attained. It is influenced by category development and is often expressed in terms of share of market. See *brand potential index*, *headroom*.

market profile A summary of the characteristics of a market, including information on typical purchasers and competitors and often general information on the economy and retailing patterns of the area.

Market Research Corporation of America (MRCA) A consumer research organization specializing in continuous syndicated reporting of food and drug buying habits and usage patterns on the basis of diaries kept by a consumer panel.

market response The sales consequences of the stimulation provided by marketing spending.

market segment See *segment*.

market segmentation See *segmentation*.

market share The percentage of a product category's sales, in terms of dollars or units, obtained by a brand, line, or company.

market structure study A market research study that seeks to isolate the critical factors (demographic, attitudinal, etc.) that determine the patterns of consumer behavior toward a category of goods. See *market mapping study*.

market testing The selection of a geographic location (or locations) to test the viability of a product or service before full-scale marketing is begun. See *sales area test, test market.*

markup 1. The difference between the price at which a product is purchased for resale and the price at which it is sold, figured either in dollars or as a percentage of the purchase price. 2. An increase in price. 3. See *margin.* 4. The written instructions to a typesetter on manuscript copy for typeface, size,width, etc.

marriage See *composite.*

marriage split An arrangement between or among advertisers to purchase jointly a certain space in different regional editions of a nationally distributed periodical, with the advertisements of each appearing in the copies delivered to their respective areas of the country.

masked-identification test A test of advertising memorability in which respondents attempt to identify advertisers or brands in advertisements in which brand names and trademarks are masked out.

masking shot See *matte shot.*

mask out To cover an area or detail so that it will not appear in a photograph.

mass display A display of a retail product set up in a store, apart from the product's usual shelf display.

mass magazine A magazine edited for the general public.

mass market A large number of undifferentiated prospective consumers of products or services.

mass media The various vehicles used for sending advertising messages and general news and information to a mass audience, including radio, television, cable television, magazines, newspapers, etc.

Mass Media Bureau A division of the Federal Communications Commission, formed by the merger of the Broadcast Bureau and the Cable Television Bureau.

mass merchandiser A retail outlet or chain handling three or more general merchandise lines in a store of at least 10,000 square feet of space. They often evolve from discount stores; such outlets cultivate a discount image through advertising, promotion, and pricing policies.

mass publication A periodical with a large, general circulation.

mass transportation A system of public conveyance such as buses, streetcars, trains, subways, and rapid transit.

master A film, videotape, disc, etc., of all elements of a performance in complete and final form to be used as an original for reproduction and release.

master contract See *blanket contract.*

master control The central control facility of a television or radio station.

master copy 1. A recording made in as few generations as possible and used as the highest quality finished product available. 2. Artwork that is camera ready.

master newspaper list A complete list of daily newspapers or of those newspapers used by an advertiser, for planning or ordering advertising space; usually includes rate and circulation data. See *mock newspaper schedule.*

master of ceremonies (emcee) (MC) An individual who acts as a host on a radio or television program.

master positive A positive film print from which duplicate negatives are made.

master script See *shooting script.*

master station A network origination control point.

master tape An edited audiotape or videotape complete with all elements to be recorded on quantity prints or dubs.

masthead The standing heading of a newspaper or magazine, usually located on the editorial page, that contains the name, ownership, management, subscription rates, place of publication, and so on. See *flag*.

mat 1. A cardboard cutout used to mount artwork. 2. See *matrix*. 3. See *matte*.

mat board Illustration board with a matte finish used for graphics.

match In direct mail, the typing of addresses, salutations, or inserts onto letters with other copy imprinted by a printing process.

match action cutting The editing of camera shots so that continuity is maintained between the shots.

matchbook covers An advertising medium employing the exterior and occasionally interior faces of the safety card used on matches; usually dispensed at no charge.

match dissolve A dissolve in which the principal figures or objects in the close of the preceding scene appear in the same positions in the new one.

matched groups Groups used for testing purposes that have similar demographic characteristics. See *control group*.

matched sample A statistical sample identical to one or more others in significant respects.

material terms 1. The factors that are significant in defining the operation of a contest. 2. The omission of pertinent facts, misleading information, and so on.

matrix 1. A sheet of fibrous material used as a mold for casting a letterpress plate for a print advertisement. It is less expensive to mail to a number of publications than an actual duplicate plate. Also **mat**. 2. A mold from which a letterpress type character is cast. Also **mat**. 3. An array of numbers arranged in rows and columns.

matrix algebra A system of mathematical axioms and operations used for work with matrices; essential in the development and understanding of multivariate statistical analysis.

mat service A company that produces matrices for advertisements, borders, pictures, public relations material, and so forth, and supplies them to newspapers.

mat shot See *matte shot*.

matte 1. Not glossy; without strong highlights (a matte finish). 2. See *mat*.

matte out To eliminate a portion of a picture.

matte shot A camera shot made with a matte or mask in part of the frame to allow another shot to be printed in the opaque area (a shot taken through a keyhole uses this technique). Also **masking shot**, **mat shot**.

mature stage See *product life cycle*.

maxiline See next.

maximil The milline rate of a newspaper before any discounts. Also **maxiline**. See *minimil*.

maximum depth requirement The maximum length of a periodical advertisement of less than a full column length allowed to pay less than a full column space rate.

MBM See *market-by-market allocation*.

MC See *master of ceremonies*.

MCEI See *Marketing Communications Executives International*.

McKittrick's Directory A quarterly guide to advertising agencies, their personnel, and their accounts.

MCU See *medium close-up*.

MDI See *market development index*.

MDT Mountain Daylight Time. See *time zone*.

mean The arithmetic mean, the most common of the three means (arithmetic, geometric, and harmonic); a value computed by adding the values in a group together and dividing the resulting total by the number of values in that group. See *average, median. mode.*

measure See *line length.*

measurement technique A method used to measure radio and television audiences, such as a meter, diary, telephone coincidental, and so on.

measuring stick See *line gauge.*

mechanical A final layout of art, copy, and so on, ready for the engraver or printer; camera ready copy. See *keyline, pasteup.*

mechanical animation See *animation.*

mechanical binding A plastic spiral, metal ring, or other device used to bind pages of a catalog, notebook, and the like.

mechanical department The department of a magazine or newspaper that sets type, makes plates, and prints the issue or edition.

mechanical requirements The layout and makeup specifications of a periodical to which prepared advertising printing material must conform.

media Plural of **medium**; vehicles used to convey information, entertainment, news, and advertising messages to an audience. Includes radio, television, cable television, newspapers, magazines, outdoor boards, car cards, and so on.

media association An organization of individuals or companies formed to promote a particular mass medium, such as the National Association of Broadcasters and the American Newspaper Publishers Association.

media buy The purchase of time or space in an advertising medium.

media buyer An advertising agency employee who recommends time, availability, and space in media schedules for clients and buys advertising space or time in communications media. Also **buyer**.

media coverage The reach of an advertising schedule, expressed as a percentage of the target audience.

media department An advertising agency department that schedules advertising campaigns and buys the appropriate space or time.

media director An employee of an advertising agency responsible for supervising the selection and purchase of space and time in communications media for a client's advertising efforts.

media generation The people who have grown up with the media; those who cannot remember the time before television.

media kit An advertising sales folder; usually contains a rate card, survey results, information about the station or periodical, and other sales literature.

media market The geographic area covered by the medium being used or measured. See *market.*

Mediamark Research, Inc., (MRI) A company that provides a widely used, nationally syndicated consumer database; a source of information about demographics, media exposure, and product consumption.

media mix 1. The use of two or more of the mass media to advertise or promote a product or service. 2. A record of the media time or space bought during a campaign or specific period. Also **media schedule**.

median A measure of central tendency; that value above which and below which half of the values in the set fall. See *average, mean, mode.*

media objectives The statement of specific goals of an advertising campaign.

media plan A sales plan designed to select the proper demographics for an advertising campaign through proper media selection. See *marketing plan*.

Media Records, Inc. A research organization that publishes reports of major advertisers' advertising volume in daily and Sunday newspapers, given by newspaper in agate lines and total dollar expenditures (by brand, if indicated).

media representative A salesperson who works for a newspaper or magazine, radio or television station or network, or outdoor company. Also **media salesperson**. See *station representative*.

media salesperson See previous.

media schedule See *media mix*.

Mediastat See next.

Media Statistics, Inc. (Mediastat) An audience research organization.

media strategy A plan of action by an advertiser or its agency for bringing advertising messages to the attention of consumers through the use of appropriate media.

media survey A survey of the extent to which specific communications media reach specific markets and audiences.

media synergism The use of the electronic media to add impact to the message of the print media, or vice versa.

media translation An adaptation of a media spending plan from a national to a local level, or vice versa, as for testing purposes. See *as-it-falls method, correct increment method, little America method*.

media vehicle See *vehicle*.

Mediawatch An electronic monitoring system devised by the Arbitron Company that measures network, spot, and syndicated programming and cable television

commercial spots 24 hours a day in the top 75 markets.

media weight The number and size or length of advertisements, or the total audience delivery level, produced by an advertising effort.

medium See *media*.

medium close shot See next.

medium close-up (MCU) A camera shot between a close-up and a medium shot. Also **medium close shot**.

medium long shot (MLS) A camera shot between a medium shot and a long shot.

medium shot (MS) A camera shot approximately halfway between a close-up and a long shot. Also **mid shot**.

mental set A pre-existing attitude or belief that conditions a person's responses to new situations and ideas.

merchandise mix 1. The basic variety of stock of a distributor. 2. By item or sales, the various products and package sizes of a given brand, category, or marketer. Also **mix**. See *product line*.

merchandise pack A package of a retail product that offers a premium, which is usually enclosed. See *in-pack premium*.

merchandising 1. A sales or promotional activity directed toward stimulating interest in a product or advertising campaign. 2. The activity of a station or network or periodical that helps an advertiser promote a product or service in addition to the advertising. 3. The solicitation of salesperson and retailer support for a marketing effort. The term *merchandising* is often used interchangeably with *marketing*.

merchandising allowance See *promotion allowance*.

merchandising committee A committee appointed by a store chain, wholesaler, etc., to decide on the acceptance of new products, manufacturer's promotions, etc. Also **buying committee**.

merchandising director An employee of a manufacturer, advertising agency, distributor, or retailer responsible for planning and implementing retail selling efforts.

merchandising service A service offered, usually free of direct charge, by a communications medium to help in promoting an advertiser's products or ad campaign to distributors or retailers or to gather marketing information of interest to the advertiser.

merge-purge To join different mailing lists and automatically remove identical names.

message research An analysis of print or broadcast mass media content.

meter A device used for recording the periods when a television set is in use, and, usually, the channel to which it is tuned. See *Arbitron*, *Audimeter*. 2. A device used in research for measuring consumer and audience behavior in terms of mechanical or physiological responses.

metered market service A meter-based local market television audience measurement service that A.C. Nielsen operates in New York, Los Angeles, Chicago, San Francisco, Philadelphia, Detroit, and other markets.

methodology The study and principles underlying development of research design and analysis.

metro See next.

metro area A Metropolitan Statistical Area as defined by the Office of Management and Budget; sometimes refers to an area geographically broader or narrower than the corresponding MSA. Used in estimating household ratings and audience shares. Also **metro**. See *Metropolitan Statistical Area*.

metropolitan area See previous.

metropolitan daily A daily newspaper published in a large city.

Metropolitan Statistical Area (MSA) An urban area with a population of at least 50,000. Designated by the Office of Management and Budget for statistical reporting purposes and used in audience measurement studies. MSA is generally synonymous with the former term Standard Metropolitan Statistical Area. See *Consolidated Metropolitan Statistical Area*, *Primary Metropolitan Statistical Area*.

metro rating A rating computed for the households or individuals in a well-defined metropolitan area; normally, the Metropolitan Statistical Area.

metro rating area (MRA) A separate reporting area where Arbitron reports television household ratings, shares, and households using television.

metro share The television households in the metro area tuned to a specific station as a percentage of metro area television households with a receiver turned on.

metro survey area (MSA) An area generally corresponding to a metropolitan statistical area and subject to exceptions dictated by historical industry usage and other marketing considerations.

middle break 1. A commercial break in the middle of a radio or television program. 2. A station identification made at or near the midpoint of a radio or television program.

middle majority The lower-middle and upper-lower classes of American society; constitutes about two-thirds of the total population.

middleman A selling factor involved in the distribution chain between growers, fabricators, or manufacturers, and consumers; especially wholesalers. Also **intermediary**.

middle management The executives who are responsible to senior management for the day-to-day administration and operation of an organization.

middle-of-the-road (MOR) A radio station format characterized by popular music other than country and western, folk, jazz, rock, and so on. See *format*.

midpoint The halfway point of a number of steps in statistics into which a total range of values has been divided. See *median*.

mid shot See *medium shot*.

milking strategy A marketing strategy designed to extract greatest possible profit, rather than sales potential, from a product or service; usually designed to generate funds to be invested in other ventures believed to have greater long-range profit potential. Also **profit-taking strategy**.

millimeter (mm) A metric unit equal to one-thousandth of a meter or 0.03937 inch; standard size films are measured in millimeters of width.

milline An agate line of advertising space in one million copies of a publication.

milline rate A figure used to determine the cost-effectiveness of advertising in a newspaper; reached by multiplying the cost per agate line by one million, then dividing by the circulation. See *tru-line rate*.

Mimeograph™ A stencil duplicating machine. Often used generically.

minimil The milline rate of a newspaper after all possible discounts for space and frequency purchases. Also **minimilline**. See *maximil*.

minimilline See previous.

minimum depth requirement A newspaper requirement that advertisements have a certain proportion of depth to width, usually one inch per column.

minimum frequency A level of exposure to or scheduling of advertising that is believed to represent the lowest level at which the advertising will be effective in attaining its ends, while permitting the greatest degree of advertising continuity.

minimum reporting standards The standard minimum requirements (minimum amounts of listening during a survey) that a radio or television station must meet in a given market to be listed in the report of that market.

minor sponsor A sponsor who presents only one of the commercials on a radio or television program.

minuscule A small or lowercase letter. See *majuscule*.

minute-by-minute profile An estimate of the varying numbers of listeners to a radio or television program at closely spaced periods during the program; used to determine the most advantageous times for scheduling commercials.

mirror shot A camera shot of an image in a reflecting surface.

misleading advertising See *false advertising*.

misprint A typographical error made by a typesetter. See *printer's error*.

misredemption The redemption of coupons presented either by persons who have not made the purchases the coupons are intended to promote, or by retailers who have not redeemed the coupons in the normal course of business with properly qualified customers.

missionary salesperson 1. A sales representative employed by a marketer to make contact with prospects who currently are not purchasing its products. Also **pioneer salesperson**. 2. Loosely, a detailer.

mist shot A camera shot taken through gauze or one that is slightly out of focus.

mix 1. The selection of different media for an advertising campaign. 2. The re-recording of separate visual and audio elements on a film or tape to produce a master. 3. The number of original performances and reruns of a television series included in a contract. 4. See *merchandise mix*. 5. To combine electrically any two sound or video sources.

mix-and-match sale A sale at which the customer is allowed to select a certain number of assorted items for a fixed price.

mixdown A technique used to reduce multitrack recordings to one track.

mixed media The use of two or more media in a program or presentation, such as slides and tapes or sound effects, rear screen projection, live performers, and so on. Also **multimedia**.

MLS See *medium long shot*.

mm See *millimeter*.

MNA See *multinetwork area*.

mnemonic An acronym, symbol, or other mental device used to assist human memory.

MOAL See *Mail Order Action Line*.

mobile unit 1. A car, truck, or trailer equipped with facilities to originate a remote broadcast. Also **remote unit**. 2. Research facilities that can be moved to desired interviewing sites, such as shopping centers.

mock newspaper schedule A selective list of daily U.S. newspapers, chosen for their high milline rate and coverage and arranged in the population order of their communities; used to facilitate mass purchasing of advertising space. See *master newspaper list*.

mock-up A full-scale representation of an object, building, room, commercial product, and so on; often used in the making of television programs and motion picture.

mockup 1. A rough sketch or design for artwork. See *rough*. 2. A layout for a brochure or booklet. See *dummy*, *rough*.

mode 1. That point in a statistical measurement where the greatest number of values lie. 2. The highest point of a histogram or bar graph; a measure of central tendency. See *average*, *mean*, *median*.

model 1. A more or less closely imitative representation of an object, scene, etc., at reduced scale, often used for planning camera shots and talent movement. 2. A person retained to appear on camera or before a live audience to demonstrate a process or merchandise, especially apparel. 3. A mathematical representation of a set of relationships or principles.

modeling light An illumination that reveals the depth, shape, and texture of a subject.

model release See *release*.

modular agency See *à la carte agency*.

moiré 1. A wavy, patterned effect in a halftone illustration, often caused by making a halftone from a halftone print. 2. A design produced by the irregular pattern of two superimposed, regularly patterned screens. So named because of its resemblance to the light and dark patterns seen in watered silk fabric.

molding A trim strip of metal, wood, or plastic surrounding an outdoor advertising panel.

monaural Pertaining to single-channel audio, as opposed to stereophonic or quadraphonic. Also **mono**.

monitor 1. A high-quality television receiver used in a control room or studio to review a performance in progress. 2. To check the timing, program content, and commercial content of a television or radio show. 3. Loosely, to inspect periodically.

mono See *monaural*, *monotone*.

monochromatic Pertaining to a single color.

monotone See *black and white*. Also **mono**.

montage 1. A combination of juxtaposed or superimposed images, used in photography, layout design, motion pictures, and television as a means of giving a succinct impression of a complex subject, of time elapsed, etc. See *photomontage*. 2. A rapid sequence of varying sounds.

month's supply The size of a marketer's (especially a retailer's) inventory of a product, stated as the number of months of sales at current sales rates that inventory on hand alone could provide; as defined by A.C. Nielsen Co.

mood commercial A commercial message designed to establish a particular atmosphere.

mood music The music used to establish an audience attitude or intensify atmosphere. Also **background music**, **program music**.

mood programming See *block programming*.

MOR See *middle-of-the-road*.

morning drive See *daypart*.

mortality 1. The rate of failure to complete interviews in a survey. 2. The loss of respondents to a continuing survey over a period of time.

mortise 1. A cutout made in a halftone plate so that type matter or another picture may be inserted. See *notch*. 2. To make a cutout in a halftone plate.

motion picture A series of pictures photographed with a camera on a thin, flexible plastic film and projected in a rapid sequence so as to give the illusion of motion. Also **movie**.

motivation An internal psychological state that serves as the basis for action. Also **motive**.

motivational research (MR) The application of research techniques in advertising and marketing to determine the base of brand choices and product preferences.

motive See *motivation*.

movie See *motion picture*.

Moviola™ A film-editing machine. The term has become generic and is applied to many devices that are capable of synchronizing pictures and sound.

MPA See *Magazine Publishers Association*, *multiple product announcement*.

MPS See *mail preference service*.

MR See *motivational research*.

MRA See *metro rating area*.

MRCA See *Market Research Corporation of America*.

MRI See *Mediamark Research, Inc*.

ms. See *manuscript*.

MS See *medium shot*.

MSA See *Metropolitan Statistical Area*, *metro survey area*, *Nielsen Market Section Audiences*.

mss. Manuscripts.

MST Mountain Standard Time. See *time zone*.

MSU A Canadian term for 1,000 standard units; used as an arbitrary measurement for the wholesale sale of a product in various unit sizes.

mug shot See *head shot*.

multimedia See *mixed media*.

multimedia survey A survey that secures information from a respondent about the activity of a household or individual with respect to two or more media.

multinetwork area (MNA) A compilation of television markets used by Nielsen's Television Index to provide estimates of television audiences on a geographic base where all three national networks have approximately comparable facilities.

multinetwork area rating An audience rating given by A.C. Nielsen to network program performance in those cities where all three networks are represented.

multiple correlation See *correlation*.

multiple insertion The use of two or more enclosures in a direct mailing.

multiple pricing The offering of more than one retail unit for sale at a single unit price (e.g., two for $1).

multiple processing The Nielsen procedure used to remove duplicate viewing within the same household for program or HUT computation.

multiple product announcement (MPA) A commercial in which two or more products or services are presented as a unit. See *integrated commercial, piggyback unit*.

multiple regression analysis A statistical method for predicting variation in a dependent variable through analysis of a number of independent variables involved with it.

multiple-set television households (multiset TVHH) An Arbitron estimate of the number of television households with more than one television receiver, based on information obtained from diaries.

multiple sound track A group of sound tracks recorded side by side; used for stereophonic, quadraphonic, or multiple audio track recording.

multiple sponsorship The dividing of the cost of a television or radio program between or among different, noncompetitive advertisers. See *sponsor*.

multiple unit sale A sale involving more than one item.

multiplex Relating to a system of transmitting several messages simultaneously on the same circuit or channel.

multiset household A household with two or more radio or television receivers. See *multiple-set television households*.

multiset TVHH See *multiple-set television households*.

multispot plan A package rate for commercials on radio or television.

multistation lineup A group of radio or television stations in a single market area that carry the commercials of an advertiser.

multivariate analysis The simultaneous measurement and assessment for interference of statistical relationships within or between sets of variables.

Multi-Vision See *Tri-Vision*.

musical clock A type of radio program consisting of music, news, weather reports, and frequent references to time. Usually broadcast in the early morning.

musical format A radio station format under the general heading of music. Subheadings vary, and few agree about definitions; they may include middle-of-the-road, top 40, rock, easy listening, classical, country and western, religious, jazz, rhythm and blues, and so on. See *format*.

musical ID See next.

musical logo A musical signature associated with a product, advertiser, program, or station. Also **musical ID, musical signature**. See *logotype*.

musical signature See previous.

music and effects track See *M and E track*.

music bed A musical background used for commercials, transitions, station breaks, and so on. See *bed*.

music bridge   A musical transition.

music clearance   The securing of rights to use a copyrighted musical selection. See *clearance*.

music track   The optical or magnetic track of a film or videotape on which music is recorded.

mutton quad   See *em quad*.

n The number of respondents in a sample or subsample.

NA See *no answer, not available.*

NAB See *National Association of Broadcasters, Newspaper Advertising Bureau, Inc.*

NAB code A code of standards for commercial time, program content, etc., established by the National Association of Broadcasters.

NAC See *national audience composition, net advertising circulation.*

NAD See *National Advertising Division, national audience demographics report, Nielsen Audience Demographic Report.*

NAEA See *Newspaper Advertising Executives Association.*

name A single entry on a mailing list.

name acquisition The technique of soliciting response to obtain names and addresses for a mailing list.

nameplate See *flag.*

name removal service A portion of the mail preference service offered by Direct Marketing Association; consumers fill in and return a form requesting that their names be removed from all mailing lists used by participating members of the DMA and other direct mail users.

NARB See *National Advertising Review Board.*

NARTB See *National Association of Radio and Television Broadcasters.*

NASA See *National Advertising Sales Association.*

national advertising Advertising serving a common objective, delivered to a nationwide market, and generally placed by an advertising agency.

national advertising rate A periodical or broadcast advertising rate charged by local media for advertising placed by national advertisers; customarily higher than the rate for local advertisers.

National Advertising Review Board (NARB) An advertising industry organization that provides self-regulatory review and approval of advertising proposed for use in any medium.

National Advertising Sales Association (NASA) An organization for the promotion and development of newspaper advertising, founded in 1907. Formerly the American Association of Newspaper Representatives, Inc.

national Arbitron rating A television rating of national audience size made by the Arbitron Company.

National Association of Broadcasters (NAB) A major voluntary commercial broadcasting association founded in 1923. NAB promulgates self-regulatory codes, represents the industry to government, and offers services to members.

National Association of Radio and Television Broadcasters (NARTB) The former name of the National Association of Broadcasters.

National Association of Television Program Executives (NATPE) An organization that seeks to contribute to the improvement of television programming by providing a forum for discussion of ideas and exchange of information concerning programming, production, and related fields.

National Association of Transportation Advertising See *Transit Advertising Association*.

national audience composition (NAC) A *Nielsen Television Index* persons sample that provides estimates of audiences to television and network programs.

national audience demographics report (NAD) A statement from *Nielsen Television Index* that provides estimates of television usage and sponsored network program audiences in terms of both households and persons by household market divisions.

National Business Publications (NBP) See *American Business Press*.

National Cable Television Association (NCTA) The major association of cable television operators in the United States, founded in 1952.

National Editorial Association (NEA) The former name of the National Newspaper Association.

National Industrial Advertisers' Association (NIAA) An association of advertisers, agencies, and communications media formed for the purpose of promoting industrial advertising and marketing.

National Newspaper Association (NNA) An organization of small-town newspaper editors, founded in 1885; formerly National Editorial Association.

National Opinion Research Center (NORC) An academic research organization at the University of Chicago that investigates public opinion; occasionally conducts studies for private clients.

National Outdoor Advertising Bureau (NOAB) A cooperatively owned national organization used by advertising agencies to buy and service outdoor advertising campaigns. It maintains a national field staff to inspect outdoor advertising structures.

national plan A strategy for a nationwide marketing effort.

national rate The rate charged by a communications medium for advertising nationwide. Also **general rate**. See *local rate*, *regional rate*.

national rating A rating calculated for a television or radio network or program across the United States.

National Research Institute (NRI) An audience research organization.

national sales The purchase of time by national advertisers on a local radio or television station through advertising agencies or station representatives. See *local sales*.

national spot 1. The advertising time purchased by a national advertiser. 2. The broadcast station availability sold through national sales.

NATPE See National Association of Television Program Executives.

NBI See *Nielsen Broadcast Index*.

NBP National Business Publications. See *American Business Press*.

NCH See *Nielsen Clearing House*.

NCS See *Nielsen Coverage Service*.

NCSA See *noncommercial spot announcement*.

NCTA See *National Cable Television Association*.

NDI See *Nielsen Drug Index*.

NEA See *National Editorial Association*.

near pack display A receptacle used to hold and display near pack premiums.

near pack event A promotion making use of a near pack premium.

near pack premium A premium item offered free or for a discounted price with the retail purchase of another product and positioned close to, but not touching, this product at the point of sale.

negative appeal An advertising message that does not promote the good qualities of the product or service, but rather intimidates the audience with the consequences of not using the product or service.

negative correlation See *correlation*.

negative option A buying plan in which a customer or club member receives regular announcements of records, tapes, books, or other products and agrees to accept and pay for them or notify the company not to ship within a reasonable time after each announcement.

negative space The white space around artwork or in photographs.

neighborhood showing A closely spaced group of posters advertising a product or service available in the same neighborhood.

nemo An acronym for **not emanating main office** or **not emanating main origination**. A remote broadcast.

neon See *neon light*.

neonized bulletin An outdoor advertising display using neon tubes.

neon lamp See next.

neon light A transparent tube filled with an inert gas such as neon which, when electrified, emits a brightly colored light; usually bent tubes are used to form advertising signs. Also **neon, neon lamp, neon tube**. See *neonized bulletin*.

neon tube See previous.

nesting In direct mail advertising, placing one enclosure within another before the contents are inserted into an envelope.

net A quantity remaining from a gross amount after suitable deductions. See *gross, net cost*.

net advertising circulation See *net circulation*.

net audience See *reach*.

net circulation The total number of persons passing an outdoor advertisement in a given period who face the advertisement easily. Also **net advertising circulation**. See *gross circulation*.

net controlled circulation The number of purchased and unpurchased copies of a controlled-circulation publication that are actually distributed to the intended readership.

net cost 1. The cost of a service provided by an advertising agency, aside from the agency commission. Also **net**. 2. An advertising rate applied after deduction of applicable discounts, the agency commission included. Also **net, net plus**.

net effective distribution See *effective distribution*.

net name arrangement An agreement between a list owner and a list user at the time of ordering, or before, in which the list owner agrees to accept adjusted payment if fewer than the agreed-on number of names are shipped.

net orders processed (NOP) See *net sales*.

net paid The number of copies of a newspaper or magazine, less the number unsold, held back, defective, and so on, that are actually paid for.

net paid circulation The net circulation of a periodical for which not less than 50 percent of the newsstand or subscription price has been paid; a minimum set by the Audit Bureau of Circulations.

net plus See *net cost*.

net profit The difference between the price obtained by the seller of an item and all costs incurred by the seller for the transaction, including the cost of purchasing or producing the item sold; expressed in terms of dollars or as a percentage of dollar sales, before or after taxes. See *margin*.

net rating The percentage of the total potential audience to which a television or radio program, commercial, etc., is exposed, as expressed after audience duplication is deducted. See *reach*.

net rating point (NRP) A single percent of the cumulative audience, a specified group of either television households or individuals residing in a specified area estimated to be in the audience at least once during two or more time periods; used in expressing a net rating. See *gross rating point*.

net reach The number of different people reached by a given schedule. Availabe through Arbitron Information on Demand, net reach is reported for single station and multiple station schedules. See *cumulative audience, reach*.

net sales The quantity of items sold, or the amount received for these items, after all adjustments and returns. Also **net orders processed**.

net unduplicated audience The actual number of persons exposed to advertising, regardless of how many exposures each person may have. See *cumulative audience, gross audience, reach*.

net weekly audience The number of persons or households that tune in at least once a week to a television or radio program that is aired more than once a week.

net weekly circulation The number of persons or households that have tuned in to a specific radio or television (noncable) station for at least five consecutive minutes in a given week. See *significantly viewed*.

network 1. A national or regional organization distributing radio or television programs for a substantial part of each broadcast day to stations for simultaneous broadcasting, generally by interconnection facilities. 2. A group of independent and generally noncompeting advertising agencies that exchange ideas, information, and services. Also **agency group**, **agency network**.

network affiliate See *affiliate*.

network clipping The illegal practice of a broadcast station deleting the end of a commercial or network program.

network compensation The money paid to affiliates by radio and television networks for carrying programs and commercials. See *reverse compensation*.

network continuity department A television or radio network's continuity acceptance department.

network feed The transmission of a network program to affiliated stations by microwave or wire. The feed may be aired live or taped for later broadcast.

network franchise See *franchise*.

network identification An announcement identifying a television or radio network, made at the beginning or end of a network broadcast; also used as a cue to affiliates.

networking The organization of television or radio stations and the scheduling of programs for the purpose of network broadcasting.

network option time See *option time*.

network program A program delivered simultaneously to more than one broadcast station, regional or national, commercial or noncommercial.

Network Program Analysis (NPA) An Arbitron term for an analysis of the network television programs broadcast during the major sweep periods.

network programming The programming supplied by a national or regional network, whether commercial or noncommercial.

network programs by DMA report A compilation by *Nielsen Station Index* of the market-by-market audience estimates for network programs.

network station See *affiliate*.

network time See *option time*.

neuro-linguistic programming A theory of communication, used in consumer research, stating that people use various modes to understand the world: the visual mode, the sound mode, and the kinesthetic (emotional) mode. Researchers read what type a respondent is by calling up childhood memories and observing eye movements, breathing patterns, and other signals.

new business rep 1. An advertising agency employee or principal responsible for developing new agency clients. 2. A salesperson responsible for making initial sales. Also **pioneer salesperson**.

new product 1. In law, a product that has been in distribution, available to its ultimate consumer, for less than six months. 2. A product bearing a new brand name, or a newly introduced flanker item or line extension; occasionally used loosely to refer to an improved product of an existing brand, or a new size.

news hole The amount of space available in a newspaper for news after the space necessary for advertising has been determined.

newsletter A periodical, usually letter size and without advertising.

newspaper 1. A periodical that contains news, opinions, features, advertising, and so on, usually distributed on a daily or weekly basis. 2. An organization that publishes a newspaper.

Newspaper Advertising Bureau, Inc. (NAB) An association of daily newspapers that promotes the use of newspapers and supplements as an advertising medium.

Newspaper Advertising Executives Association (NAEA) The former name of the International Newspaper Advertising Executives.

newspaper chain See next.

newspaper group An organization that owns two or more newspapers in different markets. Also **newspaper chain, newspaper syndicate**.

newspaper syndicate See previous.

newsprint An inexpensive, machine-finished paper usually made from soft, coarse wood pulp and used for newspapers.

news release See *release*.

newsstand circulation The sale of a periodical through retail outlets, rather than by subscription; usually considered with respect to the total number of issues sold in this manner, or the percentage of the total relative to total circulation.

next to reading matter (NR) (NRM) The position of advertising matter placed next to text instead of other advertising. See *preferred position*.

NFI See *Nielsen Food Index*.

NG No good; a notation used in editing rejections, as of a recording on film or tape. See *OK*.

NHI See *Nielsen HomeVideo Index*.

NIAA See *National Industrial Advertisers' Association*.

***Nielsen Audience Demographic Report* (NAD)** A publication of A.C. Nielsen that gives data on television audiences, analyzed according to sex, age group, and other demographic characteristics, for each program or time period.

Nielsen Broadcast Index (NBI) The Canadian counterpart of the *Nielsen Station Index* in the United States.

Nielsen Clearing House (NCH) A division of A.C. Nielsen that administers the processing of store-redeemed coupons for contracted clients.

Nielsen Company See *A.C. Nielsen Company*.

Nielsen Coverage Service (NCS) A service of A.C. Nielsen that supplies audience data for television stations on a county-to-county basis.

Nielsen Drug Index (NDI) A syndicated market research service of A.C.Nielsen that measures product distribution, inventories, sales, and share of market on a bimonthly basis in drug and mass merchandising stores, on a nationally projectable basis.

Nielsen Food Index (NFI) A syndicated market research service of A.C. Nielsen that measures product distribution, inventories, sales, and share of market on a bimonthly basis in retail food stores, on a nationally projectable basis.

Nielsen HomeVideo Index (NHI) A division of Nielsen's Media Research Group responsible for syndicated and nonsyndicated measurement of cable, pay cable, VCRs, video discs, and other television technologies.

Nielsen Market Section Audiences (MSA) A report by *Nielsen Television Index* that provides estimates of U.S. television household usage and program average audiences for the total country and by a variety of market sections.

Nielsen Post-Buy Service (NPBS) A special analysis facility of the *Nielsen Station Index* that enables agency/advertiser clients

to analyze the audiences achieved by their network or spot schedules.

Nielsen rating A percentage of U.S. television households tuned to a particular network program during the average minute of a particular telecast, as reported by *Nielsen Television Index*.

Nielsen Station Index (NSI) A service of A.C. Nielsen's Media Research Group that provides syndicated local market television audience measurement.

Nielsen Television Index (NTI) A service of A.C. Nielsen's Media Research Group that provides audience estimates for all sponsored U.S. network television programs.

night See *daypart*.

ninety A radio or television commercial that is 90 seconds long; often noted as :90.

ninety-day cancellation The right to cancel advertising on 90 days' notice, as in outdoor advertising.

nixie An undeliverable piece of mail.

NNA See *National Newspaper Association*.

NOAB See *National Outdoor Advertising Bureau*.

no answer (NA) In research, a reason for the absence of data from a questionnaire.

no-change rate A media space or time rate offered to an advertiser that uses the same copy repeatedly.

non-ABC Referring to a periodical that does not subcribe to the Audit Bureau of Circulations.

non-ADI station A broadcast station that is not located in the major market of an Area of Dominant Influence.

non-air commercial A commercial not intended for broadcast use, such as non-broadcast audience reaction commercials, copy testing, or client demonstrations.

noncommercial broadcasting Radio and television programming that receives no advertising revenue and that is designed to serve the educational, cultural, and other needs of the community.

noncommercial program See *sustaining program*.

noncommercial radio See *noncommercial broadcasting*.

noncommercial spot announcement (NCSA) A public service announcement.

noncommercial television See *noncommercial broadcasting*.

nondirective interview An interview in which respondents' answers are unrestricted and unprompted. See *directive interview*.

non-DMA station A station that is not located in the major market of a Designated Market Area.

nonduplication The FCC rule that prohibits two commonly owned stations in the same market from programming the identical material.

nonilluminated Pertaining to an outdoor poster panel that is not artificially lighted.

nonparametric Pertaining to a set of statistical techniques not requiring rigid or stringent adherence to distribution assumptions in hypothesis testing.

nonprobability sample A nonscientific sample from which legitimate conclusions may not be drawn. Also **nonrandom sample**. See *convenience sample*.

nonprogram material A broadcast item, such as a billboard, commercial, credits in excess of 30 seconds, or a promotional announcement. Not included, usually, are public service announcements and promotional announcements for the same program.

nonrandom sample See *nonprobability sample*.

nonresponse (NR) A missing response to a survey question, or a respondent who, for any reason, fails to respond to a questionnaire in a predetermined sample. See *bias of nonresponse*.

nonresponse error A survey error that occurs if respondents differ in some characteristics from nonrespondents. Increases in sample size will not lessen any bias that is due to nonresponse error. See *bias of nonresponse, nonsampling error*.

nonresponse rate The percentage of respondents to a survey who fail to respond, either totally to a questionnaire in a predetermined sample, or to an individual question in a survey.

nonsampling error The result of imperfect survey procedures caused by one of several factors: nonresponse error, interviewing bias, prestige bias, and response error. Also **procedural bias**. See *sampling error*.

nonstructured interview An interview in which the respondent talks freely, with little or no guidance about subject matter.

nonverbal communication The sending and receiving of messages without the use of written or spoken words.

NOP Net orders processed. See *net sales*.

NORC See *National Opinion Research Center*.

norm A mean, median, or mode; an average.

normal curve See next.

normal distribution curve A frequency distribution curve in statistical measurement that produces a unimodal and symmetrical plot with the mean, median, and mode at the midpoint. Also **bell curve, Gaussian curve, normal curve**.

normal lens A camera lens that approximates the view of the human eye.

nostalgia radio A radio format characterized by reruns of vintage programs and by musical standards. See *format*.

not available In research, a reason for missing data in a table.

notch An opening cut into a side or corner of a printing plate or the like to receive special type or a cut; differs from a mortise is not being surrounded on all four sides by the original plate. Also **outside mortise**.

noted The number of persons who have seen the studied advertisement in a certain periodical; the term is used by the research firm of Starch & Associates. See *read-most, seen/associated*.

noted score The percentage of ad-noters for a certain issue of a certain periodical. The term is used by the research firm of Starch & Associates. See *ad-noter*.

not emanating main office See *nemo*.

not emanating main origination See *nemo*.

noter See *ad-noter*.

notification date A radio or television deadline for notification by an advertiser of intention to exercise an option for new or continued sponsorship.

novelty format An attention-getting direct mail size and/or shape.

novelty printing The printing of advertising slogans or names on pens, pencils, badges, matchbooks, and other inexpensive items.

NPBS See *Nielsen Post-Buy Service*.

NPA See *Network Program Analysis*.

NR See *next to reading matter, nonresponse*.

NRI See *National Research Institute*.

NRM See *next to reading matter*.

NRP See *net rating point*.

NSI See *Nielsen Station Index*.

NSI area A group of counties, including the metro or central area of a given market and additional counties to encompass approximately 95 percent of the average quarter-hour audience to the stations in that market. This is not a reported area but constitutes the area that must be sampled each time a given market is measured and reported. It is not a basis for calculating station total audiences.

NSI Plus A computerized analysis service for clients of *Nielsen Station Index*. Provides such studies as audience flow, reach and frequency, audience duplication, and exclusive viewing using standard or specially tailored geography.

Nth name selection A fractional unit that is repeated in sampling a mailing list. For example, in an "every 10th" sample, you would select the 1st, 11th, 21st, and so on, names after you selected the starting point at random.

NTI See *Nielsen Television Index*.

numbers Usually referred to as "the numbers"; the all-important radio and television ratings.

nut 1. The total cost of a radio or television program, production, or sponsorship. 2. See *en*. 3. See *quad*.

nut quad See *en quad*.

OAAA See *Outdoor Advertising Association of America, Inc.*

O and O Owned and operated. The major market radio and television stations, which are owned and operated by the networks. Also **O&O**.

OAT See *on air test*.

OBC See *outside back cover*.

objective 1. A goal of a business firm, process, or program, usually for a stated time. 2. Pertaining to an attitude of dispassionate, fair-minded evaluation; usually required of the best advertising agency service.

objective-and-task method A method for establishing a marketing budget by setting total appropriations at a level judged adequate to cover the cost of tasks that will allow attainment of objectives.

objective research See *quantitative research*.

observational method A technique of behavior research that uses observation of subjects' actions rather than questioning to derive findings.

obtained score The actual percentage of respondents who prove recall of a printed advertisements; a Gallup and Robinson term.

OC See *on camera*.

occasion A radio or television time interval intended or used for a commercial announcement. Also **commercial occasion**.

occupational classification The categorization of persons, e.g., periodical sub-

scribers, in terms of their business, profession, or position within a company.

OEM See *original equipment manufacturer*.

OFC Outside front cover. See *first cover*.

off air See *off the air*.

off camera Pertaining to an image outside the field of a television or motion picture camera.

off camera announcer A television announcer whose voice is heard but who does not appear on camera. Also **off screen announcer**.

off card Pertaining to advertising time sold at a special rate, not shown on the television or radio rate card.

offensive spending The purchase of advertising or other marketing support intended to expand one's sales. See *defensive spending*.

offer 1. The terms under which a specific mail order product or service is promoted. 2. A premium or prize an audience may compete for or receive by submitting labels, facsimiles, and so on.

off invoice A deduction from an invoice from a manufacturer or wholesaler to a retailer made in exchange for the retailer's promotional efforts. Also **off invoice allowance**.

off invoice allowance See previous.

off label 1. Referring to a specially reduced retail price marked over the regular label of an item. See *price pack*. 2. An inferior grade of a brand, discount priced and specially labeled.

off mike Referring to a sound directed away from a microphone as to give the effect of distance. See *on mike*.

off register Pertaining to a printing plate that is not aligned properly and that smears or prints slightly off center.

off scene Not visible to an audience. See *off camera*.

off screen announcer See *off camera announcer*.

off screen narration See *voiceover*.

offset 1. See *photo offset lithography*. 2. An unwanted deposit of ink from the surface of a freshly printed sheet to the back of a sheet placed on top of it; often prevented by inserting a nonprinted slip sheet between printed sheets.

offset lithography See *photo offset lithography*.

offset paper Paper designed for use in offset printing; available coated or uncoated, in a variety of finishes.

offset printing See *photo offset lithography*.

offset scrapbook A book of camera ready copy in a scrapbook format, reproduced for promotional purposes. See *scrap*.

offset sheet See *slip sheet*.

off shelf display A display of merchandise in a store or location other than the customary position for such merchandise on the store's shelves.

off the air Pertaining to television or radio material not broadcast, or facilities not used in the process of broadcasting. Also *off air*.

OK A notation used in editing to indicate a film shot, take, or sound that is considered acceptable for use. See *NG*.

OK wc See next.

OK with corrections (OK wc) Pertaining to signed approvals of art, keyline, or proof material where corrections, usually minor, have been noted as needed.

old-line wholesaler A wholesaler who sells and delivers merchandise only, having no affiliates and offering limited, if any, services.

on air See *over the air*.

on air test (OAT) A test of a commercial or program that uses a real broadcast of the test material on television or radio as the stimulus for a measurable audience response, such as recall, attitude change, purchase interest change, interest, or audience size.

on camera (OC) Pertaining to an image or scene by a television or motion picture camera.

on camera narration Narration in which the narrator is seen on camera. See *voiceover*.

one-cent sale A sale of two retail items for the regular price of one, plus one cent.

on sheet poster An outdoor poster consisting of a single sheet, 28 by 42 inches or 30 by 46 inches, used especially on subway and railroad station platforms.

one-time-buyer A mail order purchaser who has not ordered a second time from a given company.

one-time rate The basic cost for a single advertisement; one that does not earn a frequency discount. Also **basic rate**. See *open rate, transient rate*.

one-time use A common stipulation in a mail order list usage, list reproduction, or list exchange agreement that the mailer will not use the names on the list more than one time without the specific prior approval of the list owner.

one twenty A commercial that is two minutes (120 seconds) long; rare. Also noted as :120.

on mike Pertaining to a performer who is within the beam of maximum sound acceptance of a microphone. See *off mike*.

on order Pertaining to time on a network affiliate that has been ordered by an advertiser but that has not yet been cleared.

on-pack coupon A coupon attached to or part of the exterior of a product package.

on-pack premium A premium affixed in some manner to the exterior of a product's package.

on spec Pertaining to photography, artwork, advertising campaigns, and so on, that are made without a contract but with some expectation that an agreement to use the material will be reached. Also **on speculation**.

on speculation See previous.

on the air 1. Referring to the period of a radio or television transmission. 2. Pertaining to a performer who is on camera or mike. 3. Pertaining to material that is broadcast. 4. Pertaining to facilities that are used in the process of broadcasting. See *off the air*, *over the air*.

on the log Having been entered in a daily journal of events, as a log of television or radio broadcasts.

on the shelf See *in the can*.

opacity The property of paper that determines whether print from one side will show through to the other. The opposite of *transparency*.

opaque projector A device that will project an image of opaque material, such as a printed page. See *overhead projector*.

op ed Opposite editorial; the page facing the editorial page in a newspaper. Also **page opposite**.

open 1. The beginning of a broadcast program. See *opening billboard*. 2. Pertaining

to artwork or page make-up that has a large amount of white space.

open distribution The distribution of a product within a certain territory by any dealer choosing to carry it. See *exclusive distribution*.

open end 1. A recorded commercial that has time left at the end for a tag. 2. A program furnished to a station with time left for the local insertion of commercials. 3. A radio or television program that has no specified time to end.

open-end diary A broadcast audience research journal that does not list specific time segments. See *closed-end diary*.

open-ended question A question for which the possible anwers are not listed on a questionnaire, and that therefore does not restrict the respondent to any predetermined choice of answers.

open-end transcription 1. A recorded television or radio program, usually syndicated, with free time for local announcements. 2. A recorded commercial with free time for a local announcement. See *open end*.

open face A category of display type having open letters defined with strokes of uneven thickness that give a three-dimensional effect. See *inline*, *outline*.

opening billboard An introduction to a television or radio show; usually includes a mention of the sponsors. Also **open**. See next.

opening credits The credits that appear at the beginning of a television program or motion picture. See *opening billboard*.

opening shot The first camera shot used in a production.

open left To begin a camera shot with the subject to the extreme left; a direction to a television camera operator.

open negotiation A negotiation between a broadcast station or station representative and a buyer, in which they ultimately agree on a price for an advertising campaign at a specified rating.

open rate The highest rate for advertising charged by a medium. Also **base rate**. See *card rate, one-time rate*.

open right To begin a camera shot with the subject to the extreme right; a direction to a television camera operator.

open-side envelope An envelope with a lengthwise flap.

open space An outdoor advertising availability; poster or bulletin space not under contract and for sale.

operating sheet See *program log*.

operations research (OR) The application of such mathematical methods as models to a system of variables, to project probable changes in the system resulting from changes in one or more variables.

opinion A judgment or view about a particular matter.

opinion leader A person with media exposure who influences the attitudes or opinions of others.

opinion research Research that concentrates on the opinions of respondents rather than on facts.

Opinion Research Corporation (ORC) A research firm in Princeton, New Jersey, that conducts a variety of projects useful to business with relation to public, stockholder, and employee attitudes.

opportunity of exposure The amount of reasonable expectation that an advertisement will be seen or heard.

optical 1. A special visual effect done with a camera or other piece of television or motion picture equipment. Also **optical effect**. 2. See next.

optical answer print A print of a commercial in which all color corrections and optical effects have been incorporated; used to obtain final approvals for commercial production. Also **optical**.

optical center The point on a page where a reader's eye naturally falls when turned to the page; slightly above the geometric center.

optical effect See *optical*.

optical house A laboratory that specializes in producing special effects for film.

optical print See *answer print*.

optical track A sound track recorded by optical means on the margin of motion picture film at least 16mm in width. See *magnetic track*.

optical weight The visual impact that a page makes on a reader or a viewer.

optical window A portion of a television picture containing a second or alternate message; often used in commercials.

option time 1. A contract, arrangement, or understanding, express or implied, between a radio or television station and a network that prevents the station from scheduling programs before the network agrees to use the time during which such programs are scheduled, or that requires the station to clear time already scheduled when the network seeks to use the time. Also **network option time, network time**. 2. The portion of the day during which, by contract between a network and affiliated station, one or the other may exercise control over programming.

OR See *operations research*.

orange good A product that is consumed and replaced at a moderate rate; usually in fairly broad distribution, requiring moderate service, and with a moderate to good margin (e.g., dress clothing). See *red good, yellow good*.

orbit A method of scheduling commercials in a variety of programs or time periods to reach the greatest number of different members of the audience.

ORC See *Opinion Research Corporation.*

order 1. A prospect's agreement to make a purchase. 2. A seller's document used to record and implement the terms of a purchase. 3. A service package, product, or group of products exchanged in a sales transaction.

order book A catalog used as a reference in ordering merchandise.

order card A reply card used to initiate an order by mail.

order form A printed form on which a customer can provide information to initiate an order by mail.

order letter A preliminary letter of agreement between an advertising buyer and a communications medium specifying terms of purchase of advertising space or time; sent by the buyer.

order-process department A department of a television or radio network that prepares cost estimates and initiates contracts for advertisers.

ordinate The vertical coordinate of a graph. Also **y-axis**. See *abscissa.*

organizational chart A table, usually of lines and boxes, depicting lines of reporting and authority, subordinate to superior, and showing how people or departments relate to each oher in a hierarchical organization.

organization marketing The public relations activities of a company in service of its marketing objectives.

organizer 1. A printed sheet presenting the main points of a salesperson's argument and around which the sales pitch is organized. 2. The binder in which such sheets are carried.

orientation shot An establishing shot.

original 1. A piece of camera ready copy, as a photograph, drawing, painting, etc., for photomechanical reproduction. Also **finished art**. 2. The first photoengraving or film reproduction made from camera copy, as opposed to electrotypes or other duplicate materials made from such copy. 3. Not copied or reproduced.

original equipment manufacturer (OEM) A manufacturer of devices and/or components that sells its products to other manufacturers for marketing under their own names.

original purchase unit An actual purchase of or subsccription to a periodical; used in readership surveys.

original sample The estimated number of households originally drawn for a survey.

original tape A videotape accepted for transmission or reproduction.

originate To produce and transmit a television or radio program or other material, especially when fed to other stations.

origination point The location from which a program is fed, either by a network or a station. See *feed.*

ornament A decorative design or character used in printing.

orphan An isolated line of type left at the bottom of a page; often the first line of a paragraph that is continued on the next page. See *widow.*

OTC Over the counter. See *proprietary pharmaceutical.*

outdoor advertising The use of posters, painted displays, billboards, spectaculars, and other display advertising along highways, on walls, roofs, and so on. See *transit advertising.*

Outdoor Advertising Association of America, Inc. (OAAA) An organization of outdoor advertising plant operators, founded in 1891 to maintain industry-wide standards and provide its members with information and services.

outdoor advertising company A firm that specializes in building and maintaining outdoor advertising space on a national and/or local basis.

outdoor plant See *plant*.

outdoor service The maintenance and repair of outdoor advertising structures.

outdoor space buyer An advertising agency employee who is responsible for buying outdoor advertising space.

outflow The portion of the audience that changes channels at the conclusion of a television program. See *inflow*.

outgoing Pertaining to outdoor advertising poster panels or bulletins that expose the advertiser's message to traffic leaving the central business district of a town or market; now becoming obsolete because of the development of many cities into complexes of adjacent urban areas.

outlet 1. A network affiliate. 2. The market for a commodity.

outline 1. A display type having open letters defined with strokes of even thickness. See *inline*, *open face*. 2. A sketch without shading.

outline cut See *silhouette*.

out-of-focus Pertaining to a photograph or motion picture that is not sharp; fuzzy.

out-of-focus dissolve A dissolve in which the camera taking one shot is slowly put out of focus, after which the camera for the next shot is slowly brought into focus. Also **defocusing**.

out-of-home Pertaining to the mass media that are consumed away from home as opposed to home consumption, such as in a car, in an office, on a train, in a hotel, etc.

out-of-market traffic The traffic originating beyond the area in which an outdoor advertising plant operates.

out of pocket 1. Pertaining to costs for services or merchandise provided to an organization by an outside supplier, rather than being developed by the organization's own production capability. 2. Referring to expenses incurred in completing a job other than normal, chargeable expenses and that may entail the outlay of cash, e.g., special travel, entertainment, etc.

out-of-service Pertaining to an outdoor structure temporarily or permanently unavailable for advertisers.

out-of-stock Pertaining to merchandise not presently available, especially for retail sale, beause of inadequate supply or insufficient distribution support.

out of sync 1. Lacking synchronization between a transmitted and received television picture, usually resulting in a vertical roll. 2. Lacking synchronization between sound and picture. See *in sync*.

out period See *hiatus*.

out point The videotape or film frame selected as the ending point of a scene. See *in point*.

outro (*sl.*) The ending of a program. See *intro*.

outsert A piece of printed material attached to, rather than inserted into, a package. Also **package outsert**. See *package insert*.

outside back cover (OBC) An advertising space position in a periodical.

outside broadcast See *remote*.

outside front cover See *first cover*.

outside mortise See *notch*.

outside station A station that is not classified as "home" to a market but is receivable in a market other than its home market. Superstations (outside their home market) and cable services are treated as outside stations.

outtake A scene or shot that is edited out and not used in the production. See *keep-take*.

overage See *overrun*.

overcommercialization An excessive number of, amount of time devoted to, or interruptions by commercial matter in a television or radio program. See *clutter*.

over frame See *voiceover*.

overhang See *extended cover*.

overhead The general expenses of a business that cannot be charged directly to a product or production, such as rent, lighting, office expenses, depreciation, taxes, and so on.

overhead projector A device that projects an image of a horizontal transparency on a vertical screen. The transparency may be a copy of printed material, illustrations, diagrams, and so on, or it may be writing done with a special pen directly on transparent material. See *opaque projector*.

overhead shot A camera shot from a position directly above the action or object.

overlap 1. A period in which two successive television or motion picture images appear together (e.g., during a lap dissolve). 2. See *extended cover*.

overlapping circulation The circulation to the same subscribers of two or more periodicals under consideration for use by an advertiser. See *duplication*.

overlay 1. A sheet, image, printed matter, etc., superimposed on an existing design or piece of artwork. 2. A plastic sheet used to protect artwork. 3. See *snipe*.

overline A caption placed above a cut.

overmatter See *leftover matter*.

overnight 1. Referring to a report on television program audience size delivered the day following a broadcast. 2. See *daypart*.

overprint 1. To print on top of another print. Also **surprint**. 2. See next.

overrun 1. A number of additional copies of a magazine, collateral piece, etc., printed in excess of those required for general circulation, distribution, or quantity ordered. Also **overage, overprint**. 2. The excessive production of items, creating a manufacturer's overstock. 3. To move words from one line to the next because of an insertion or deletion.

overs See next.

overset A portion of type matter set but not used, usually because of a lack of space. Also **overs, runovers**. See *leftover matter*.

overset matter See *leftover matter*.

overshoot To take a wider camera shot than intended.

overstock To order more merchandise than can be handled or sold.

over the air Referring to broadcasting as opposed to cable transmission. Also **on air**.

over the counter (OTC) See *proprietary pharmaceutical*.

overwire hanger See *banner*.

owned and operated See *O and O*.

PAAA See *Premium Advertising Association of America, Inc*.

package 1. A television or radio show or series ready for broadcast that is offered to an advertiser, usually for a lump sum. 2. A combination of television or radio programs or commercial spots offered together to an advertiser, usually at a discount, by a network or station. Also **plan, package plan**. See *plan rate*. 3. The exterior appearance of a single unit of a product. 4. The assembled enclosures of a mailing effort; includes an envelope, letter, reply device, and so on.

package band A promotion offer or other announcement printed on a paper band wrapped around a retail package.

package cut An advertising illustration showing a package or carton, usually provided by manufacturers' sales representatives to cooperating distributors for retail advertising.

package design 1. The graphic design used on a package for a unit of product. 2. A marketing services professional specialty, consisting of the art and study of creating effective product packages.

packaged good A product wrapped by the manufacturer; especially a small item used broadly and frequently consumed, such as packaged food, health and beauty aids, etc.. Typically sold through food, drug, and mass merchandiser retail stores.

package enclosure A premium or brochure enclosed in a product's package. See *in-pack premium, package insert*.

package insert A promotional piece placed in a package, such as a coupon for a refill or replacement or for a different product, or an order form for a special premium. See *outsert, package enclosure*.

package outsert See *outsert*.

package plan See *package*.

package program A complete television or radio program lacking only commercials that is furnished to a sponsor, network, or station. Also **package show**. See *package*.

packager A person or organization that puts together television or radio programs and offers them for sale to networks, stations, or sponsors. Also **syndicator**.

package rate See *plan rate*.

package show See *package program*.

package test A test of the elements, in part or in their entirety, of one mailing piece against another.

pad To add material to a commercial or television or radio program only so it does not end too soon or sound too empty of content.

page 1. The printed area of a periodical page; a basic space unit in advertising and advertising rate calculations. 2. Type that is set and ready to print. 3. The matter that is printed on a page. 4. To turn pages, as page through.

page break The point in a periodical, book, manuscript, etc., at which type matter is carried over to the next page.

page opposite See *op ed*.

page proof A printer's proof of a completed page, with or without illustrations in place. See *galley, proof*.

page size The size of a full-page, nonbleed advertisement in a periodical.

paid cancel A person who completes a basic buying commitment. Also **complete cancel**.

paid circulation The distribution of a publication to persons or organizations that have paid for a subscription. See *controlled circulation*.

paid spot A radio or television commercial.

paint bulletin See next.

painted bulletin A large, outdoor advertising structure (commonly 14 by 48 feet) on which an advertising message and illustration are painted directly. Also **bulletin**, **paint bulletin**. See *billboard, poster panel*.

painted display An advertisement on a painted bulletin.

painted display plant An outdoor advertising company that owns and maintains bulletins.

painter's guide A line rendering with color overlays indicating the forms and colors for a painted bulletin.

paint out To obliterate copy on an outdoor advertising painted bulletin in preparation for a change in design. Also **coat out**. See *blank out*.

paired comparison A statistical comparison of a number of things that have a common point or points of similarity. Along one dimension, each thing is compared with and rated with regard to all the others on a two-by-two basis.

pamphlet A booklet, usually promotional or informational, with pages of printed matter —generally eight or more—and a paper cover. See *brochure, leaflet*.

pan 1. To make a shot in which the camera moves in a horizontal or vertical arc. 2. See next.

panchromatic Pertaining to black-and-white film that registers all visible colors in gray values falling between white and black. Also **pan, pan film**.

P and H See *postage and handling*.

panel 1. A permanent group of respondents for investigations of consumer opinions, attitudes, reactions, etc., who are surveyed either continuously or periodically. 2. An outdoor advertising display board, whether regular or illuminated; usually of billboard size. 3. A block o type or an illustration that is indented from the margins, sometimes with rules at top and bottom.

panel number A code given to outdoor advertising panels to aid employees in painting or posting them.

pan film See *panchromatic*.

pan master A fine-grained panchromatic black-and-white film or slide made from a color original, used as the source for subsequent printing.

panoramic shot See next.

pan shot A shot in which the camera pans a scene. Also **panoramic shot**.

pantry audit A consumer research survey of items actually found in respondents' homes. Also **pantry check, pantry inventory**.

pantry check See previous.

pantry inventory See *pantry audit*.

paper 1. Thin, light sheets made from wood, rags, straw, or other fibrous material, manufactured by hand or machine. Better grades of paper are made from linen rags; lesser grades from groundwood pulp. Also **paper stock**. 2. A periodical such as a newspaper. 3. A general term for photographic printing and enlarging stock. 4. Informally, money or financing for credit. 5. To use paper to cover a surface or wrap an object.

paperboard A heavy, paper-like material made from wood pulp, waste paper, or straw.

paper stock See *paper*.

papier-mâché A mixture of wood and paper fibers with a paste of clay and rosin, molded into various forms; used for making matrices.

parallel location The location of an outdoor advertisement parallel to a street or road, or with both ends within 6 feet of a line parallel to a street or road.

parallel single (PS) An outdoor advertising panel that is the only panel visible to approaching traffic, or the only panel visible for 25 feet along the line of travel with no other painted display visible within 50 feet.

parameter A statistical characteristic of a population, which is subjected to measurement among a random sample of the population and subsequent analysis in research.

parent station A television station that supplies programming and commercials to another station to expand the coverage of the parent.

partial self-liquidator See *semi-liquidator*.

partial sponsorship The sponsorship of a television or radio program by more than one advertiser, each having a separate segment. Also **segment sponsorship**.

participating advertiser An advertiser who buys time for commercials within a television or radio program.

participating agency An advertising agency that has a commercial announcement on a radio or television program but is not the agency of record.

participating announcement A television or radio commercial from one of several sponsors of a program. Also **participation**.

participating sponsor One of two or more sponsors of the same television or radio program.

participation See *participating announcement*.

participation program A radio or television program designed to carry the commercial messages of a number of advertisers. See *announcement program*.

participation spot The time reserved by a station for a commercial.

part-time station A television or radio station restricted by the FCC to a limited broadcast schedule each day. See *daytime station, limited-time station, sharing time*.

pass-along audience The number of persons who receive a periodical from the original subscriber or purchaser; does not include others in the homes of such persons. Also **pass-along circulation, pass-along readers, secondary readership**.

pass-along circulation See previous.

pass-along readers See *pass-along audience*.

passive media The mass media that require the consumer to do nothing except watch or listen, as in radio, television, cable television, and direct broadcast satellites.

pasteup A camera ready layout of type proofs, photostats, artwork, etc., pasted in the proper position on paperboard; used for reproduction purposes. Also **mechanical, pasteup dummy**.

pasteup dummy See previous.

PA system See *public-address system*.

PAT See *Product Acceptance Test*.

patch 1. A section of a printing plate or keyline that has been corrected or revised by new material stripped in or pasted over the original material. 2. To repair a pasteup by inserting new material.

patent   A grant issued by the U.S. government that gives the inventor or discoverer of a new and useful process, machine, manufacture, composition of matter, or any new and useful improvement of these items the right to exclude all others from making, using, or selling the invention. See *copyright*. 2. To obtain this right with regard to an invention. 3. Pertaining to the body of law covering such protections, which include trademarks and product designs.

patent infringement   The illegal use of an invention or process registered to another person or corporation.

patent medicine   See *proprietary pharmaceutical*.

patent pending   A notice to the public that an application for patent has been filed in the U.S. Patent and Trademark Office.

patronage dividend   A check or credit voucher from a wholesaler to a retailer, made as part of a profit-sharing system. Also **deferred discount**.

patronage rebate   A check or credit voucher from a wholesaler to a retailer as a credit for large-quantity purchases or as a promotion allowance.

pay cable   The television programs distributed on a cable television system and paid for on an individual basis in addition to the monthly cable charge. See *pay television*.

pay cable channel   A cable television system channel that carries a pay cable network, channel, or pay-per-view channel.

pay cable household   A household that subscribes to one or more cable television premium services.

pay cable network   A cable television service, usually delivered to the cable television system by satellite.

payback   See *payout*.

payola   The undisclosed money, service, or anything of value directly or indirectly paid or promised to a radio or television station employee for the broadcast of any matter. Payola has often been received for the promotion of records on radio stations. See *plugola*.

payout   A profit return on an investment, especially an investment of marketing expenditures. Also **payback**. See *investment spending*.

pay out   To return a profit on an investment.

pay-per-view (PPV)   Pertaining to a pay cable or subscription television service that charges viewers for each program watched.

pay television   A system of distributing television programs, motion pictures, and so on, over the air or by cable, for which subscribers pay on an individual per-program basis. Pay television systems scramble either sound or picture signals to prevent reception by nonsubscribers. Also **pay TV, payvision, premium television, subscription television, toll television, toll video**. See *cable television*.

pay TV   See previous.

payvision   See *pay television*.

pay window   The length of time a program or motion picture is available for broadcast on pay cable television.

PBS   See *Public Broadcasting Service*.

PCA   See *Program Cumulative Audiences*.

PD   See *public domain*.

PDT   Pacific Daylight Time. See *time zone*.

PE   See *printer's error*.

peak time   A British term for prime time.

peel-off label   A self-adhesive label attached to a backing sheet that is attached to a mailing piece. The label is intended to be removed from the mailing piece and attached to an order form or card.

penalty cost The differential efficiency of media coverage provided by national media versus the equivalent local media; a factor in preparing media plan translations for test markets.

penetration 1. The effectiveness of advertising in reaching and persuading the public. 2. The percentage of households in a given area that have a television or radio receiver. Also **saturation**. 3. The percentage of households in a given area that have subscribed to cable television. 4. The relationship of the number of individuals or families on a particular mailing list (e.g., in total, by state, by zip code, by SIC) compared to the total number possible.

penny saver An inexpensively printed tabloid, usually distributed weekly at no charge, that contains no editorial matter, only local classified and display advertising.

people meter (PM) A home television audience measurement device that requires interaction by the members of the family to record audience composition. See *Arbitron*, *Audimeter*.

percentage-of-sales method A technique of determining marketing budgets based on a predetermined percentage rate of spending relative to anticipated dollar sales.

percent distribution The proportion of total survey area television households specified survey areas viewing a home market station (or all home market stations, in the case of total percent distribution).

perception The ability of the human mind to receive sensory impressions and give them meaningful interconnection and interpretation.

perceptual mapping See *connotative mapping*.

perceptual mapping study See *market mapping study*.

per diem A cost, allowance, or fee calculated on a daily basis, as for services or travel and entertainment expenses.

perfect binding A form of book binding in which the edges of the signatures are scuffed and then glued to the backbone or binding edge, eliminating wire staples.

perforate To pierce a sheet with small, closely spaced dots or slits to facilitate even tearing, as in printed advertising pieces with coupons, reply forms, etc.

performance allowance A rebate of a portion of the purchase price of goods provided to retailers who agree to perform cooperative merchandisng services. See *cooperative advertising*.

performing right A right granted through the payment of fees to ASCAP or BMI to play the recordings of a composer and/or lyricist associated with that company.

performing rights society An association or corporation, such as ASCAP, BMI, or SESAC, that licenses the public performances of nondramatic musical works on behalf of the copyright owner.

per inquiry advertising (PI) Advertising for which the proprietor of a communications medium is paid according to the number of inquiries or completed sales that result.

periodical A publication, such as a magazine or newspaper, that appears at regular intervals. In advertising, generally refers to a magazine.

Periodical Publishers' Association (PPA) An organization founded in 1900 to support good relations within the periodical publishing industry and to verify the credit standing of advertising agencies.

perk See next.

perquisite An item or privilege granted by an employer in addition to wages or salary (e.g., stock options, automobiles, residences, free tickets, vacations). Also **perk**.

personal diary See *individual diary*.

personal endorsement See *testimonial*.

personal influence The personal, face-to-face interactions of consumers bearing directly on purchase decisions; includes personal sales contacts, opinion leader influences, and word-of-mouth advertising.

personal interview A research method in which a sample of respondents is interviewed individually, face-to-face.

personality A person selected for use in an advertisement due to the public recognition and reputation he or she enjoys.

personalized letter See next.

personalizing Adding the name or other personal information about the recipient to direct mail pieces.

personal letter A direct mail letter containing the recipient's name in the salutation and personally signed by the sender.

personal sales Sales made on the basis of a face-to-face contact, personal telephone call, personal letter, etc., from a salesperson to a prospect.

person marketing The activities directed to modify public attitudes and behavior regarding a specific person, such as a political candidate, celebrity, or prospect for a position.

persons-per-diary value The numeric value assigned to each in-tab diary for the process of projecting audience estimates to the entire population in a market. It reflects the number of persons in the geographic age/sex group represented by each in-tab diary after sample balancing has been performed.

persons ranking The ranking of television programs (highest to lowest) based on the number of persons reached, by selected age groups.

persons reached See *individuals reached, reach*.

persons-using-radio rating See *individuals-using-radio rating*.

persons using television (PUT) The percentage of persons in a given demographic category in the survey area who are viewing television during a specific period. See *persons viewing television*.

persons-using-television rating See *individuals-using-television rating*.

persons viewing television (PVT) The number of persons in Canadian television homes by network area or DMA using their receivers for more than five minutes in each quarter hour, expressed as a percentage of the network area or DMA persons in television households. See *persons using television*.

persuasiveness The ability of advertising to influence audience or prospect attitudes, especially purchase intent and corporate perception, in the manner intended by the advertiser. See *believability*.

P&H See *postage and handling*.

phantom section A drawing or rendering showing the exterior of an object as if it were transparent, to reveal interior detailing. Also **ghosted view**.

phone list A mailing list compiled from names listed in telephone directories.

photo agency A commercial organization that sells photographs from an extensive picture library. Also **stock house**.

photoboard A set of still photographs made from a television commercial, accompanied by a script, and printed on a single sheet of paper; used primarily for recordkeeping or merchandisng purposes.

photocomposition A method of setting type by exposing negatives of the characters on film or photographic paper. Also **photographic typesetting** (when only type is being composed), **phototypesetting, phototypography**. See *photo offset lithography*.

photocopy 1. A photographic copy of a page, advertisement, picture, and so on, made directly on sensitized paper, especially automatically. See *xerography*. 2. To make such a copy.

photoengraving 1. The process of making letterpress printing plates by photochemical means. 2. A picture printed from a plate made by such a process.

photogenic Pertaining to physical characteristics, especially facial features, which make a person an attractive photographic subject.

photographic typesetting See *photocomposition*.

photography The art or process of registering and fixing visual images by means of a camera on light-sensitive photographic film.

photolettering A technique for supplying reproducible display copy in the form of a photographic positive of letters developed on film or paper; the letters are enlarged to the desired size in printing the positive. See *photocomposition*.

photolithography See *photo offset lithography*.

photomatic A television commercial produced from filming a sequence of still photographs; usually used only for test purposes. See *animatic*.

photomechanical A process that combines photographic and mechanical means to produce a printing plate. See *intaglio, lithography, photoengraving*.

photomontage A single picture composed of two or more other, smaller pictures or portions of pictures. See *montage*.

photo offset lithography A planographic printing process in which a photographic image is transferred from a printing plate or cylinder to a rubber blanket, which prints the image to paper. Also **offset, offset lithography, offset printing, photolithography, photo offset printing**. See *dry offset, letterpress, lithography*.

photo offset printing See previous.

photoprint A print made of a page by any photographic copying process.

photo proof See *reproduction proof*.

photo release See *release*.

Photostat™ 1. A photocopying machine. 2. A type of high-contrast photographic negative or positive made on paper. Also **stat**. 3. To copy as a Photostat.

phototype A printing plate or block made from a photograph.

phototypesetting See *photocomposition*.

phototypography See *photocomposition*.

physical distribution The marketing activities intended to move products from manufacturer to purchaser.

physical inventory A record of saleable merchandise on hand at a given time, with its sale or replacement value.

PI See *per inquiry advertising*.

PIB See *Publishers' Information Bureau, Inc.*

pica 1. A size of type; 12 points. 2. A standard measure for the width of a line of type; 6 picas equal 1 inch. 3. A unit of type height equal to 1/6 of an inch. 4. A typewriter font one pica deep and with ten characters per inch. See *elite*.

pica rule See *line gauge*.

pica stick See *line gauge*.

pickup See *pickup material*, *remote*.

pick up To use pickup material in an advertisement.

pickup material The advertising material created for one advertisement and used in some form in a different advertisement. Also **pickup**.

picture dupe negative A film negative printed from a master positive or from a picture negative. See *dupe*.

picture master positive A film print used to produce a picture dupe negative.

picture negative A film that produces a negative image, whether camera original or print.

picture print A positive print made from a picture negative.

picture safety The border around the essential area of a picture.

piggyback A direct mail offer that is included for free with another offer.

piggyback commercial A commercial used in a piggyback configuration. Also **split commercial**.

piggyback coupon A pop-up coupon so inserted in a periodical as to lie across advertising of other advertisers on the page following.

piggyback unit A presentation of two unrelated commercials by the same sponsor, one immediately after the other; usually purchased as a single unit. See *integrated commercial*, *multiple product announcement*.

pilot A videotape or film of a proposed television series prepared for presentation to prospective sponsors, networks, and advertising agencies. Also **pilot film, pilot program**.

pilot film See previous.

pilot print See *answer print*.

pilot program See *pilot*.

pilot study A small-scale trial research study, as of consumer attitudes, conducted to provide a basis for judging the promise of a large-scale survey on the same lines. Also **pilot survey**.

pilot survey See previous.

pilot test A screening of a television pilot in which members of the audience, who are often pulled in off the streets, evaluate the potential of the program.

pioneer salesperson See *missionary salesperson*, *new business rep*.

pipeline 1. The processes through which merchandise passes from manufacturer to consumer. 2. A direct channel for information.

pitch 1. An informal term for an advertising agency's presentation to a new business prospect. 2. An appeal to an audience or sales prospect. See *character pitch*.

placement call See next.

placement interview The initial contact with a member of a household to secure an agreement to participate in a survey and to gain permission to install a people meter or diary in the home.

plan See *creative strategy*, *marketing plan*, *package*.

planned-no-viewing households The television households in a Nielsen survey that indicated at the time of diary placement that no television viewing would occur during the survey week and that did not return a usable diary.

planography A printing process in which the printing surface is flush with the non-printing surface, e.g., lithography. See *intaglio*, *letterpress*, *relief printing*.

plan rate The charge to an advertiser who buys time in quantity; based on the number of spots. Also **package rate**.

plans board An advertising agency management committee for review of creative strategies and approval of proposed advertising.

plans committee A management committee or organization for determining company policy and making long-range general plans for sales, advertising, product development, expansion, etc.

plant 1. A factory or workshop designed to produce equipment or products (e.g., a printing plant) 2. The outdoor advertising structures in a given town or area, operated by an outdoor company or plant operator. Also **outdoor plant**.

plant capacity In outdoor advertising, the number of 100 showings available in a plant, determined by dividing the total number of panels in a plant by the number of panels that make up the 100 GRPs or 100 showings.

plant operator An individual or company that operates and maintains outdoor advertising structures.

plastic plate A letterpress plate formed of plastic with raised characters, used for making castings rather than for printing; supplied to a newspaper by a mat service in place of a matrix.

plateau A level that is reached and maintained, such as in newspaper subscriptions audience ratings, advertising agency billings, cable penetration, etc.

platen 1. An element in a printing press that presses the sheet to be printed against the printing surface. 2. The roller of a typewriter. 3. A sheet of heavy glass used to hold animation cels flat and still during shooting.

plate size The size of a printed advertisement; must take into account the publication's mechanical requirements and other restrictions.

playback 1. The set of answers given by a respondent to interviewer questions in a survey. Also **protocol**. 2. The recounting of the content of a specific commercial by a respondent in an interview. 3. The process of playing a tape.

play theory A theory that the user of mass media does so primarily to derive pleasure rather than receive information.

plot plan See *floor plan*.

plotter 1. A device for producing hard copies of graphic materials. 2. A device that mechanically draws computer-driven graphs, charts, drawings, and so on.

plow-back method A way of determining an advertising appropriation based on the use of all anticipated net profits from a specific period; used especially in aggressive advertising of new products. See *investment spending*.

plug 1. A free on-air mention of a product, service, or personality that has advertising value. 2. A slang term for a television or radio commercial. 3. To promote an advertiser, product, program, station, and so on.

plugola The promoting of products on the air for which the radio or television station does not receive payment; record plugola, song plugging, or "accidental" mentions of products by performers for which payment is received. See *payola*.

PM See *people meter, push money*.

PMA See *primary marketing area*.

PMB See *Print Measurement Bureau*.

PMSA See *Primary Metropolitan Statistical Area*.

PNR See *proved name registration*.

pocketpiece (PP) A biweekly rating report, designed to fit in a coat pocket, issued by *Nielsen Television Index*.

point 1. A unit of measure of the height of printing type; in the United States, equal to 1/12 of a pica or 1/72 of an inch. 2. A measure of cardboard thickness, equal to 1/1000 of an inch. 3. See *gross rating point*. 4. A period used as in punctuation as in "decimal point."

point-of-purchase (POP) The place at which a customer encounters a retail item. Also **point-of-sale**.

point-of-purchase advertising The advertising, promotional matter, or display structure, usually prepared by the manufacturer, for use on the retailer's premises.

Point-of-Purchase Advertising Institute, Inc. (POPAI) A nonprofit organization of makers of point-of-purchase advertising displays and the advertisers and retailers who use them.

point-of-sale See *point-of-purchase*.

point system A system for the vertical measurement of type; adopted in 1886 by the United States Type Founders Association and based on a then-standard pica type body. One point is .013837 inches. See *point*.

pole piece An advertising display in a retail store, mounted on a pole for greater visibility. Also **spectacular**.

political advertising The use of commercials and advertisements to influence elections and government by persuading voters and government officials to behave voluntarily in a recommended manner.

pollster 1. An organization that conducts public opinion polls and/or surveys. 2. An individual who works for a polling organization.

polyphase method An audience measurement method in which listeners, after being favorably tested for adequate ability to recall television or radio programs, are asked to maintain diaries on their broadcast media program selections.

pony spread A periodical page arrangement in which an advertisement occupies a portion of each of two facing pages. Also **junior spread**.

pony unit See *junior unit*.

pool See *commercial pool*.

pool out To develop one or more commercials for use in a commercial pool.

pool partner A commercial used in a commercial pool; usually in reference to a two-commercial pool or a newly developed commercial.

POP See *point-of-purchase*.

POPAI See *Point-of-Purchase Advertising Institute, Inc.*

pop-in A brief television or radio commercial making one point about something advertised; a program may have several.

pop-off A sudden departure of something from on camera to off camera in a television show. Also **pop-out**.

pop-on A sudden emergence of something on camera in a television show.

pop-out See *pop-off*.

popular music The music that is currently most in demand as shown by record, tape, and CD sales, juke box plays, radio station programming, and so on.

popular press The print media publications, especially newspapers that contain more entertainment than information, that are geared toward the less educated segment of the population.

population The whole number of persons or things under study; usually represented by a sample. See *population density*, *statistical population*.

population density The average number of persons in a square mile.

pop-up A die-cut folder containing a paper construction that pops up to form a three-dimensional illustration when the fold is opened.

pop-up coupon A tear-off perforated coupon stitched into the binding of a periodical as a separate, small space unit. Also **preclipped coupon**. See *bind-in card*, *blow-in card*.

porta-panel A mobile outdoor advertising poster panel that is wheeled from location to location. Frequently used for merchandising purposes at retail outlets.

portfolio test A test of periodical advertising using a dummy magazine containing the advertising being tested as well as other advertising used as a control.

position 1. The consumer perception of a product's or service's benefits in comparison to its competition, which the advertiser attempts to create and encourage as part of its marketing strategy. Also **product position, purchase proposition**. 2. The placement of an advertisement in a publication in terms of page number, side, proximity to editorial, etc., or the location of a commercial in a radio or television program. 3. A statement of philosophy by an advertiser or advertising agency with regard to a proposed advertising campaign. 4. To locate an advertisement or commercial in a specific way in a periodical or program.

position request A request by an advertiser, or its agency, for a certain location in a periodical or time on a television or radio program, if available. See *preferred position*.

positive correlation See *correlation*.

post The condition of a subject or respondent in a research experiment after a test treatment has been applied. Also **posttest**. See *pre*.

postage and handling (P and H) (P & H) A charge presumably made to cover the costs of postal delivery and preparation for such a shipment by mail of an order; made in addition to the purchase price of the item.

postage-saver An envelope mailed third class with a sealed top flap but an ungummed end flap permitting postal inspection.

postal card A card sold by the U.S. Postal Service, having a printed indicia and sent as first-class mail. Also **postcard**.

postal service prohibitive order A communication from the U.S. Postal Service to a company indicating that a specific person or family considers the company's advertising mail to be pandering. The order requires the company to remove all names listed on the order from its own mailing list and from any other lists used to promote that company's products or services. Names listed on the order are to be distinguished from names removed voluntarily by the list owner at an individual's request.

post-buy analysis An evaluation based on the audience viewing levels at the time a commercial ran; used to determine the effectiveness of an advertising buy.

postcard See *postal card*.

postcard mailer A booklet or packet containing business reply cards from a number of advertisers, for selective return to order products or obtain information. Often distributed by trade, business, and industrial publications as a service to advertisers.

post choice The percentage of a sample audience that chooses a certain brand of product after exposure to an advertisement for the brand; used in tests of the persuasiveness of advertisements. See *pre-to-post*.

posted bulletin A large outdoor advertising structure; the most common size is 14 by 48 feet.

poster A printed paper advertisement that is pasted, tacked up, or inserted into a permanent frame in a public place. Also **bill**. See *outdoor advertising*, *transit advertising*.

poster frame A framed panel used for holding a poster on or in a bus, terminal, station, store, bank, and so on.

posterize To design a poster or advertisement in a style characteristic of outdoor advertising posters; all elements are eliminated except for the ones that identify the product.

poster panel An outdoor billboard on which advertising is displayed on printed paper sheets rather than by being painted. The standard poster panel is approximately 25 by 12 feet; the image is printed in sections on 24 or 30 sheets. See *billboard*, *painted bulletin*.

poster plant An outdoor advertising plant specializing in posters and poster panels.

poster showing An outdoor advertising showing consisting of a number of posters.

posting The physical placement of an outdoor advertisement.

posting date The date on which an outdoor advertising showing is scheduled to begin. See *posting leeway*.

posting instructions The detailed information sent to an outdoor advertising plant operator for the display of a particular poster design.

posting leeway A grace period, customarily five working days after an outdoor advertising scheduled posting date, allowed to a plant operator to complete the posting of a showing without penalty.

posting listing The selection of individual panels that will comprise an outdoor advertising poster showing under contract.

posting period The length of time during which one outdoor advertising poster design is displayed; usually one month. Figured as 30 days for the purpose of costing and credits.

postmark advertising An advertising slogan or design printed by a postage meter.

postsync See next.

postsynchronization The recording of dialogue or other sound to match the existing lip movements on the picture track of a film or tape. Also **postsync, postsynchronized sound**.

postsynchronized sound See previous.

posttest See *post*.

posture The relative aggressiveness of an advertising campaign.

potential audience The number of persons or households capable of exposure to a medium by virtue of ownership, presence, or use of the medium in question.

potential viewer (PV) A projection of the maximum number of persons who have the opportunity to see an outdoor advertising poster.

pounce pattern A method of preparing large painted bulletins from relatively small art masters using projection and tracing.

powerhouse See *clear-channel station*.

pp See *pocketpiece*.

PPA See *Periodical Publishers' Association*.

PPV See *pay-per-view*.

PR See *public relations*.

PRD See *product research and development*.

pre The condition of a subject or respondent in a research experiment prior to the application of a test treatment. Also **pretest**. See *post*.

prealerted survey A survey in which respondents are notified of their selection for the survey in advance of the actual data collection; usually by telephone or mail.

precancelled stamp A postage stamp bearing the cancellation mark of a post office when sold; used for third-class, fourth-class, and bulk-rate mail.

pre-choice The percentage of a sample audience that uses a product before exposure to an advertisement for the brand; used in tests of the persuasiveness of advertisements. See *pre-to-post*.

precision sample See *probability sample*.

preclipped coupon See *pop-up coupon*.

predate A publication printed before its release date, such as a morning newspaper printed the previous night.

predesignated sample A sample of respondent households or individuals selected before a survey begins; some units may ultimately turn out to be nonrespondents.

preempt To replace a regularly scheduled television or radio program or commercial with another program or commercial. Sometimes due to a special or political broadcast. See *preemption*.

preemptible 1. Pertaining to a commercial occasion sold at a discount but subject to preemption pending its later sale at a higher rate. See next. 2. Satellite service that is not guaranteed and may be canceled. See *protection*.

preemptible rate The amount charged on a radio or television station for commercial time that is not guaranteed. The time may be sold to another advertiser who is willing to pay the full rate for the time. The pre-emptible rate is usually sold at a discount. See *fixed rate*.

preemptible spot A radio or television commercial time period that is subject to cancellation.

preemption 1. The cancellation by a network or station of a regularly scheduled program in order to substitute a special program. 2. See *preemptible spot*. 3. The cancellation of a network program by an affiliate.

preemptive claim An advertising claim making first use of a benefit or support for a benefit that competitors could also advertise but presumably will not rather than appear imitative.

prefade To roll back-timed music at a predetermined time so that it will end on time. The music is then faded in when needed.

preferred position A location for an advertisement in a periodical or television or radio schedule that an advertiser demands for strategic reasons and for which a higher than usual rate is charged. See *fixed position*, *run-of-paper*.

premiere The first public performance of a show or commercial. See *preview*.

premium 1. An item offered free or at a nominal price as an inducement to buy or obtain for trial the advertised product or service. See *giveaway*. 2. An extra charge or higher total cost, as for a preferred advertising position or for special treatment of advertisements. Also **premium price**. 3. A token cash payment mailed with survey diaries to serve as an inducement for households to participate in the survey and return the diary.

Premium Advertising Association of America, Inc. (PAAA) An organization of users of premiums in sales promotion founded in 1911. The PAAA conducts surveys relating to the use of premiums.

premium buyer A person who buys a product or service to get another product or service, usually free or at a special price, or who responds to an offer of a special product (premium) on the package or label, or sometimes in the advertising, of another product.

premium container A container for a retail product which, being reusable after the original contents are gone, functions as a premium.

premium pack A package of a product offering a premium, usually in either in-pack or on-pack form.

premium price See *premium*.

premium rate An above normal amount paid to a radio or television station to secure a special time period on the air.

premium television See *pay television*.

prepack display A display case or bin that arrives at a retail store containing the merchandise it is to display already in place. Also **prepack shipper**.

prepack shipper See previous.

prepasting Applying paste to outdoor advertising posters in the plant rather than in the field. The method uses a conveyor belt for paste application; posters are then sealed in plastic bags and stored until the posting date.

preprice To mark an item with its retail price before delivery to a store.

preprint 1. A printing of periodical advertising matter on separate sheets before actual publication; done by an advertiser for special purposes, e.g., to serve as retail displays or to gain support from retailers. 2. An advertising insert printed in advance and supplied to a newspaper or magazine; printing may be on one side only, allowing the periodical to print its own material on the reverse side. 3. See *hi-fi insert*.

preprint order form A form listing wholesalers' items constantly in stock; used by a retailer for ordering.

preproduction Pertaining to planning and organizational activities for a television, radio, or film production.

presentation A formal, face-to-face exposition of information, plans, visual material, etc., regarding a subject or a proposed course of action; used, for example, by advertising agencies to solicit new business and to sell a client a proposed advertising campaign.

presentational Pertaining to a form of delivery wherein the announcer or speaker talks to the camera as if it were the audience.

press 1. A machine for transferring words and images to paper using ink. Also **printing press**. 2. Originally the print media, now includes the electronic media. 3. Loosely, journalists and journalism.

press agent A person hired to promote and publicize performers, politicians, or other individuals or organizations through the use of free publicity obtained from the mass media. Also **drumbeater, flack, publicist**.

press clipping An item of interest removed from a publication by a reader or a clipping bureau.

press kit A portfolio of news releases, pictures, background information, and so on, distributed to the press for publicity purposes.

press proof One of the first copies of a press run; used for checking.

press release See *release*.

press revise The final proof made before a press run.

press run See *run*.

pressure sensitive Pertaining to any adhesive backing that holds firmly to a surface when pressed against it; protected by a paper covering that is peeled off at time of application; used on decals, posters, mailing labels, etc.

prestige bias A survey error that results if the respondent unconsciously or consciously tries to upgrade his or her social image or cultural level by reporting what he or she believes are more desirable preferences or activities. See *bias, nonsampling error*.

pretest 1. To test before use, as an advertisement on an audience sample. 2. See *pre*. 3. A preliminary tryout of a survey questionnaire to evaluate its workability and suitability. Also **field test**. See *post*.

pre-to-post 1. An observation, especially a measurement, of subjects' or respondents' behavior preceding and following a test treatment. 2. A measure of respondents' change in desire or purchase intent for a product or service before and after exposure to an advertisement. Also **pre-to-post choice, pre-to-post purchase intent**.

pre-to-post choice See previous.

pre-to-post purchase intent See *pre-to-post*.

preview 1. To watch a commercial before it is broadcast. 2. A viewing of a commercial before it is aired. 3. A pilot. 4. A performance of a scheduled broadcast performed for a studio audience before the broadcast. See *premiere*.

preview report An optional advance report that provides basic audience data on the early weeks of a regular report period, available in certain major markets from *Nielsen Station Index*.

price 1. The amount of money a seller receives or asks in exchange for a product or service; from the prospective buyer's viewpoint, the cost of the product or service. A key variable in marketing strategy and marketing mix. 2. To determine the amount of money a seller requests or receives in exchange for a product or service.

price cut 1. A reduced retail price marked on an item. 2. A reduction in price for goods or services.

price pack A retail package offering a temporary reduction from the standard price, used as a promotional inducement to purchasers. Also **cents-off**.

primary audience 1. The potential audience for a single advertising message. 2. The persons or places to which a periodical is sold or delivered for use. 3. The persons to whom the editorial content of a periodical is directed. Also **primary readership**. 4. The total number of primary readers of a periodical.

primary circulation The recorded circulation of a periodical, based on subscription and newsstand sales figures.

primary household A household that includes a subscriber or purchaser of a periodical.

primary marketing area (PMA) 1. The principal area of editorial and advertising coverage of a newspaper. 2. The principal area of sale for a product, service, or category whose sales are sharply skewed regionally. Also **heartland**.

Primary Metropolitan Statistical Area (PMSA) A geographic area containing a population of more than one million. See *Consolidated Metropolitan Statistical Area, Metropolitan Statistical Area*.

primary reader A person residing in a primary household who has looked at the content of a periodical.

primary readership See *primary audience*.

primary research Research that collects original data as opposed to using data from other studies.

prime time 1. The broadcast periods viewed or listened to by the greatest number of persons and for which a station charges the most for air time. 2. See *daypart*.

prime time access rule (PTAR) A ruling of the Federal Communications Commission limiting television network feeds in order to stimulate local prime time broadcasting.

principal 1. An owner or partner of an advertising agency or broadcast station. 2. A proprietor, partner, or major officer in a business.

Principal Register The main federal government register of trademarks kept under the provisions of the Trademark (Lanham) Act of 1946. Marks ineligible for registration may be eligible for inclusion in the *Supplemental Register*.

principle of closure A theory in psychology that a subject tends to mentally complete an object, action, etc., perceived as incomplete. Also **law of closure**. See *cloze procedure*.

printed bulletin An outdoor advertisement using printed sheets in a space usually used for painted bulletins.

printed word media The advertising media prepared by printing, e.g., periodicals, posters, shopping bags, and matchbooks. See *print media*.

printer's error (PE) In proofreading, a type error or undesirable feature of a proof that is deemed to be the fault of the typesetter and is therefore not charged to the advertiser or advertising agency in correction. See *author's alteration, editorial alteration*.

printing broker A person who locates printing facilities needed by a client. May be an advertising agency, for a fee included in the price quoted.

printing press See *press*.

Print Measurement Bureau (PMB) A Canadian organization of periodical publishers, advertisers, and advertising agencies formed to ensure standardized periodical readership figures.

print media The mass media that are not broadcast: newspapers, magazines, periodicals, and direct mail. See *printed word media*.

prism shot A photographic image taken through an image-multiplying prism so as to reproduce the same image many times.

private brand See next.

private label A wholesaler's or retailer's label bearing its own company name or another name it owns exclusively.

private mail Mail handled by special arrangement with a private delivery company other than the U.S. Postal Service.

prize broker One who arranges barters of merchandise given as prizes on television or radio shows in return for mentions of the brand names of the merchandise donated. See *barter broker*.

probability In sampling, the degree to which the frequencies occurring in data from a sample of a population may be expected to conform to the total population.

probability sample A statistical sample in which all population members in the universe being measured have an equal chance to be included. Results of a survey using a probability sample are projectible to the universe. Also **precision sample**.

probe A survey question asked as a follow-up to a previous question to elicit additional information or response.

problem-solution advertising A format for advertisements involving depiction of a consumer problem and demonstration of how the advertised product can solve the problem.

procedural bias See *nonsampling error*.

process color See *color separation*.

process plate A photoengraved plate that prints one of four separated colors in reproducing an original full-color illustration. See *color separation*.

process screen See *rear screen projection*.

process shot A shot in which foreground action is filmed against a front or back projection containing a previously filmed scene.

produce 1. To create the physical material (film, plates, tapes, etc.) to be used by a medium as an advertisement. 2. To manage the development of a planned event. See *producer*, *production*.

producer 1. An advertising agency employee responsible for the production of commercials, including selection of a production supplier, cost control, and quality control. See *production director*. 2. An individual who is ultimately responsible for a production, commercial, television series, and so on. Sometimes the financial backer of a production. 3. A third person to whom a commercial has been sold, assigned, transferred, leased, or otherwise disposed of.

producer-director An individual who handles the combined functions of a producer and a director.

producer goods See *industrial goods*.

product A physical item, especially one to which value has been added, offered for sale. Consists of a **tangible product** (a physical object or service package seen as the thing to be sold), an **extended product** (the unseen services and ancillary features such as packaging that accompany a tangible product), and the **generic product** (the essential benefit sought by the buyer in the product).

product acceptance test (PAT) A test of the absolute or relative rate or amount of acceptance of a product by consumers.

product awareness A measure of audience familiarity with or knowledge of a commercial product.

product copy 1. The portions of the prose in an advertisement devoted to product and claims. 2. All copy, sets, etc., used for a specific television or radio program.

product identification The ability of individuals to identify a radio or television program with a program sponsor or a commercial with a well-known line or logo.

product image The relative quality of a commercial product as perceived by an audience. See *brand image*.

production 1. A single radio or television program or commercial. 2. The process of organizing, writing, casting, designing, rehearsing, taping, and so on, of a show, program, or commercial. 3. The transformation of an idea into a finished product, such as an advertising campaign, book, and so on. 4. A show, especially with regard to the lavishness of effort and expense in producing it. 5. The processes of a company that ready a product for marketing.

production aids The stock music, sound effects, props, equipment, and so on, available for a production.

production company See *production house*.

production department 1. A station, network, or advertising agency department that designs and executes programs or commercials. 2. An advertising agency department that supervises the setting of type, the preparation of offset film and engravings, and the printing of print advertising materials. 3. The composing room and pressroom of a newspaper or magazine.

production director A person in charge of production, as for a publishing house, advertising agency, or television station. See *producer*, *production manager*.

production house An organization that specializes in making television commercials, although it may produce programs as well. Also **production company**.

production manager 1. The person responsible for the development of advertising materials (usually print) for an advertising agency. 2. The person responsible for the final reproduction in print of a periodical, book, or collateral printed piece. See *producer*, *production director*.

product life cycle A marketing theory that products or brands are like organisms in following a sequence of stages from conception to expiration. In the **introductory stage**, sales are derived primarily from first-time trial purchases. In the **growth stage**, sales increase from new trial, and repeat purchases serve as a base. In the **mature stage**, sales level out as new trial is offset by cessation of purchase, and rates of repeat purchase fluctuate. In the **declining stage**, sales diminish as cessation of purchases becomes the dominant mode.

product line An array of forms and sizes of a product or products sold under a single label or brand, or sold by a single manufacturer. Also **line**. See *merchandise mix*.

product manager See *brand manager*.

product position See *position*.

product programming An expanded presentation of product information in greater detail than a normal advertising time span allows. Also **infomercial**.

product protection The amount of time or space that a communications medium guarantees to advertisers between the broadcasting of competing commercials or the physical proximity of printed advertisements for competitive products. See *protection*.

product research 1. Research into consumer attitudes toward competing products' features. 2. Research into the physical properties and characteristics of product formulations or designs either employed by competitors or being considered for future use.

product research and development (PRD) A corporate process and personnel group using product research to further corporate marketing objectives. Also **research and development**.

product usage information Information about the consumers of different product types and brands, usually categorized demographically or psychographically.

product use study A survey conducted to determine if there is a difference in total product use or frequency of use between viewers and nonviewers of a commercial message or campaign.

professional journal A journal written primarily for a specific group of individuals, such as lawyers, physicians, or journalists.

professional magazine A publication for members of a specific profession or related professions. See *consumer magazine*, *trade press*.

profile A delineation of audience, reader, or buyer demographic or psychographic characteristics. See *audience profile*.

profit-taking strategy See *milking strategy*.

program 1. A complete, self-contained broadcast presentation, either commercially sponsored or sustaining. Also **show**. 2. One episode of a series. 3. A plan for a public relations campaign. 4. The instructions given to a computer to perform specific tasks. 5. To write instructions for a computer.

program analyzer A machine for recording audience reactions to television or radio commercials or programs. See *black box*.

program balance The arrangement of the various program elements to provide the desired audience reaction.

program basis An estimate of the actual cost of a television show, considering the discounts earned by the show based on the number of times it is telecast, but not any discounts earned by an individual sponsor; used by A.C. Nielsen.

program billboard See *billboard*.

program campaign An advertising campaign using programs, as opposed to spots.

program compatibility The appropriateness of advertising to a television or radio program, and vice versa.

program coverage factor The percentage of television households in a market able to receive a network program from fewer than three stations.

Program Cumulative Audiences (PCA) A report on the four-week cumulative home audiences for specific television programs, along with frequency distributions over the same period for each; issued five times a year by A.C. Nielsen.

program delivery rating The estimated percentage of households in a given area that are tuned in to a television or radio program at a given moment.

program effectiveness 1. A measure of audience acceptance as determined by ratings. 2. A measure of sponsor acceptance as determined by sales of advertising time.

program exclusivity See *exclusivity*.

program following The television or radio program following another. See *lead-out*.

program length commercial A pitch program of unspecified length consisting of a continuous demonstration or sales presentation.

program log A radio or television station log listing the time of programs, classification, source, commercial matter, station identification, and so on. Also **operating sheet**.

program music See *mood music*.

program opposite A radio or television program that is on the air at the same time on another station.

program practices See *continuity acceptance*.

program preceding The radio or television program that is broadcast immediately before another. See *lead-in*.

program profile 1. A graphic summary of audience reaction to a television or radio program in terms of minute-by-minute viewing levels or other measures. 2. The demographic or psychographic characteristics of a program's audience.

program rating See *rating*.

program rating summary report (PRS) See *household tracking report*.

program selector The individual with the greatest control over the others in a household regarding choice of television programs.

program station basis (PSB) The percentage of radio or television receivers in a coverage area tuned in to a given program at a given moment, taken as a basis for a rating of the program's success against all individual competition. See *rating*.

program use The airing of a commercial on two or more interconnected stations. See *dealer use, wild spot*.

projectall A device used to project opaque slides.

projected audience A rating expressed in terms of households reached by applying universe estimates.

projected audience size 1. The number of persons or households predicted for the audience of a commercial or a television or radio program. 2. The size of an audience as estimated on the basis of a sample.

projection 1. The statistical process of estimating unknown figures on the basis of existing ones, usually with known probability for error. 2. A figure estimated in this way. 3. The attribution of one's feelings and attitudes to another. See *identification*. 4. The process of reproducing a film or videotape image on a screen.

projection television A method of casting a television image on a large screen by using mirrors and lenses. May be either front or rear projection.

projective technique A psychological technique for determining underlying attitudes, topics of concern, etc., in which a subject is encouraged to give a spontaneous association in response to ambiguous pictures, shapes, or phrases.

projector An optical or electronic device used to project film, slides, video signals, etc., onto a screen or other surface.

promo 1. An announcement that plugs a network, station, sponsor, product, and so on. 2. An announcement that identifies the sponsor of a future television or radio program beyond the mention of the sponsor's name. Also **promotional announcement**, **promotion spot**.

promotion 1. An effort, usually temporary, to create interest in the purchase of a product or service by offering extra values; includes temporary discounts, allowances, premium offers, coupons, contests, sweepstakes, etc. Also **sales promotion**. 2. Loosely, any effort to encourage the purchase or use of a product or service. 3. The techniques designed to attract and retain listeners, viewers, readers, and so on, to one of the mass media, through attempts to demonstrate that the station or publication is superior to the competition.

promotional announcement See *promo*.

promotion allowance A price reduction by a manufacturer or its agent to a wholesaler or retailer who agrees to promote the product purchased under allowance. Also **merchandising allowance**.

promotional period See *drive period*.

promotion department A network, station, publishing firm, or other body's department concerned with audience and sales promotion.

promotion drive period See *drive period*.

promotion manager The individual in charge of a company's promotion department and its activities.

promotion period See *drive period*.

promotion spot See *promo*.

prompter card See *cue card*.

proof 1. An impression on paper of type, an engraving, or the like, for the purpose of checking the correctness and quality of material to be printed. Also **proof sheet**. 2. A trial print made from a negative. 3. See *proof of purchase*.

proof of performance The certification that an outdoor advertising service has been delivered.

proof of purchase A piece of evidence that a consumer has purchased a product or service (e.g., a receipt, label, package, or portion thereof); usually furnished to manufacturers, often by mail, in compliance with the terms of a sales promotion.

proofread 1. To read a printer's proof to check the correctness of the typesetting or page makeup and of adding corrections and alterations. See **proofreading marks**. 2. To find and eliminate errors in typography, punctuation, spelling, and grammar in printed material. May include the use of spelling and punctuation checkers using a computer word processing program.

proofreader's marks See *proofreading marks*.

proofreading marks The symbols used by proofreaders in correcting copy, normally indicated in the margins rather than on the copy itself. Also **proofreader's marks, proofreading symbols**.

PROOFREADER'S MARKS

ℒ	Take out
∧	Left out, insert
#	Insert space
℮	Turn inverted letter
⊗	Broken letter
⌄	Push down space
⊏	Move left
⊐	Move right
‖	Align type
=	Straighten line
⊙	Insert period
⌃	Insert comma
⌃	Insert colon
⌃	Insert semicolon
⌄	Insert apostrophe
⌄⌄	Insert quotation marks
=/	Insert hyphen
⌃	Insert inferior figure
⌄	Insert superior figure
ℒ	Set in small capitals
ital	Set in italic type
rom.	Set in roman type
bf	Set in bold face type
stet	Let it stand
out sc	Out, see copy
⊕	Spell out
¶	Start paragraph
no ¶	No paragraph

proofreading symbols See previous.

proof sheet See *proof*.

prop An object appearing in a photograph or motion picture or on a stage or television set to lend a realism to the setting or action. Also **property**.

propaganda A communication intended to influence belief and action, whether true or false information is contained in such communication.

property See *prop*.

proprietary pharmaceutical A product containing a drug sold at retail without a doctor's prescription. Also **over the counter, patent medicine**.

prospect A person who can be considered eligible for the purchase of a product or service by virtue of circumstance and interest.

prospecting Obtaining leads for further sales contacts rather than to make direct sales.

protected rate A cost for goods or services that a supplier agrees to maintain for a purchaser, despite later cost increases for other purchasers.

protection 1. A duplicate made in case the original is lost or damaged. 2. Satellite service that is guaranteed and may not be canceled. See *preemptible*. 3. The amount of time before and after the assigned mailing date during which the list owner will not allow the same names to be mailed by anyone other than the mailer cleared for that specific date.

protocol See *playback*.

proved name registration (PNR) The proven recall of a printed advertisement elicited by the display of the brand name, as used by Starch & Associates.

proven recall A respondent's recall of the content of advertising that is demonstrated by a repetition of the content.

PRS Program rating summary report. See *household tracking report*.

PRSA See *Public Relations Society of America*.

PS See *parallel single*.

PSA See *Photographic Society of America*, *public service announcement*.

PSB See *program station basis*.

PST Pacific Standard Time. See *time zone*.

psychogalvanic skin response See *galvanic skin response*.

psychogalvanometer In advertising research, an instrument used to measure a respondent's galvanic skin response. Also **galvanometer**. See *arousal method*, *galvanic skin response*.

psychographic Pertaining to the study of the personalities, attitudes, and life styles of individuals and groups, especially in quantitative terms; based on the belief that such readily measurable, descriptive characteristics serve as better predictors of behavior than do demographic characteristics.

PTAR See *prime time access rule*.

PUAA See *Public Utilities Advertising Association*.

public A group of persons, especially one that is interested in or affected by a particular action or idea. See *audience*, *market*.

public address system An audio system used to deliver messages to large numbers of people, usually by nonbroadcast means. Also **PA system**.

publication 1. The state of being published. 2. A format published, especially a periodical.

publication date The date on which a book, periodical, or other publication becomes available for sale to the public.

publication-set type Printing material for an advertisement that is prepared by the periodical in which it is run rather than supplied camera ready by the advertiser or its agency. Also **pub-set**. See *composition-set type*.

Public Broadcasting Service (PBS) A private organization for the selection and distribution of programs to noncommercial television stations.

public domain (PD) The realm of all publications, art works, songs, etc., that are not copyrighted and can therefore be appropriated by anyone.

publicist See *press agent*.

publicity Information regarding a person, corporation, product, etc., released for non-paid use by the mass media; often disguised as news.

publicity director An advertising agency or advertiser employee responsible for obtaining publicity for clients or the employer. Also **public relations director**.

publicity release A news story distributed by a press agent concerning a client. Also **blurb**. See *news release*, *publicity*, *puff*.

publicity still A photograph taken of a person or product to be used for publicity.

public opinion A range of viewpoints regarding an issue held by an interested group of persons.

public opinion survey A scientific sampling of the expressed attitudes of the public. See *survey*.

public relations (PR) 1. The process of influencing the attitudes and opinions of a group of persons in the interest of promoting a person, product, idea, institution, and so on. 2. The degree to which such entities have obtained understanding and goodwill from their publics.

public relations director See *publicity director*.

Public Relations Society of America (PRSA) A professional organization formed in 1948 to provide professional development and placement services for members.

public service advertising The commercials or advertisements placed in a medium with or without charge in the interest of promoting the general welfare and goodwill of its audience.

public service announcement (PSA) An announcement for which no charge is made and that promotes programs, activities, or services of federal, state, or local governments or nonprofit organizations, and other announcements regarded as serving community interests, excluding time signals, routine weather announcements, and promotional announcements.

public service copy Advertising copy of a civic or philanthropic nature posted on an outdoor advertising structure in the interest of community welfare.

public station A radio or television station that receives programming or funds from the Corporation for Public Broadcasting.

Public Utilities Advertising Association (PUAA) A worldwide association of public utility companies formed to foster advertising and public relations practices among members that will serve industry goals.

publish To print and disseminate printed matter, such as newspapers, magazines, and books.

publisher 1. A person or organization who issues, or causes to be issued, printed matter such as periodicals, books, music, etc. 2. The owner or designated chief executive officer of a newspaper or other periodical.

Publishers' Information Bureau, Inc. (PIB) A firm that publishes syndicated reports on the advertising schedules and expenditures, by product or service, of advertisers in consumer magazines. See *Leading National Advertisers–Publishers' Information Bureau*.

publisher's interim statement A sworn circulation statement issued at optional intervals by a periodical publisher between the regular circulation statements. See *Audit Bureau of Circulations*.

publisher's representative A person who solicits the purchase of advertising space from advertisers on behalf of a periodical publisher. See *representative, salesperson*.

publisher's statement A sworn statement made by a publisher as to the circulation, geographic distribution, etc., of a publication. See *Audit Bureau of Circulations*.

pub-set See *publication-set type*.

puff A publicity release containing more than the usual number of superlatives. Also **puff piece**.

puffery The extravagant praise lavished on a product by an advertiser that stops just short of deception.

puff piece See *puff*.

pull The degree of demand for a product or service from purchasers. See *push*.

pulling power The effectiveness of an advertisement or radio or television program in persuading the public to buy a product, watch a program, send in coupons, or take some other positive action.

pullout A self-contained section of a newspaper designed to be removed.

pulp 1. A disintegrated fibrous material, as wood or cloth, for making paper. 2. A popular magazine, appealing to an unsophisticated mass audience, printed on comparatively coarse, cheap paper, often newsprint. See *slick*.

pulp magazine See *pulp*.

Pulse, Inc. A broadcast audience survey organization founded in 1941.

pulsing The use of heavy advertising in cyclical or intermittent periods.

purchase-privilege premium A self-liquidator or semi-liquidator premium.

purchase proposition See *position*.

purchaser A person who buys a product or service, usually at retail. See *consumer*.

pure program rating An estimate of television or radio audiences for a program during a survey period, excluding any program preemptions that have occurred.

purge To eliminate duplicates or unwanted names and addresses from a mailing list.

push The force employed in convincing wholesalers and retailers to purchase a product. See *pull*.

push money (PM) A special reward given by manufacturers to agents' or dealers' employees for encouraging the sale of their goods rather than a competitor's; usually paid on each sale, whether pushed or not. Also **spiff**.

PUT See *persons using television*.

PV See *potential viewer*.

PVT See *persons viewing television*.

pylon 1. A support for an outdoor advertising display. 2. A tall outdoor sign.

pyramid See *pyramid makeup*.

pyramiding A method of testing mailing lists by starting with a small quantity and, based on positive results, continuing with larger and larger quantities until the entire list is mailed.

pyramid makeup A newspaper page composition in which advertisements are positioned from bottom to top in diminishing size so that they form steps from the bottom to the top outside. Also **pyramid**.

q & a See *question and answer*.

q and a See *question and answer*.

QC See *quad center, quality control*.

QL See *quad left*.

Q rating A rating of the percentage of television viewers or radio listeners who are aware of a given program and regard it as a favorite.

Q sort A research procedure in which a respondent sorts printed statements into piles that represent the degree of truth the respondent finds in the statements.

quad In typesetting, a measure of indentation equal to one em (**em quad** or **mutton**) or to a half em (**en quad** or **nut**). See *quadraphonic*.

quad center (QC) A centered line of type. See *quad left, quad right*.

quad left (QL) Less than a full line of type, positioned flush left. See *quad center, quad right*.

quadraphonic Pertaining to audio signals recorded in a manner permitting their playback as four separate information channels; used to better simulate the experience of live music. Also **quad**. See *monaural, stereophonic*.

quad right (QR) Less than a full line of type, positioned flush right. See *quad center, quad left*.

qualified circulation See *controlled circulation*.

qualified issue reader A person who qualifies for examination on his or her reactions to a periodical advertisement by giving evidence of having read the issue in which the advertisement appeared. Also **qualified reader**.

qualified reader See previous.

qualified respondent A person who has met the standards established for respondents in a consumer or audience research project.

qualified viewer A person who qualifies for examination on his or her reaction to a television commercial by giving some evidence of having watched the show on which the commercial was presented.

qualitative research Research involving differences of kind or condition rather than of amount or degree; usually used to broaden insight and develop hypotheses. Also **subjective research**. See *quantitative research*.

quality circulation Readership demographics that are highly desirable to the newspaper or magazine and its advertisers.

quality control (QC) An organizational process for maintaining product or service quality at a designated standard.

quality demographics The middle- to upper-income households containing individuals in the age bracket of late 20s to 50 years.

quantitative audience measurement See next.

quantitative research Statistical research involving differences of amount or degree rather than kind or condition; usually used to reach conclusions. Also **objective research, quantitative audience measurement**.

quantity discount 1. See *frequency discount*. 2. A discount for large purchases of goods, made either at one time or over an extended period.

quantity prints 1. Multiple film or videotape prints of a commercial prepared to permit its simultaneous airing on a number of networks or stations. 2. Multiple glossy prints of a still photograph, made from an original negative and used for mailings, sales kits, press kits, or the like; usually 8 by 10 inches.

quarter One-fourth of a fiscal or calendar year; three months.

quarter-hour audience An estimate of the average audience having viewed a station for a minimum of five minutes in a specific quarter hour. These quarter-hour total audiences, when accumulated over larger time periods, become **average quarter-hour (AQH)** audiences.

quarterly A publication that is issued every three months.

quarterly measurement A broadcast audience survey taken for a period of 12 consecutive weeks. See *sweep*.

quarter run See *quarter showing*.

quarter service See next.

quarter showing In transit advertising, the placement of car cards in one-fourth of the available vehicles in a given area, or one-fourth of those required for full service. Also **quarter run, quarter service**.

quartile One of four statistical parts into which the whole population of a sample is divided, the parts being arranged in some meaningful numerical order.

queen size poster A 30-by-88-inch transit advertising poster used on the sides of buses and other vehicles.

question and answer (q and a) (q & a) 1. A format for advertising copy in which consumers pose questions answered by advertisers or spokespeople. 2. An interview format. 3. A format for meetings, in which a spokesperson presents material in response to questions.

questionnaire A form that lists a series of closed-ended or open-ended questions to be answered and filled out by the respondent. See *schedule*.

quintile One of five statistical parts into which a whole population of a sample is divided, the parts being arranged in some meaningful numerical order.

quota 1. A sales goal set for an individual, usually expressed either in total dollars or as a percentage. 2. A media plan goal set in terms of, for example, individuals or households to be reached. 3. A number or proportion to be reflected by one element in a population sample; intended to produce a suitably balanced sample. See next.

quota sample A statistical sample in which the characteristics of those represented are selected in predetermined proportions, often based on census data. See *probability sample, random sample*.

quote A price estimate given for supplies, printing, equipment, and so on. See *estimate*.

R See next.

® Registered. A symbol used to identify a registered trademark. Also **R**. See *copyright*, *register*, *trademark*.

RAB Se *Radio Advertising Bureau, Inc.*

rack A system of shallow shelves, hanger hooks on pegboard, or hoppers for the storage and display of retail merchandise. See *shelf*.

rack focusing The focusing of a camera on a performer or object, keeping the background or foreground out of focus, in order to concentrate a viewer's attention. Also **selective focusing**.

rack folder An advertising or informational folder intended for display in and dispensing from a rack.

rack jobber A service wholesaler who, by exclusive agreement with a retailer, prices and stocks a department of specified footage (usually of nonfood items in a grocery store). Also **rack merchandiser**.

rack merchandiser See previous.

rack sale The sale of newspapers from unattended open racks or boxes, payment dependent on the honesty of the takers. Seldom seen now.

RADAR See *Radio's All-Dimension Audience Research*.

RADI See *Radio Area of Dominant Influence*.

radio 1. A mass communications medium consisting of audio signals carried by radio waves created by licensed broadcasting stations to listeners interested in the information or entertainment contained in such signals; often a medium for advertising. 2. The electromagnetic waves used to transmit audio and video signals to properly equipped receivers. 3. A radio receiver.

Radio Advertising Bureau, Inc. (RAB) A trade association of radio stations and networks, established to promote radio as an advertising medium.

Radio Area of Dominent Influence (RADI) A market description used by Pulse for counties where most of the radio reception is of programs from home stations.

Radio Expenditure Report (RER) A syndicated quarterly report on national expenditures for advertising time, by advertiser.

radio family See *radio household*.

radio format See *format*.

radio home See *radio household*.

radio household A household that owns any type or model of radio, even when the radio is temporarily out of order, being repaired, or not being used for any other reason. Also **radio family**, **radio home**.

Radio Information Center (RIC) An organization that tracks radio formats on a monthly basis.

radio rating point A unit of radio audience size equal to one percent of the radio-owning households in the area under study.

Radio's All-Dimension Audience Research (RADAR) An audience research project funded by the four national radio networks. See *All Radio Methodology Study*, *Cumulative Radio Audience Method*.

ragged Pertaining to type that is set with an even right margin but an uneven left margin (**ragged left**) or, more commonly, an even left margin but an uneven right margin (**ragged right**). See *justification*.

rag paper A high-quality book or typing paper composed wholly or in part of linen or cotton fibers instead of wood fibers.

railroad showing A bulletin or poster used alongside a railroad track or in a station. Also **station poster, transportation display poster**.

rain lap The pasting of outdoor poster sheets from the bottom row of paper up, thus covering the top edge of the bottom sheets with the sheet above; done to prevent rain from seeping between the poster and the panel face and thus peeling the sheets from the board.

R and D Research and development. See *product research and development*.

R and F See *reach and frequency*.

random access A method of obtaining data from computer storage on a nonsequential basis.

random digit dialing (RDD) A procedure for sampling all telephone households in an area using a random digit sample, which includes unlisted numbers. See next.

random digit sample (RDS) A random sample of possible telephone numbers made without the use of a telephone book in order to obtain a representative sample containing unlisted as well as listed numbers.

randomization A process used to ensure that a statistical sample will be selected at random from the total population.

randomness 1. A characteristic of any phenomenon that is devoid of measurable

regularity. 2. An equalized probability of any member of a population being selected for a sample.

random sample A sample taken from a population, each member of which has an equal chance of being selected. Also **unrestricted sample**. See *probability sample*, *quota sample*.

range The difference between the highest and lowest measurements in a study.

rank 1. The relative status of one thing with relation to another, e.g., the effectiveness of one advertisement with relation to another. 2. To arrange in order of importance, desirability, use, or value.

rank order correlation The establishment of the relationship of variables that are scored according to rank rather than by quantity.

rate 1. The amount, per unit of space or time purchased, charged by a communications medium to an advertiser. 2. To estimate media audience size based on a research sample.

rate base 1. A minimum guaranteed circulation used as a basis for determining advertising space rates. 2. A minimum audience size guaranteed by a medium in return for a stated advertising rate.

rate book 1. A book giving advertising rates for a number of communications media. See *Standard Rate and Data Service, Inc.* 2. A sales representative's manual of prices for products or services.

rate card A card listing advertising charges and other information for a communications medium.

rate class The type of rate in effect during a specific period of the television or radio broadcast day. See *class rate*.

rate cutting The practice of selling time or space for less than the price set on the rate card, or the offering of bonus space or time.

rated Pertaining to an outdoor advertising structure that has been evaluated for visibility, competition, direction of traffic (incoming or outgoing), type of area, and circulation.

rated exposure unit (REU) A measure of an advertising medium's value.

rate differential The difference in rates charged by local media to local and national advertisers. Also **differential**.

rate holder A printed advertisement or broadcast spot that is run specifically to maintain the rate of a long-term advertising contract.

rate inclusions The facilities and personnel available without extra charge to the advertiser at rate card prices.

rate of response See *response rate*.

rate of return See *response rate*.

rate protection A guarantee of continuation at a former rate, made to an advertiser having a contract with a communications medium that raises its rates while the contract is in effect.

rating A figure establishing the popularity of a television or radio program or the exposure obtained by the advertising it carries, usually measured as a percentage of the households able to receive a program that actually are tuned to it for a given period. Also **program rating**. See *audience, average audience rating, households-using-radio rating, households-using-television rating, individuals-using-radio rating, individuals-using-television rating, instantaneous audience rating, national rating, program delivery rating, sets-in-use rating, share, station rating, total audience rating*.

rating distortion An activity by a broadcast station that may affect the way survey respondents or diary keepers record or report their listening or viewing without changing their actual listening or viewing.

rating point One of the theoretically possible 100 points on a rating scale. See *gross rating point*.

rating scale A scale of degrees used to measure a survey respondent's attitudes regarding a subject under investigation, such as product preference or purchase intent.

rating service A research organization that performs quantitative and/or qualitative audience measurements. See *A.C. Nielsen Company, Arbitron, Pulse, Inc., Trendex, Inc., Videoprobe Index, Inc.*

ratio scale A statistical measurement scale with known and equal intervals between points and a known true zero point.

raw stock Unexposed and unprocessed film. See next.

raw tape Unused audiotape or videotape. Also **blank tape, uncut tape, virgin tape**.

R&D Research and development. See *product research and development*.

RDD See *random digit dialing*.

RDS See *random digit sample*.

reach 1. The estimated number of households or individuals in the audience of a television or radio program, group of programs, or announcement, at least once over some specified period. Also **net audience, unduplicated audience**. See *circulation, cumulative audience, frequency*. 2. The percentage of the population or households covered by an outdoor advertising campaign.

reach and frequency (R and F) A criterion for evaluating the level of cumulative audience exposure to an advertising effort on the basis of the percentage of all persons or households who are exposed to the advertising (**reach**), and the average number of exposures for each (**frequency**), over a stated period. Gross rating points are equal to the product of reach and frequency.

reaction shot   A cut to a camera shot showing the effect of action or dialogue on a character.

readability   The relative ease of comprehending a written text. See *legibility*.

reader   A person who has read the material in question, as a periodical or advertisement.

reader ad   A printed advertisement, usually all type, that appears to be news or editorial matter; often required to be marked as advertising.

reader confidence   The loyalty of a regular readership to a periodical.

reader exposure   See *exposure*.

reader impression study   A study to determine the significance of a periodical advertisement to ad-noters; conducted by the research firm of Starch & Associates.

reader interest   1. The interest in a company's periodical advertising on the part of readers, measured either by the numbers interested in one advertisement or by the number of readers of one periodical interested in the advertising for that particular product or service as opposed to that for others. 2. A newspaper or magazine feature evoking a response from a reader.

reader profile   A demographic description of the readers of various print media.

reader response   The actions taken by readers of a publication, especially letters, coupon requests for more information, or orders prompted by a print advertisement.

reader service card   A return postal card bound into a magazine containing numbers corresponding to various advertisers from whom information may be requested by

circling the proper number(s) and returning the card. Also **bingo card**.

readership   The total number of people actually reached by a publication; the primary and pass-along audiences combined. See *circulation*.

readership study   1. A survey of the characteristics of the readership of a periodical. 2. A survey of a publication's readers about their attitudes toward the publication and its content.

readers per copy   A ratio of a publication's readership to its circulation; usually stated as an average number of readers per copy.

reader traffic   The pattern of attention shift from one part of a periodical to another on the part of its readers.

read in   A cutline or head that leads (reads in) to the head or text that follows. See *read out*.

reading days of issue exposure   The total readership of a periodical multiplied by the average number of days the average individual is exposed to its contents.

reading diagonal   The path a reader's eyes follow on a page; from upper left to lower right.

reading matter   In a newspaper, editorial and news matter as opposed to advertising matter.

reading notice   A brief, all-text newspaper advertisement set in the form of editorial matter but labeled "advertisement" to prevent deception. See *reader ad*.

reading time   The average time spent by the average reader of a periodical on any given issue.

read most   The number of persons who read more than half of an advertisement in a periodical; the term is used by the research firm of Starch & Associates.

read out A subordinate head that leads (reads out) to the text that follows. See *read in*.

real time The time required for a television or radio performance according to the script, without lengthening or shortening.

rear projection (RP) See next.

rear screen projection (RP) The projection of images from the side opposite the audience onto a translucent screen, in order to create a background scene. Also **process screen, rear projection**.

reason why An advertising statement or advertisement offering specific, objectively stated arguments in support of claimed benefits.

rebate 1. A refund of payment, as one by an advertising medium to an advertiser because of a discount earned beyond that originally anticipated. 2. To make such a payment.

rebroadcast 1. To repeat a broadcast, or segment of one, as to present it at a more favorable time in a time zone different from that of the original broadcast. 2. See *repeat*.

recall 1. To remember the content of a program, periodical, or advertisement. 2. The content or extent of such recollection. See *day-after recall*. 3. A request for a return of a product for service or replacement, usually from manufacturers to owners.

recall interview A research method in which the interviewer asks respondents to remember their behavior at some time in the past. Recall interviews may be either aided or unaided. See *coincidental interview*.

recall method A method of testing the effectiveness of advertising through the ability of respondents to recall advertisements.

recency The latest purchase or other activity recorded for an individual or company on a specific customer mailing list. See *frequency*.

recency-frequency-monetary-value ratio (RFMVR) A formula used to evaluate the sales potential of names on a mailing list.

recent reading technique A method employed by *Target Group Index* for analyzing magazine readership by asking respondents whether they have read any issue of a certain magazine in the last week or month.

recognition 1. The ability of research subjects to recall a specific advertisement or commercial message. 2. An agreement by a communications medium to regard an advertising agency as bona fide, competent, and ethical and thus entitled to discounts. Also **agency recognition**. See *recognized agency*.

recognition method An aided recall method for determining whether a respondent in a survey has been exposed to an advertisement.

recognized agency An advertising agency that is allowed agency commissions from the media because it meets certain industry standards. See *recognition*.

recommendation The approval of an advertising agency by a communications medium for recognition by its members. Also **agency recommendation**.

recommended agency An agency that is a member of a standards-setting media association.

record 1. A collection of data. 2. A phonographic disc or electrical transcription containing recorded audio signals. 3. To store an audio performance or information on a phonographic disc or electrical transcription.

recorded program A broadcast program primarily featuring discs, transcriptions, or tapes.

recorder An electronic device used to make a permanent record of audio or video information, such as a tape recorder, videotape recorder, or wire recorder.

Recordimeter™ An electronic device used by A.C. Nielsen to record, for national audience composition research, the times that a television set is in use, but not which channels. See *Audimeter*.

recording 1. The process by which audio or video information is stored for later playback. 2. A disc or tape on which audio or video signals are stored.

recording error See *response error*.

recording medium A medium capable of storing information for later playback, such as a tape, disc, or film.

recording supervisor The individual in charge of servicing clients or other employees in a recording company, postproduction facility, and so on.

red book An informal name for the *Standard Directory of Advertising Agencies* and for the *Standard Directory of Advertisers*.

redeem To fulfill the requirements of a consumer promotional offer, as a coupon or trading stamps, in a prescribed manner resulting in receipt of goods at reduced price or gratis.

redemption 1. The cashing in of coupons or trading stamps to obtain discounts or premiums. 2. The percentage of coupons or trading stamps issued that are cashed in. Also **redemption rate**.

redemption rate See previous.

red good A product that is quickly consumed and has a high rate of replacement; usually broadly available, requiring little service, and priced with a low gross margin (e.g., food products). See *orange good, yellow good*.

reduce To decrease the size of a picture, artwork, type, and so forth, during reproduction.

reducing glass A double-concave lens that is mounted in a frame to be used for reducing the apparent size of an image to judge its effect at a smaller size.

reduction negative A film negative made from a larger negative.

reduction print A film print made from a larger negative.

reestablishing shot A return to the camera shot that established the scene originally. See *establishing shot*.

reference group A population group with which an individual identifies himself or herself, regardless of actual membership in the group.

reference medium A publication of statistical and other useful information issued periodically for commercial use.

reflection button A small glass or plastic reflector, used in combination with others to create letters or designs in unilluminated outdoor advertisements. See next.

reflector A round button, visible at night by reflected light, used to form letters and designs on outdoor signs.

refund 1. A return by the seller to the buyer of some or all of the money exchanged for the purchase of goods or services, when the buyer is legitimately dissatisfied, for one of a number of reasons, with the purchase.

region A geographic area, usually including several states, designated for analytic or administrative purposes. See *unit, zone*.

regional chain A group of affiliated retail stores in a specific geographic area.

regional channel station An AM radio station broadcasting to an entire region rather than to an urban area after sundown, but allowed less power than that of a clear-channel station.

regional edition An edition of a national periodical distributed in one geographic area; its advertising space can be purchased separately.

regional feed 1. A feed from a network to a region of the country. 2. A feed of an announcement to a group of network-affiliated stations in a region. Also **sectional feed**.

regional network A radio or television network broadcasting to one region of the country.

regional publication A magazine designed to appeal to regional tastes and life styles.

regional rate A rate offered by some radio and television stations to regional advertisers at less than the national rate but more than the local rate.

regional split See *split run*.

register 1. The correct superimposition of each color plate of an illustration; the print is "in register" if properly printed and "out of register" if not. 2. To cause a trademark, patent, copyright, etc., to be recorded by a government agency to establish a claim to its exclusive use. 3. The proper alignment of two or more images on separate animation cels.

register mark An indicator, usually in the shape of a plus, printed in the margins of pages to assist in proper registration.

regular Pertaining to an outdoor poster panel or billboard without illumination; a casual designation for "unilluminated."

regular audit An audit of a periodical's circulation conducted at established intervals.

related 1. Pertaining to two or more advertisements, by two or more advertisers, that are published in such a way as to support one another's message. 2. Pertaining to retail items that are generally used together and are thus appropriate to sell or promote together.

related display A retail display of dissimilar but related items.

relay station A retransmitting station used to link a remote station and a broadcast station. Also **satellite**.

release 1. An informational document on a recent or current event, as within a business organization, distributed to broadcast stations, newspapers, and magazines for public relations purposes. Also **news release**, **press release**. 2. A legal contract assigning a person's rights to use of his or her name, likeness, ideas, or property to another party in return for a stated consideration (e.g., a photo release). Also **model release, release form**.

release date The earliest date on which advertising or publicity sent to media may be used.

release form See *release*.

release print A print of a television film or motion picture intended for distribution.

reliability The consistency of a research test design, measured by its ability to produce repeatedly similar results under similar conditions (**test-retest reliability**), and by the ability of one part of the design to produce results compatible with those from the remainder (**split-half reliability**).

relief See next.

relief printing A method of printing from inked surfaces that are raised from the base of the plate, as in letterpress printing. Also **relief**. See *intaglio, letterpress*.

remainder A unit of product, especially a book, remaining unsold at the regular price after demand for the product at that price level has expired; usually sold at a discount. See *overstock, second*.

remarketing A campaign designed to reach the prospects who did not respond to the first effort to sell a product or service (e.g., periodical subscriptions, book clubs, or cable television services).

remembrance advertising See next.

reminder advertising 1. A campaign of brief mentions of a product or service that is assumed to be familiar to the audience. Also **remembrance advertising**. 2. Advertising intended to remind the audience about benefits of a product or service or the immediacy of their need for such benefits.

remnant space The magazine advertising space that is sold at a discount, usually in regional editions, to ensure that it will be used.

remote A broadcast that originates from outside a station. Also **field pickup, field production, outside broadcast, pickup, remote pickup**. See *nemo*.

remote pickup (RP) (RPU) See *remote*.

remote unit See *mobile unit*.

rendering An advertising layout or rough illustration.

renewal 1. An extra outdoor poster used to replace one that is damaged. The number of posters printed for renewal purposes varies from 10 to 20 percent of the total order. 2. A renewed periodical subscription. 3. The extending of a contract on or before its expiration date.

renewal right See *first refusal*.

rental See *mailing list rental*.

rep See *representative*.

repeat 1. To run the same advertisement more than once. 2. A repeated broadcast of a television or radio program. 3. A periodic broadcast of a specific, single show over a number of years. Also **rerun**.

repetition The reiteration of an advertisement, slogan, or theme to strengthen its impression.

replacement medium A local communications medium used in place of a national medium, as for advertisement testing or market expansion in the area.

reply card A sender-addressed card included in a direct mailing on which the recipient may indicate his or her response to the offer.

reported spending See *traceable expenditure*.

reporting error See *response error*.

Report on Syndicated Programs (ROSP) A supplementary report by *Nielsen Station Index* that contains a comprehensive profile of the audiences, competition, and lead-in programs to more than 300 syndicated shows.

reportorial Pertaining to a style or format for advertisements imitating factual, objective editorial.

reposting charge An additional cost incurred for posting a change of design to an outdoor advertising poster before the expiration of the display period.

representative 1. A person who solicits the purchase of advertising space or time on behalf of a medium. Also **rep, sales representative**. See *station representative*. 2. A salesperson for an agent.

representative sample A form of quota sample in which percentages of various elements of a population are included that are regarded as representative of the whole population. See *quota sample*.

reprint A proof or copy of an advertisement printed in addition to those reproductions printed in a publication. Generally printed in quantity, and often used for merchandising purposes.

repro See next.

reproduction proof A camera ready, carefully checked page of copy used to make a printing plate. Also **enamel proof, photo proof, repro, repro proof, slick**.

repro proof See previous.

reproportion To change only one of two dimensions when enlarging or reducing flat copy. Normally employed when adjusting ads to fit various newspaper column widths without changing column lineage.

RER See *Radio Expenditure Report*.

rerun See *repeat*.

resale price maintenance The maintenance of a minimum retail price agreed with or imposed by a manufacturer.

rescale See *resize*.

reschedule 1. To select a new time period to broadcast a radio or television program that was not aired, for any reason, in its original time slot. 2. To select a new issue of a periodical in which to run an advertisement that could not run as planned.

research 1. A process of systematic scientific investigation designed to develop information or products of use to marketers. 2. A group of employees in an organization responsible for conducting such investigations. 3. To conduct such investigations.

research and development (R and D) (R&D) See *product research and development*.

research department An advertising agency department that collects and analyzes data on products, markets, advertisers, and the media.

research director An advertising agency or advertiser employee responsible for procurement, analysis, and dissemination of information on factors influencing the market for goods. Also **director of research, marketing research director**.

residual A fee paid to talent for reruns of commercials, programs, announcements, narration, and so forth, according to a scale usually established by union agreements. Also **reuse fee, SAG fee**.

resize To alter the dimensions of an advertisement for use in a periodical space other than that for which it was originally designed. Also **rescale**.

resolution The clarity of a television image as received by a set.

respondent A person who makes solicited answers to questions in a survey.

respondent set 1. The body of attitudes held by a survey respondent regarding matters relevant to the survey, e.g., to being questioned, or to the product or advertising that is the subject of the survey. 2. The total number of people who respond to a consumer promotion offer, as a premium or refund; used to calculate such promotion costs when multiplied by the individual cost of such offers.

response 1. A reply to an interviewer's question. 2. An action prompted by an advertisement. See *reader response, return*.

response device In direct mail, any card or envelope used to respond to the offer, such as a business reply card.

response error A survey error that occurs if a respondent or interviewer fails to record information according to the instructions. Also **recording error, reporting error**. See *nonsampling error*.

response list A compilation of names of individuals who have purchased an item as a result of direct mail advertising.

response rate The proportion of a designated sample of persons who provide usable data to a survey. The calculation of response rates involves adjustments to account for unusable samples and for incomplete and otherwise unusable diaries or questionnaires. Also **cooperation rate, rate of response, rate of return, success rate**. See *bias of nonresponse, call-back, nonresponse*.

restock To order additional quantities of a retail product to maintain stock at a satisfactory level. 2. To stock a product again that has been allowed to go out of stock.

restricted 1. Pertaining to sales items not to be legally sold in certain geographic areas. 2. Pertaining to items to be sold in certain geographic areas only under special legal restrictions.

retail advertising 1. Advertising designed to promote local merchants and their goods and services. 2. Advertising placed by local merchants. Also **local advertising**.

retail cooperative A cooperative wholesale purchasing organization owned by retailers.

retailer-owned wholesaler A wholesale organization owned by a retail cooperative. Also **cooperative wholesaler**.

retailer's service program A program of services provided by a wholesaler to enable independent retailers to compete with chain stores.

retail man See *detail rep*.

retail rate 1. A television or radio station time rate for local retailers. 2. The space rate charged local advertisers in local print media. See *local rate, national advertising rate*.

retail rep See *detail rep*.

retail trading zone The area beyond an urban area whose residents regularly trade in the urban area.

retouch 1. To alter a photograph or artwork by hand to emphasize or introduce desired features or eliminate undesired ones. 2. To alter film negatives or positives to correct imperfections or achieve desired reproduction.

retrospect See *flashback*.

return 1. A direct response by a consumer to an advertiser in consequence of a sales offer, contest, or coupon promotion. See *response*. 2. The mail received by a broadcast station or advertiser as the result of a commercial or campaign.

return card A self-addressed postcard sent with advertising to encourage customer inquiries or orders. See *response device*.

return envelope An addressed reply envelope, either stamped or unstamped, as distinguished from a business reply envelope that carries a postage payment guarantee; included with a mailing.

returns per thousand circulation A figure used in gauging the effectiveness of an advertising campaign in a given communications medium by the percentage of direct responses to an advertisement.

REU See *rated exposure unit*.

reuse fee See *residual*.

revamp To give a new look or form to old copy without rewriting the material. See *rewrite*.

reverse 1. The mirrorlike inversion of the elements on a printing plate or the like in relation to their order on the surface printed from it. Also **reverse plate**. See *flop*. 2. A photographic print in which values are inverted from the state in which they appear on a negative, as white type reversed out of a dark background. See *reverse type*.

reverse angle A camera shot taken from the opposite side of the original shot. Also **reverse shot**.

reverse compensation Payment for television programs by an affiliated television station to the network. See *network compensation*.

reverse kicker See *barker*.

reverse plate See *reverse*.

reverse shot See *reverse angle*.

reverse type Type that is printed the opposite from normal, such as white letters on a dark background. See *reverse*.

revise 1. A proof taken to determine if corrections on a previous proof were properly made. Also **revised proof**. 2. To make corrections as on a proof, layout, copy, etc.

revised proof See previous.

rewrite To write copy again to improve it. See *revamp*.

RIC See *Radio Information Center*.

ride the boards See next.

ride the showing To inspect the outdoor advertising panels that comprise an advertising buy. Also **ride the boards**.

right of first refusal See *first refusal*.

right of publicity The concept that well-known persons should have control over the use of their names for commercial or advertising purposes.

right to refuse The right of the media to refuse advertising or any other material.

river A conspicuous chain of white space running down a page of print because of poorly positioned word spacing from line to line; may distract the reader.

roadblock To present simultaneously the same commercial on all television or radio stations in a given geographic area; obtains maximum reach in a given period.

Robinson-Patman Act An act of Congress passed in 1936 that forbids unfair trade practices such as price and payment discrimination in interstate commerce.

rocker (*sl.*) A radio station with a rock format.

rock format See *format*.

role playing technique An interview technique in which respondents are encouraged to imagine the part they would play in an imaginary situation as a way of determining their attitudes.

roll 1. To play a videotape or film. 2. See *roll-out*.

roller caption See next.

roller title A device used to move titles up, down, or across in front of a television or film camera. Also **roller caption, roll title**.

roll-in 1. An insertion and integration of a commercial into a television or radio broadcast. 2. To insert and integrate a commercial into a television or radio broadcast.

rolling sample An audience measurement technique that averages samples taken over time.

rolling split A cumulative purchase of space in syndicated newspaper supplements on a market-by-market basis in such a way that full national advertising coverage is obtained.

roll-out 1. To mail the remaining portion of a mailing list after successfully testing a portion of that list. 2. To advertise a product, often new, in a limited geographic area before committing to a national campaign. Also **roll**.

roll title See *roller title*.

roman The standard text type, characterized by upright thick and thin strokes with serifs. See *italic*.

roof bulletin An outdoor advertising bulletin built on the roof of a building.

ROP See *run of paper*.

ROP color See *run-of-paper color*.

ROS See *run of schedule*.

ROSP See *Report on Syndicated Programs*.

roster recall   A method of testing audience recall of television or radio programs that uses lists of the programs given to respondents. Also **roster study**. See *aided recall*.

roster study   See previous.

rotary plan   See next.

rotate   1. To move an advertisement from one outdoor board location to another to give it wide exposure. Used if a showing is scheduled for more than 30 days. Also **rotary plan**. 2. To move older retail items to the front of the shelf to sell them first. 3. To present a series of advertisements in a regular order of repetition.

rotating bulletin   The process of moving an advertiser's message from one outdoor advertising location to another at stated intervals to achieve a more balanced coverage of a market. See *set showing*.

roto   See next.

rotogravure   1. An intaglio printing process using a copper cylinder into which the printing image is etched. 2. A newspaper supplement with a magazine-like format printed by this process. Also **roto**.

rough   An unfinished layout or dummy, showing only the general conception of a design. Also **rough dummy, rough layout, visual**. See *comprehensive layout, layout*.

rough cut   A preliminary arrangement of film or tape shots in the early stages of editing. See *answer print, final cut*.

rough dummy   See *rough*.

rough layout   See *rough*.

rough mix   A preliminary joining of music, effects, and dialogue on one track.

rough print   An uncorrected film print that is used primarily to check shot composition and timing. Also **sample print, slop print**.

round robin   An interconnecting circuit between or among television or radio sta-

tions that allows instantaneous switching between origination points.

route list   A list of local retail stores, with notes regarding volume of business and operating methods, especially for use by salespeople.

RP   See *rear projection, rear screen projection, remote pickup*.

RPU   Remote pickup. See *remote*.

rub off   See next.

rub on   Pertaining to letters, numerals, and symbols that can be affixed to paper or other materials by rubbing; used for layout and graphics. Also **rub off, transfer letters**.

rule   A straight, type-high border or divider line, either plain or decorative, used around advertisements to separate or visually enhance them.

run   1. The total number of copies of printed jobs, newspapers, magazines, collateral pieces, etc., that are printed as ordered. Also **press run**. 2. A complete showing of all the episodes of a television series. 3. See *showing*. 4. To use an advertisement in one or more issues of a periodical.

runaround   See next.

run-around   A block of type, where a portion is set to less than full measure to leave space for an illustration, large initial, and so on. Also **runaround, set around**.

rundown   A producer's list of the intended order of shots and effects to be used in a television or motion picture production.

run in   To set a piece of copy as a direct continuation of the previous copy, without beginning a new paragraph. Also **run on**.

running text   The main text on a printed page, as opposed to its display lines.

running time   The time that a television or radio commercial or program is expected to take on actual presentation.

running title See *crawl*.

run of book 1. Pertaining to the positioning of advertising at the discretion of the magazine instead of the advertiser. 2. The status of an advertisement positioned at the publisher's discretion. See *fixed position*, *run of paper*.

run of paper (ROP) 1. Pertaining to the positioning of advertising at the discretion of the newspaper instead of the advertiser. 2. The status of an advertisement positioned at the publisher's discretion. Also **run of press**. See *fixed position*, *run of book*.

run-of-paper color (ROP color) 1. Color advertising run anywhere in a newspaper that is convenient. 2. Color advertising run in the main section of a paper rather than in a supplement.

run of press See *run of paper*.

run of schedule (ROS) The status of a television or radio commercial for which a specific day, or specific hour, has not been reserved by the advertiser, but rather the broadcast station is left to select the time. Also **floating time**, **run of station**. See *best time(s) available*.

run of station See previous.

run on See *run in*.

run out To set the first line of an indented paragraph full measure while indenting the remainder, creating a hanging indentation.

runovers See *overset*.

run-through A preliminary rehearsal of a television commercial or television or motion picture performance with all elements present.

rural station A broadcast station having exclusive coverage of a rural area.

rushes The rough, unedited prints of motion picture film shot the previous day, shown for evaluation and selection. Also **dailies**.

rush print See previous.

SAA   See *Specialty Advertising Association*.

saddle stitch   A type of magazine or booklet binding using staples along the center fold between the pages. See *side stitch*.

safe area   See next.

safety   1. The distance between a magazine's page edge and printed copy (type and/or illustrations) not intended to be trimmed off in a full or partial bleed advertisement. 2. A second original or dub of an audiotape or videotape made in case of damage to the original. Also **safe area**, **safety area**.

safety area   See previous.

SAG   See *Screen Actors' Guild*.

SAG fee   See *residual*.

salable sample   A product sample of trial size that is sold at a nominal price at retail.

sale   1. A transaction involving the exchange of goods or services for money or credit. 2. An offer of products or services for purchase at temporarily reduced prices, made by a retailer.

sales   1. A marketing process involving personal development and maintenance of prospects for purchases as a means of meeting marketing objectives. 2. A commercial profession or craft in which an individual seeks to develop and maintain buyers for goods he or she wishes to sell. 3. The amount of goods exchanged by an individual or organization over a stated period.

sales area test   A test market conducted in a geographic area where sales results can

be obtained speedily and conveniently, as in a sales district; can determine the advisability of extending the campaign to other areas. See *market testing*, *test market*.

sales audit   A periodical measurement of dollar and unit movement of products through retail stores; commonly done by establishing store inventories at the opening and closing of the audit, and totaling receipts of merchandise for the period.

sales call norm   An organization's estimate of the number or length of sales calls a salesperson should make over a stated period, by account or in total.

sales contest   A competition open to a company's sales personnel or to customers and prospects, structured to reward superior performance or unusually large purchases. See *sales incentive*.

sales control   The continuous and systematic inspection of a firm's sales results in order to develop effective plans.

sales deficit   The difference between the actual sales volume and the sales par in a given sales area.

sales department   1. The department at a radio or television station, magazine, newspaper, or outdoor company concerned with the sale of time or space to advertisers and advertising agencies. 2. The department at a manufacturing company or organization concerned specifically with the sale of product or service.

sales effectiveness test   A test of the effectiveness of a communications medium or advertising campaign in selling a product.

sales force The group of employees of a company that is responsible for developing sales and sales prospects. See *sales department*.

sales forecast An estimate of the sales volume for a specific future period.

sales incentive A reward in excess of salary or commission provided to a salesperson in return for achieving a stated sales goal. See *sales contest, salesperson's premium*.

sales letter A letter on a company's letterhead mailed to a sales prospect.

sales life The period during which an item available for retail sale is likely to retain its original quality and may thus be sold. Also **shelf life**.

salesman See *salesperson*.

sales management The planning, coordination, and control of sales operations and the recruitment and supervision of salespeople.

sales manager (SM) An employee of a marketer responsible for sales management.

sales meeting A meeting sponsored by an organization with members of its sales force, for informational, training, and motivational purposes.

sales network A linking together of a number of media outlets for the purpose of selling joint time or space at a discounted rate.

sales par The amount of sales a particular area should contribute to a company's total sales in an average selling effort.

salesperson 1. A person designated by an organization to sell products. 2. See *space salesperson*. 3. See *time salesperson*.

salesperson's premium A reward to a salesperson for extraordinary effort or for leadership in the amount sold. See *sales incentive*.

sales portfolio A manual of information carried by a salesperson for reference or display.

sales potential 1. The maximum sales likely to be achieved by a company's products in a given period. 2. See *headroom*.

sales presentation See *presentation*.

sales promotion See *promotion*.

sales promotion department 1. The department of a manufacturing or wholesaling company responsible for the planning and implementation of all promotional activities. 2. A department of an advertising agency responsible for devising promotion plans for clients.

sales quota A figure, usually either the number of unit sales to be made or the sales revenue to be received, set as a goal for a salesperson or agent in a stated future period.

sales representative See *representative, salesperson*.

sales service A service, usually offered by a retail-owned wholesaler, that provides sales visits to retailers on behalf of and for a fee paid by manufacturers.

salting The placement of decoy or dummy names in a mailing list to trace unauthorized list usage and delivery. Also **seeding**.

same size (ss) An instruction to a photographer, printer, and so on, to reproduce an image without changing its size.

SAMPAC See *Society of Advertisers, Music Producers, Arrangers, and Composers*.

sample 1. A group of individuals, regarded as representative of a whole population, that is selected for a study or interviewing. 2. A small quantity or single portion of a product distributed gratis or at a reduced price to induce the recipient to buy the product steadily.

sample area   The geographic area in which a survey respondent sample is obtained.

(sample) cell   A small, homogeneous group within a larger statistical sample. See *cell*.

sample copy   A free copy of a publication distributed to a prospective subscriber or advertiser.

sample error   See *sampling error*.

sample in-tab   See *in-tab sample*.

sample package   An example of the mailing piece to be mailed by a list user to a particular list. Such a mailing piece is submitted to the list owner for approval prior to commitment for one-time use of that list.

sample print   See *rough print*.

sample reel   See *demo reel*.

sample size   The number of elementary units in a survey that supply information that is used in tabulations. Also **in-tab sample size**.

sampling   1. The technique of using a mathematically selected portion of a statistical population to describe or evaluate the entire statistical population. 2. The distribution of product samples in retail merchandising.

sampling error   The deviation between the observed characteristics of a sample and those of the population from which it is drawn; inherent in all samples and inversely related to sample size. Also **sample error**, **sampling variation**. See *nonsampling error*.

sampling rate   The ratio of the sample size to the size of the statistical population.

sampling unit   A geographic area used for research purposes, normally consisting of a county or independent city. Some counties, however, may be divided into two or more sampling units due to topography or ethnicity.

sampling variation   See *sampling error*.

sandwich   1. See *donut*. 2. A radio or television network program that is scheduled between two local programs, or vice versa; often news.

sandwich board   An advertising poster suspended from the shoulders of a person walking in the street; usually there is one board in front, one in back.

satellite   1. See *relay station*. 2. A relay station placed into orbit around the earth. See *satellite station*.

satellite broker   An individual or company that purchases time on communications satellites for resale.

satellite communication   The transmission of information in which a satellite is at least one link in the signal path.

satellite news vehicle   A mobile van or truck with uplink equipment for feeding transmissions from a remote site to a satellite for relay to a television station or network. Also **star truck**.

satellite station   A station that has a rebroadcast arrangement with a primary broadcaster to service an area not normally covered by the parent station. See *relay station*.

satellite store   1. A small store, close to and competing with a large one. 2. A store close to but not part of a shopping center.

saturation   1. An amount of advertising well above the normal levels of frequency and coverage. Also **saturation campaign**, **saturation schedule**. 2. See *penetration*. 3. A property of color determining its difference from white (e.g., strong red, light red, pink, white). See *chroma*.

saturation campaign   See previous.

saturation schedule   See *saturation*.

saturation showing   An outdoor advertising showing well above 100 intensity.

Saturday morning television A term that has its roots in the child-oriented, limited animation cartoon shows that began to dominate this time slot in the 1950s but that has come to stand for this genre of mass-produced animation.

SAWA See *Screen Advertising World Association*.

scalability analysis An interview technique used to determine the tendency of a respondent to exaggerate reactions, in which stimuli of different degrees or kinds are presented successively and respondent reactions noted. Also **scalogram technique**.

scale 1. To enlarge or reduce type, artwork, etc., photographically for printing at the proper size. 2. To compute the fit of manuscript copy to type area for a given type size. 3. See *scale rate*. 4. A defined set of values.

scale rate 1. A standard cost for printing, engraving, and so on. 2. A rate of payment for talent as specified by union contract, rather than negotiated. Also **scale**.

scalogram technique See *scalability analysis*.

scan 1. One sweep of the television scanning line. 2. To sweep the scanning lines successively. 3. To examine items in a list or data file.

scan line See *scanning line*.

scanner In printing, an electronic device that is able to read colors automatically from a photograph for use in color separations.

scanning The process of analyzing successively, according to a predetermined method, the light values of picture elements constituting the total television picture area. See *scan*.

scanning line A single, continuous, narrow horizontal strip of a television picture area containing highlights, shadows, and half-tones, determined by the process of scanning. Also **scan line**.

scatter The unsold commercial time on a radio or television station or network.

scatter buying See *scatter plan*.

scatter market The unsold time on a network after the preseason up-front buying is completed. See *scatter*.

scatter plan A broadcast advertising media plan calling for a series of commercials presented at different times and on different frequencies so as to reach the greatest possible audience. Also **scatter buying**.

scenario The outline of a play, film, television show, etc. Also **synopsis**. See *treatment*.

scene 1. The locale, or visual image of such a locale, appearing in a dramatic action. 2. A sequence of a play, motion picture, television show, etc., occurring in a single place and over a continuous period.

schedule (sked) 1. A list of things occurring in a temporal sequence, stating the time at which each is to occur. Also **timetable**. 2. A list of things having a common association in a general plan, as one of advertising to be used in a communications medium or of media to be used in a campaign. 3. The times and dates the individual spots or advertisements of an advertising campaign are to be broadcast or printed. 4. A survey question-and-answer form that is filled out by an interviewer. See *questionnaire*.

schedule reach A statistical estimate of the number of different individuals (unduplicated audience) who are exposed to an advertising message.

schlock (*sl.*) Heavy, tasteless copy or advertising matter.

schmaltz Music or writing that is overly sentimental.

Schwerin Research Corporation An organization that tests the advertising effectiveness of commercials.

scientific marketing A style of marketing characterized by its use of scientific research, testing, and analytic methods as a means of minimizing risks and maximizing business opportunities.

score 1. A quantitative result of a statistical investigation. 2. A linear indentation in a sheet of paper or other material, made to ease and direct folding. 3. A musical piece, in document form, used to guide individual musicians in its performance. 4. To write music for use in a television production, motion picture, and so on.

scrambled merchandising A practice of retailers who offer for sale product lines not conventionally carried by stores of their kind.

scrap art The visual material derived from magazine and newspaper clippings, books, labels, etc., used to illustrate roughly a layout, visual, or scenic treatment.

Scratch-and-Sniff™ A microencapsulation process used to convey a specific scent to readers of print media. The scent is released by scratching a treated area to break the microscopic plastic "scent bubbles."

scratch mix See *scratch track*.

scratch off A device used in direct mail in which a surface coating is removed using a coin to reveal the message underneath; usually for a prize or a chance for a prize.

scratch track A temporary, low-quality sound track, used as a rough guide to the sound of a final recording or for television or motion picture editing and synchronization. Also **scratch mix**.

screen 1. A surface onto which the image of a slide, motion picture, or television program is projected. 2. See *halftone screen*. 3. To project photographic images. 4. To view a motion picture or videotape, often as a part of editing or evaluating it. 5. To sort or eliminate, as sales prospects, research respondents, or job applicants.

Screen Actors' Guild (SAG) A major acting union, representing professional actors and performing artists in films.

Screen Advertising World Association (SAWA) An organization promoting motion pictures as an advertising medium.

Screen Extras' Guild (SEG) A union of individuals who work as extras in motion pictures.

screening question In a questionnaire, an item designed to determine whether the following questions are to be asked of the respondent.

screening room A small projection room used primarily for screenings.

screen print See *Velox*.

script A complete sequential account of dialogue, actions, settings, etc., prepared by the author of a play, show, or program.

scriptwriter A person who writes scripts for television or radio programs.

SCSA See *standard consolidated statistical area*.

SD See *standard deviation*.

SE See *sound effects, special effects, standard error*.

seal of approval A symbol granted by a publication, especially a magazine, for use in advertising, stating that the magazine has tested the product advertised and found it satisfactory.

seasonal Pertaining to a product, service, or category normally purchased only at a certain time or times of the year.

seasonal commercial A commercial that is especially related, by audio or video reference, to a particular season, such as a Christmas commercial, Valentine's Day commercial, June bride commercial, and so forth.

seasonality index A measurement expressing the variation in sales of goods or services, for a brand or category, from an even distribution throughout the year as influenced by seasonal factors; e.g., suntan lotions have a high summer seasonality index.

second A unit of product of substandard quality, sold at a discount. See *remainder*.

secondary audience 1. The readers of a publication other than those for whom its editorial content is intended. Also **secondary readership**. 2. See *pass-along audience*.

secondary boycott A labor union boycott of a station, newspaper, magazine, and so on, wherein the union urges the public not to patronize advertisers on the station, newspaper, magazine, etc. Secondary boycotts are forbidden by the Landrum-Griffith Act.

secondary data The information collected in a survey that is not used at the time in reporting results.

secondary meaning A common word that has become identified with a specific product and is thus eligible for registration as a trademark.

secondary medium An advertising medium that is selected to supplement the advertising carried for the same product or service in another medium.

secondary readership See *pass-along audience, secondary audience*.

secondary source data The information obtained from a published study by another person or group.

second class A U.S. Postal Service mail classification for newspapers and magazines.

second cover (2C) The inside front cover of a periodical; used in ordering magazine advertising.

second season The schedule of television programs that begins in January with programs to replace those with poor audience ratings in the preceding months.

section 1. One of three levels of rates for spot television announcements. 2. See *district*.

sectional announcement A network announcement heard or seen in specific geographic areas of the country only. Also **cut in**.

sectional feed See *regional feed*.

sectional magazine A magazine intended to appeal to people in one geographic area.

see copy An instruction to a printer to compare the marked proof to the original.

seeding See *salting*.

seefee (*sl.*) Pay television.

seen/associated Pertaining to ad-noters who claim to have seen a given advertisement and to have recognized the advertiser; used by the research firm of Starch & Associates.

SEG See *Screen Extras' Guild*.

segment 1. A part of a radio or television program. 2. An identifiable subgroup of purchasers or consumers in a market who share a common characteristic or special need. Also **market segment**. 3. To divide a market by a strategy directed to gaining a major portion of the sales to a subgroup in a category, rather than a more limited share of purchases by all category users.

segmentation 1. The division of a market into demographic and geographic parts for the purpose of identifying target audiences for advertising campaigns and public relations efforts. Also **market segmentation**. 2. See *mailing list selection*.

segment sponsorship   See *partial sponsorship*.

segue   To dissolve from one musical selection or sound effect to another (pronounced "seg-way"). Also **sound dissolve**.

selected take   An approved film or videotape of a scene or shot.

selective   Pertaining to a periodical of interest to a certain type of reader rather than to the public in general.

selective attention   The conscious choice made by readers or viewers to focus attention on things that please or interest them the most, rather than equally to all things to which they are exposed. See *selective exposure, selective perception, selective recall, selective reinforcement, selective retention*.

selective clubbing   An offer to prospective subscribers of a certain number of magazines from a list at a reduced rate.

selective distribution   1. The wholesale distribution of items only to retailers who spend no less than a predetermined dollar amount or who meet certain standards in their operations. 2. The wholesale distribution of only items that have a markup of no less than a predetermined rate and yet are competitively priced.

selective exposure   The choice made by a reader, listener, viewer, and so on, of whether to read, listen to, or view a particular program, speaker, writer, and so forth.

selective focusing   See *rack focusing*.

selective magazine   A magazine published for persons with special interests. Also **special interest magazine, specialized magazine**.

selective merchandising   Merchandising that eliminates competing and redundant items.

selective perception   The predisposition of a reader, viewer, or listener to discern that information with which he or she agrees. See *selective attention*.

selective recall   The degree of memory of things experienced that is influenced by preexisting attitudes, subsequent experiences, and so on. See *selective attention*.

selective reinforcement   The conscious choice made by a reader or viewer of what to read or view that supports attitudes or opinions already held. See *selective attention*.

selective retention   The predisposition of a reader, viewer, or listener to remember information with which he or she agrees. See *selective attention*.

self-administered questionnaire   A questionnaire whose information is entered by the respondent without the aid of an interviewer.

self-cover   A pamphlet or the like whose cover is of the same paper as that of the remaining pages. Also **self-wrapper**.

self-liquidator   1. A premium whose cost is fully covered by the purchase price for which it is offered. See *semi-liquidator*. 2. A display unit provided by a manufacturer in return for payment by a retailer to cover its cost.

self-mailer   A direct mail piece folded and printed in such a way that no envelope or wrapper is required for mailing.

self-service   Pertaining to any retail operation in which customers themselves select and remove the items purchased.

self-wrapper   See *self-cover*.

sell   1. The portion of an advertisement devoted to encouraging purchase of the product or service advertised. 2. To encourage a sales transaction. 3. To complete a sales transaction. 4. To present an advertising campaign, promotional program, and so forth to an advertiser or potential advertiser.

sellathon An auction held by a public television or radio station to raise money for programs and operations.

sell-in An effort to attain distribution and build inventory for a product at retail. See *sell-through*.

selling agent A self-employed person or independent business organization who negotiates the sale of goods or services without taking title to the goods or services. See *agent*.

selling idea An advertising execution element that compellingly summarizes or expresses a creative strategy. See *slogan*.

sell-off The resale to another advertiser of advertising space or time for which one has contracted.

sellout rate The percentage of radio or television availabilities that are sold.

sell-through An effort to increase the rate at which a product is sold through retailers. See *sell-in*.

semantic differential A scale that respondents use to indicate their reactions to a research question in terms of a position between two paired, opposed, or opposite terms or adjectives.

semi-liquidator A premium that is not fully self-liquidating. Also **semi-self-liquidator**. See *self-liquidator*.

semimonthly Pertaining to a periodical issued twice a month. See *bimonthly*.

semi-self-liquidator See *semi-liquidator*.

semi-self-service Pertaining to a retail operation where not all departments are self-service.

semispectacular A painted outdoor advertising bulletin to which special lighting, animation, or three-dimensional features

have been added, but one that does not have the elaboration of a true spectacular. Also **embellished painted bulletin**.

semiweekly Pertaining to a periodical issued twice a week. See *biweekly*.

senior management See *management*.

sentence completion A method for determining preexisting attitudes or information by having a respondent in a survey complete partial sentences.

separation 1. The isolation of the three primary colors from full-color originals by means of camera filters in preparing four-color (including black key) film negatives; used in producing process printing plates. 2. A time period maintained between competing radio or television commercials.

separation filter One of the three (red, green, or blue) filters used to separate the three primary colors from one another. Used for making separation negatives.

separation negative One of the three black-and-white negatives made from the three colors of the original color film.

sepia A type of monotone film or photographic printing paper yielding brown tones instead of gray to black. Often used to imitate the tone of antique photographs.

SER Statistical error. See *standard error*.

serial A radio or television program in which a continuing story is presented in installments. See next.

series A number of television or radio programs presented at regular intervals and united by title, cast, story theme, etc. See previous.

serif In typography, a cross-stroke at the end of a main stroke of a letter.

service 1. An act or deed by one person benefitting another. 2. An organization supplying some public demand, such as banking, telephone, transportation, etc. 3.

An act performed by a seller of products to maintain the utility of the products sold.

service charge   1. A charge by a wholesaler for services other than delivery of goods. 2. A charge by a retailer for services not automatically provided the customer, e.g., deliveries, credit, or check cashing.

service fee   A fee paid by an advertiser to an advertising agency, either in the form of a retainer for general services or as special compensation for unusual services.

service literature   The booklets, folders, or specification sheets that provide the operation and maintenance procedures for products.

service magazine   See *women's publications*.

service mark   An identifying mark or symbol for the services provided by one organization; can be registered under the Trademark Act of 1946. See *trademark*.

service wholesaler   A wholesaler whose salespeople call on retailers and who offers various services in connection with the merchandise. Also **jobber**.

servicing   The steps taken to assure advertiser satisfaction after the sale of time or space in a mass medium.

session   A meeting of performing talent, such as actors, singers, or announcers, with production personnel to create some form of record of a performance.

session fee   A payment made to performers by an advertiser as compensation for performance at a session; rates are usually established by union contract. See *residual*.

set around   See *run-around*.

setback   The distance between the center of an outdoor advertisement space and the line of travel it faces.

set showing   An outdoor advertising contract in which the same locations are used for the duration of the contract. See *rotating bulletin*.

sets in use (SIU)   An obsolete term for the actual number of radio or television receivers that are being used during a given period. See next.

sets-in-use rating   An obsolete term for the percentage of some specified group of radio or television receivers that are being used during a given period.

7-1/2   The preferred speed for audiotape recording.

SF   See *soft focus*.

SFX   See *sound effects*, *special effects*.

shade   1. To eliminate false signals and exaggerated contrast from a television image. 2. To change the hue of a color by adding black.

shading tints   See *benday*.

shadow box   1. A boxlike frame for the display of retail items. 2. A device used to show two or more title cards or pictures at one time by the use of mirrors.

share   1. The percentage of the television or radio audience in a coverage area that is tuned to the program being rated. Also **share of audience**. See *rating*. 2. The percentage of total retail purchases, in terms of dollars or units, for a given category of product that is enjoyed by any one brand in that category. Also **share of market**, **share of retail sales**. See *brand share*.

shared ID   See next.

shared identification   A television station identification superimposed as a legend during a commercial. Also **shared ID**.

shared screen   A television station identification that contains the ID on a portion of the screen while the other portion is used by an advertiser or sponsor.

share of audience   See *share*.

share of market   See *share*.

share of mind   The percentage of all brand awareness or brand advertising awareness for a given category of product or service that is enjoyed by any one brand in that category; usually elicited on an unaided basis. See *top of mind*.

share of retail sales   See *share*.

share of viewing hours   The total hours that noncable television households viewed the subject station during the week, expressed as a percentage of the total hours these households viewed all stations during the period. See *significantly viewed*.

share point   A share, as of market or audience, equal to one percent of the total.

sharing time   A division of time between radio stations using the same AM channel.

sharp   Pertaining to a camera shot or print that is crisply outlined and in complete focus. See *soft focus*.

sheet   1. (*sl.*) A newspaper. 2. An outdoor advertising poster size. A one-sheet is a sheet measuring the full dimensions of an advertising poster; originally 28 by 41 inches. One-sheets were combined to make larger posters to fit different size frames. Other sizes of posters have lost their original relationship of name to sheets. For example, the 24-sheet poster was originally so designated because the complete poster was made up of 24 separate sheets. Today the number of sheets used is determined by the press size and the artwork. A 24-sheet poster is usually cut in a sheet layout known as a 10-sheet or a 12-sheet layout. A 30-sheet poster is often cut in an 11-sheet layout. In general practice, the number of separate sheets ranges from 8 to 14.

sheetage   The ratio of the surface area of a sheet to its weight.

shelf   1. A retail store's physical facility for displaying products above the floor in areas open to customers; usually a long, narrow series of horizontal tiers. See *rack*. 2. An item's current availability, as in "off the shelf."

shelf card   A display card set up on a shelf in a retail store. See *counter card, point-of-purchase advertising*.

shelf extender   A traylike extension to a retail store shelf, used for special displays or as a means of increasing the regular shelf space. Also **extender**.

shelf life   See *sales life*.

shelf marker   A tag giving the price of a retail item; usually placed in, or hung from, a channel strip.

shelf pack   A display container for retail items of sufficiently small size to permit it to be placed on a shelf with ordinary clearance height.

shelf space   The amount of space occupied by a brand or type of merchandise in a retail store; measured in terms of square feet, linear feet, or number of facings.

shelf strip   A strip of paper printed with an advertising message, attached to the front edge of a shelf. See *channel strip*.

shelf talker   A printed advertising message hung over the edge of a retail store shelf.

shelf tape   A printed adhesive tape attached to the front edge of a retail store shelf. See *channel strip, shelf strip*.

shelter magazine   See *home service book*.

shipment   A collection of products sold as a unit and transferred to the buyer together.

shirtboard advertising   Advertising printed on the white cardboard used to stiffen commercially laundered shirts.

shoehorn (*sl.*)   To add copy or visuals to an advertisement, especially one that is already crowded or pressed for time.

shoot 1. A session where performances are recorded or filmed, as for a commercial. 2. To record or film such a session.

shooting date The day scheduled to tape or film a program, scene, commercial, and so on.

shooting schedule A schedule of shots for a motion picture or television show or commercial, giving the actual chronological sequence of shots as they are to be taken rather than as they are to be assembled for the completed work.

shooting script The script from which a motion picture, television program, commercial, and so on, is made. Contains extensive details as to the action, shots, etc. Also **master script**.

shopper See *shopping newspaper*.

shopping channel A cable television channel devoted to shop-at-home services. Merchandise is displayed on the screen, and viewers are given an 800 number to call for ordering.

shopping newspaper A newspaper primarily edited for local shoppers, containing advertisements and information about stores and local events, etc. Also **shopper**, **throwaway**.

shopping service A survey service for a wholesaler or store chain in which the prices of competing stores are checked and reported.

short-handle posting A method of outdoor advertising posting in which the poster hanger works from a scaffold hung against the face of the panel and posts the paper with a short-handled brush.

short rate An additional charge incurred by an advertiser when insufficient space or time is purchased to meet the contractual obligation.

short-term subscription A periodical subscription of less than one year.

shot 1. A still photograph. 2. A single, continuous filming by a television or motion picture camera, either from one position or a moving position. Also **camera shot**. 3. (*sl.*) An outdoor advertising structure, either a poster or bulletin.

shoulder shot A camera shot of a person from the shoulders upward.

show 1. See *program*. 2. A special term display of merchandise to prospects, often in cooperation with other merchants. See *trade show*. 3. To display merchandise.

show bill A large poster advertising a play, motion picture, and so on.

show card 1. A hand-lettered poster. 2. A small advertising placard.

showing 1. A number of outdoor advertisements offered as a unit. See *intensity*. 2. A number of transit advertisements, especially car cards, offered as a unit. Also **run**. 3. The total number of panels in a contract for outdoor advertising; common weights are #100, #75, #50, and #25 showings, which relate directly to a market's population (e.g., a #50 showing will deliver 500,000 daily exposures in a market of one million people). A showing size is not a code for the number of poster panels used.

show through 1. For colors from a previous outdoor advertising poster to show through the current poster. 2. For printed matter to be seen from the back of a page because the paper is not opaque.

shrinkage 1. A measured loss of sales items or of weight in sales items, due to natural causes, pilfering, etc. 2. The reduction in size during molding and drying of a matrix from which printing plates are cast; requires overdimensioning of the original if final agate line size is to be retained.

shutter A device in a camera that admits light to the film it covers for brief intervals.

shutter speed The time interval for which a camera shutter exposes film; one of the three key variables in determining proper film exposure, the other two being f stop and film speed.

SI See *sponsor identification, station identification*.

SIA See *Storage Instantaneous Audimeter*.

side bind See *side stitch*.

side-by-side shot See *half lap*.

side position 1. A car card placement above the side window of a public transit vehicle; the common position. 2. The position of advertising posters on either side of the exterior of a public transit vehicle.

side stitch To bind a magazine, pamphlet, or booklet by stapling or sewing the folded sheets next to the edge of the fold, on the outside. Also **side bind**. See *saddle stitch*.

signage A series of signs of varying content but sharing a common design system and generally used by a single organization, company, or entity.

signal An information-bearing impulse, such as a radio wave, light wave, etc., transmitted between a sender and one or more receivers (e.g., the series of waves broadcast by a television or radio station).

signal area The geographic area in which a broadcast station's signal can be received with regularity. See *coverage*.

signal grade The degree of signal strength in various parts of a television or radio station coverage area.

signal service zone The primary service area of a radio or television station.

signature 1. A musical theme identifying a television or radio program or an advertiser's product or service. 2. A folded sheet containing 4, 8, 12, 16, and so on, pages that are printed, folded, trimmed, and bound to form a part of a book or pamphlet.

significance level See *statistical significance*.

significant difference See *statistical significance*.

significantly viewed Pertaining to television signals that are viewed in other than cable television households as follows: for a full or partial network station, a share of viewing hours of at least 3 percent (total week hours), and a net weekly circulation of at least 25 percent; for an independent station, a share of viewing hours of at least 2 percent (total week hours), and a net weekly circulation of at least 5 percent.

sign off 1. The time a broadcast day ends. 2. The announcement made at the end of a broadcast day. 3. The announcement made at the end of a program.

sign on 1. The time a broadcast day begins. 2. The announcement made at the beginning of a broadcast day. 3. The announcement made at the beginning of a program.

SII See *sponsor identification index*.

silhouette 1. An outline figure, usually of undifferentiated black against a white background. 2. A halftone in which the background has been cut away or otherwise eliminated. Also **outline cut, silhouette halftone**. See *vignette*. 3. To show a figure, as in a photograph, without a background.

silhouette halftone See previous.

SILVTR Silent videotape recording; used as a notation or direction on commercial production material.

Simmons Market Research Bureau, Inc. (SMRB) A service that reports multimedia viewership by users of products and product categories.

simple correlation See *correlation*.

simple random sample A survey sample in which each element and all possible equal-sized combinations of elements have an equal chance of selection. See *probability sample*.

simulation 1. A computerized representation of a real-time action. 2. An operation designed to model artificially a real situation.

simulcast 1. The broadcast of a single performance of the same program by both radio and television, whether or not the radio and television broadcasts are made at the same time, provided that the broadcasts take place within 21 days of each other. 2. The broadcast of a program over AM and FM stations simultaneously to provide for the two channels necessary for stereophonic reproduction; obsolete since the advent of stereo radio.

Sindlinger and Company An audience research company that utilizes telephone interviews on a national basis.

singing commercial A commercial set to music. See *jingle*.

single rate card A rate card that does not differentiate between national and local rates.

single system The process of recording both sound and picture on the same film or videotape. See *double system*.

single truck An obsolete term for a full-page newspaper advertisement.

siphoning The purchasing by cable television and pay television operations of special events, sports, movies, and so on, that originate on commercial television.

sister media The other types of the mass media in addition to the one being referred to: radio, television, magazines, newspapers, and so on.

sister station A broadcast station under common ownership with another.

sitcom See *situation comedy*.

site furnishing The appurtenances and decorations of a commercial setting.

situation comedy (sitcom) A dramatic program with continuing characters that derives its comedy from the interaction of its characters and from their reactions to normal, unusual, or ridiculous predicaments. Each episode is usually complete in itself.

SIU See *sets in use*.

six-sheet poster panel An outdoor advertising poster panel that is 5 feet 4 inches high by 11 feet 7 inches wide.

16mm A standard gauge of film.

sixty See *sixty seconds*.

:60 See *sixty seconds*.

sixty seconds A standard spot length on radio or television; others are 10, 15, 20, and 30 seconds.

sked See *schedule*.

skew 1. A concentration in excess of the average, as of sales or scores. 2. To result in, or seek, such a concentration. 3. To distort from a true value or symmetrical form. 4. More developed on one side or in one direction than another.

skewed distribution A distribution of statistical frequencies that deviates from a normal distribution in having a single mode that differs markedly from the mean.

skid A low platform for holding printed sheets or a display of merchandise.

skimming Directing advertising or programming to high-income households.

skin pack See *blister pack*.

skytyping Skywriting made with closely spaced and precisely calculated puffs of smoke, rather than with solid trails of smoke, by a number of airplanes flying in formation. See next.

skywriting The process of producing messages, symbols, etc., in the sky with trails or closely grouped puffs of smoke emitted by an airplane. See previous.

slewing The process of synchronizing videotape recorders and players during editing.

slice of life A form of television or radio commercial presenting a realistically enacted, dramatic simulation of a personal life situation.

slick A proof pulled on glossy paper, clean in appearance and suitable for reproduction. Also **reproduction proof**. 2. A popular magazine printed on glossy paper. See *pulp*.

slide A photographic transparency, usually 2 by 2 inches but may be larger, mounted on glass or in a metal, plastic, or cardboard frame to be projected on a screen; usually made from 35mm film.

slide commercial A television commercial with a video sequence composed wholly or in part of a slide or slides, rather than film.

slide projector An optical projector designed to project transparencies onto a screen or similar surface.

sliding rate A media rate for advertising that diminishes per unit of space or time as the number of units purchased increases. Also **sliding scale**.

sliding scale See previous.

slippage The percentage of purchases by people who intend to claim a promotion reward (e.g., a refund, coupon, or premium) but fail to fulfill this intent, versus purchases by people who claim such a reward.

slip proof See *galley*.

slip sheet 1. A sheet of paper placed between printed sheets to prevent offset. Also **offset sheet**. 2. To interleave freshly printed sheets of paper with porous sheets of nonprinted paper to prevent offset.

slogan A sentence or phrase used consistently in advertising to identify an advertiser's product or service. See *line*, *logotype*.

slop print See *rough print*.

slow motion The movement that appears when film is projected at a speed slower than that at which it was shot.

slug commercial See *hard sell*.

SM See *sales manager*.

SMA See *special market area*.

smaller television market The specified zone of a licensed television station that is not included in the FCC list of first fifty or second fifty major television markets.

small market A geographic area that does not contain a city; usually less than 100,000 population. See previous.

small store A retail store with annual sales of $100,000 or less, as defined by A.C. Nielsen in its retail indices.

small sweeps The television ratings that are taken in the summer.

small-town weekly A weekly newspaper published in a town physically separate from a larger city; not a suburban paper.

SMART Stop Advertising Alcohol on Radio and Television; a citizens' group.

smiley rating A research rating device in which one of an array of drawings of faces expressing feelings (e.g., frowns to smiles, hence "smiley") is selected by a respondent, most often a child, to illustrate a reaction to a question.

SMRB See *Simmons Market Research Bureau, Inc.*

SMSA See *Standard Metropolitan Statistical Area*.

smudge 1. To damage a piece of artwork, a photograph, or a freshly printed sheet in a manner that results in a blurred spot, as a fingerprint. 2. To blur a well-focused advertising idea by excessive manipulation.

sneak To slowly fade in or fade out a sound or image.

snipe 1. A sheet containing a retailer's name and/or address, usually pasted at the bottom of an outdoor poster in individual geographic locations. Also **overlay**. 2. To apply such a sheet to a poster.

SNR See *subject to nonrenewal*.

SO See *standing order*.

soap See *soap opera*.

soaper See next.

soap opera A dramatic radio or television program, usually presented daily, with continuing characters and multiple plots. The action deals with contemporary problems and continues from episode to episode. Called soap operas because many of the original sponsors were soap manufacturers. Also **daytime drama**, **soap**, **soaper**, **sudser**.

social class A level of a division of society into a hierarchy of power, prestige, and affluence groups, from lower to middle to upper classes, or finer divisions. Operationally measured by such factors as occupation, income, place of residence, affiliations, education, etc. Also **status**. See *life style*.

Society of Advertisers, Music Producers, Arrangers, and Composers (SAMPAC) A trade association of individuals involved in the creation of advertising music.

sock it To punch or emphasize a line, commercial, and so on.

SOF See *sound on film*.

soft focus (SF) Pertaining to a camera shot or print that is not well-defined and lacking in detail. See *sharp*.

soft sell The use of low-pressure techniques in commercials and advertisements. See *hard sell*.

software The programs and instructions that are used to tell a computer how to carry out its tasks.

sole sponsor An advertiser who purchases all the commercial time in a radio or television broadcast.

solid Pertaining to type lines set vertically as closely as possible; unleaded. Also **solid matter**, **solid set**.

solid matter See previous.

solid set See *solid*.

solo mailing A mailing that promotes a single product or a limited group of related products. It usually consists of a letter, brochure, and reply device enclosed in an envelope.

Sonovox An electronic device for articulating nonhuman sounds as words. See *synthesizer*.

sore-thumb display A small but conspicuous store display.

SOS See *sound on sound*.

SOT See *sound on tape*.

sound 1. The audible product of an audio system. 2. Pertaining to a film or videotape containing a soundtrack, as opposed to silent. 3. The music, disc jockeys, format, and so on, that make one radio station seemingly different from another.

sound bed A musical background, usually instrumental, over which commercials, promos, and so on, are recorded.

sound bite An audio sound effect used to enhance a video shot.

sound dissolve See *segue*.

sound editing The process of synchronizing sound and picture.

sound effect (SE) (SFX) An electrical, mechanical, recorded, or other sound, exclusive of music and dialogue, that imitates or reproduces an actual sound, such as breaking glass, dogs barking, trains whistling, etc.

sound effects library A cataloged collection of sound effects recorded on film, tape, records, and so on.

sounder A brief musical passage used on radio to identify a network, station, and so on.

sound mixer An individual who mixes sound tracks for television or film.

sound on film (SOF) A film that contains a recorded soundtrack, often single system sound.

sound on sound (SOS) The addition of new sounds to an existing soundtrack.

sound on tape (SOT) A videotape that contains a recorded soundtrack.

soundstage A large, soundproof studio used for taping or filming as well as sound recording.

soundtrack The audio portion of a film or videotape. Also **track**.

source code A unique alphabetic or numeric identification for distinguishing one mailing list or media source from another. See *key code*.

source count The number of names and addresses in a given list for the media or mailing list sources from which the names and addresses were derived.

source credibility The believability of a person who provides information; usually influenced by the informant's perception of the informer's expertise and trustworthiness with respect to the information in question.

source recorder A videotape recorder or player that is used to play back a tape for editing.

SPA See *special purchase allowance, Syndicated Program Analysis*.

space 1. The portion of a publication's pages, or outdoor or transit display areas, that may be purchased for advertising. See *white space*. 2. The distance between typographic elements.

space advertising Display advertising, as opposed to classified advertising.

space allocation The shelf space allotted to a product or group of related products in a retail store.

space buyer An employee of an advertiser or advertising agency who buys advertising space in a newspaper, magazine, and so on.

space charge The charge made by publishers, billboard owners, transit advertising companies, and so on, for advertising space. Also **space rate**.

space discount The discount offered to advertisers for the purchase of space above specified minimum amounts.

space grabber (*sl.*) A publicity agent.

space out To increase the spaces between words to fill out a line of type or between lines to extend the length of a column.

space position value (SPV) A factor used to determine the showing value in outdoor advertising. It is an index of visibility of a poster panel, based on length of approach, speed of travel, angle of the panel to its circulation, and its relationship to adjacent panels.

space rate See *space charge*.

space salesperson An individual who sells advertising space in periodicals to advertisers and advertising agencies.

space schedule A schedule of advertising space to be bought, specifying the media to be used, the dates of appearance, the size of the advertisements, the use of color,

189

positions contracted for, and the cost, submitted by an advertising agency to a client.

space spot A low-cost newspaper advertising space sold in specified quantities, to appear at unspecified intervals over a specified period.

special A single network television program that is not carried on a regular basis. Formerly called a spectacular. See *series*.

special canvass An intensive round of sales visits to a chain or association of retail stores intended to obtain support for a new brand or promotion.

special display A retail merchandising display other than that ordinarily mounted for a product on a shelf. See *display*.

special effect (SE) (SFX) An illusion generated by a wide range of processes or equipment using trick photography, optical effects, multiple images, electronics, models, miniatures, inserts, animation combined with live action, and so on.

special event A television or radio program of news interest, usually scheduled on an irregular basis, such as Senate investigations, parades, and so forth. See *special*.

special interest magazine See *selective magazine*.

specialization The use of specific formats, music, language, and so on, to attract a target audience for a broadcast or to a radio or television station.

specialized magazine See *selective magazine*.

specialized network A television network, usually pay cable, that provides programming to defined audiences, including sports, movies, and so on.

special market area (SMA) A special area measured and reported by *Nielsen Station Index*, usually for a small market that does not qualify for its own designated market area.

special opening A prepared introduction that identifies sponsors of a radio or television program.

special purchase allowance (SPA) An allowance granted by a manufacturer or wholesaler to a retailer, made in addition to a basic merchandising allowance, for the purchase of goods in a stated period.

specialty advertising Advertising accomplished by printing messages and logos on inexpensive items to be given away, including pens, matches, calendars, key rings, and the like.

Specialty Advertising Association (SAA) An association of individuals and companies involved in specialty advertising.

specialty station A radio or television station carrying religious or foreign language programming during at least one-third of the hours of the average broadcast week and one-third of the weekly hours during prime time.

specialty store A store specializing in the sale of one kind of product, often together with other products used with this basic product type.

spec sheet 1. A list of information (specifications) about a product or advertiser. 2. An equipment manufacturer's detailed description of a product.

SpectaColor™ A production technique allowing four-color newspaper advertisements preprinted on coated stock to appear in the same format in the editorial sections of all issue copies; uses electronic scanning cues to assure trimming of the roll at a uniform point, without resorting to a "wallpaper" design. See *hi-fi insert*.

spectacular 1. An outdoor advertising display, usually constructed of steel, designed for a particular advertiser on a long-term contract. The advertising copy is presented using incandescent lamps, luminous tubing flashers, caser borders, motographs, or any combination of these devices. See *semi-spectacular*. 2. A television program that is lavishly produced and usually employs well-known stars. See *special*.

spending split The percentage or dollar amounts allocated by a marketer's plans to each of the key marketing spending elements, that is, advertising, consumer promotion, and trade promotion. See *marketing mix*.

spiel (*sl.*) The continuity used in commercial copy.

spiff See *push money*.

spill-in The percentage or number of households in a home market that view stations originating in an outside market. See *spill-out*.

spill-in circulation The circulation within a given urban area of a newspaper published outside the area.

spill-in coverage The coverage of a market by a communications medium located outside the market.

spill-out The percentage or number of households in an outside market that view stations originating in a home market. See *spill-in*.

spin A promotional emphasis or idea that is attributed to a product or individual by an advertiser or press agent.

spiral wipe A basic television wipe; one picture displaces another as if a hand of a clock were accomplishing the effect.

splice 1. To join two sections of film or tape together. 2. The mechanical joining between two pieces of tape or film.

split commercial See *piggyback commercial*.

split entry A broadcast ratings company procedure for dividing the credit for listening or viewing when the reported time periods overlap for two or more stations.

split frame See *split screen*.

split-half reliability See *reliability*.

split image See *composite shot*.

split run A press run for a periodical carrying two or more different forms of an advertiser's message in different copies or issues, to test the effectiveness of one advertisement against another or to appeal to regional or other specific markets. Also **regional split**.

split run test See *split test*.

split screen 1. See *composite shot*. 2. A process used to duplicate an actor's image. Also **split frame**.

split test A technique in which two or more samples from the same list, each considered to be representative of the entire list, are used for package tests or to test the homogeneity of the list. Also **split run test**.

split thirty A 30-second television advertising spot that contains two or more related products.

spoilage 1. The printed matter spoiled in printing or binding; considered inevitable and allowed for in advance when ordering a printing quantity. 2. The rate at which any perishable product deteriorates prior to sale.

spoils Unsalable goods; reimbursement is normally claimed by the purchasing retailer or wholesaler.

spokesperson A person actively endorsing a course of action desired by an advertiser in an advertisement, especially a personality familiar to the audience. See *testimonial*.

sponsor 1. Generally, an advertiser that pays for broadcast time. 2. An advertiser that purchases an entire program. See *alternate sponsorship*, *cosponsorship*, *minor sponsor*, *participating sponsor*.

sponsored program A television or radio program paid for by one or more advertisers, as opposed to a sustaining program.

sponsor identification (SI) 1. In research, the identification by a respondent of a sponsor or its products and services with a sponsored television or radio program; established by telephone interview during or just after the program. 2. An identification announcement of a sponsor at the beginning or end of a television or radio program.

sponsor identification index (SII) The percentage of viewers who are able to identify the sponsor of a television or radio program. See previous.

sponsor relief The withdrawal from sponsorship of a radio or television program during an off-season period.

sponsorship The ownership of the advertising rights of a sponsor.

spot 1. A brief commercial or public service announcement presented on a local radio or television station. Also **spot announcement, spot commercial.** 2. The time purchased from an individual station for a spot. Also **spot sales.** 3. See *occasion.* 4. Loosely, a commercial, especially for television; usually broadcast between programs and related to neither.

spot advertising campaign A non-network advertising campaign utilizing local, regional, or national programs or announcements. Also **spot campaign.**

spot announcement See *spot.*

spot buy A purchase of commercial time on a local radio or television station.

spot campaign See *spot advertising campaign.*

spot carrier A syndicated program that is available to a number of sponsors.

spot checking The comparison of portions of an updated electronic manuscript printout with a previous version for proofreading purposes. Used to determine if a complete proofreading is advisable.

spot color Color applied for emphasis to areas of a basically black-and-white advertisement.

spot commercial See *spot.*

spot display A retail display created to be conspicuous.

spot drawing A small drawing in an advertisement or periodical page that is otherwise basically text. Also **vignette.**

spotlight 1. A luminaire with a relatively narrow beam angle designed to illuminate a specifically defined area. 2. To feature a performer on a radio or television program.

spot load The number of commercials broadcast by a radio station per hour.

spot programming The purchase of television or radio program time market-by-market from individual stations. Also **spotting.**

spot radio The commercial time purchased on local stations by national or regional advertisers. Also **spot.**

Spot Radio Rates and Data A monthly publication by Standard Rate and Data Service (SRDS) that lists the rate cards and other information about all commercial radio stations in the United States.

spot sales See *spot, spot radio, spot television.*

spot schedule The schedule of local purchases of radio or television spot time.

spot sheet A list of commercial times purchased in an advertising campaign.

spotted map A map of a market with dots (spotted) to show the placement of outdoor advertising panels or bulletins for a specific buy. Also **spotting map.**

spot television The commercial time purchased on local stations by national or regional advertisers. Also **spot.**

Spot Television Rates and Data A monthly publication by Standard Rate and Data Service (SRDS) that lists the rate cards and other information about all commercial television stations in the United States.

spotting See *spot programming*.

spotting map See *spotted map*.

spread 1. A pair of facing pages in a periodical. 2. An advertisement printed across two such pages. 3. See *double spread*. 4. See *layout*.

spread posting date The separated posting dates for a single outdoor showing, in which individual boards are posted at different times.

SPV See *space position value*.

SRA See *Station Representatives Association*.

SRP See *suggested retail price*.

SS See *same size*.

stab See *sting*.

stability The relative freedom of the characteristics of a statistical sample from chance deviation from the characteristics of the whole population; ensured mainly by taking a large sample.

stabilization curve A graphed curve illustrating the degrees of stability to be expected with various samples.

stacked Pertaining to a commercial print advertisement containing information about two or more products or services.

stacking See *block programming*.

staff opinion letter A nonbinding letter from the FTC to an advertiser concerning whether a proposed action or advertisement might violate a law or regulation.

stage left To a performer's left as he or she faces an audience; camera left is performer's right.

stage right To a performer's right as he or she faces an audience; camera right is performer's left.

stage setting The scenery, props, lighting, and costumes that help set the mood, locale, scene, and so on, for a production.

staggered schedule A schedule of advertisements in a number of periodicals that calls for their insertion on different dates.

standard (std) 1. A numeric goal, in marketing or research, intended to result from a planned course of action; failing their attainment, it is anticipated that new plans will be developed. 2. A bannerlike sign bearing the identification of an advertiser. 3. A vertical member used to support a sign. Also **upright**. 4. A popular song that has withstood the test of time. Also **evergreen**.

Standard Advertising Unit A set of uniform advertising procedures adopted by many newspapers.

standard art See *syndicated art*.

standard close A uniform close used each time a radio or television program is broadcast. Also **lock out, stock close**. See *outro, standard open*.

standard colors The ink or paint colors adopted by a medium as acceptable for use by advertisers, without the extra charge called for by custom-ordered colors.

standard consolidated statistical area (SCSA) A combination of contiguous standard metropolitan statistical areas.

standard deviation (SD) A statistical measure of the variability among a set of values. See *standard error*.

Standard Directory of Advertisers An annual series listing leading advertisers, their advertised products or services, and the positions of key management, marketing, and advertising employees; published by the National Register Publishing Company. Also **red book**. See next.

Standard Directory of Advertising Agencies An annual series listing advertising agencies, their accounts, and key employees' positions; published by the National Register Publishing Company. Also **red book**. See previous.

standard error (SE) A figure reflecting the expected variation of a particular figure, e.g., a mean or a percentage, from sample to sample. Also **statistical error**.

standard highway bulletin A painted bulletin 41 feet 8 inches long by 13 feet high.

Standard Industrial Classification (SIC) The classification of businesses in a numeric hierarchy as defined by the U.S. Department of Commerce.

Standard Metropolitan Statistical Area (SMSA) A former designation of the U.S. Office of Management and Budget, now called Metropolitan Statistical Area.

standard newspaper A newspaper of the standard size, normally 21-½ inches in depth, 14-½ inches wide, with 8 columns totaling 2,400 agate lines, or 6 columns totaling 1,800 agate lines. See *tabloid*.

standard open A uniform opening used each time a radio or television program is broadcast. Also **stock open**. See *intro*, *standard close*.

standard order blank An order form for media space and time purchases.

Standard Rate and Data Service (SRDS) A commercial firm that publishes reference volumes that quote advertising rates, production requirements, and other pertinent data for periodical, radio, television, and transit advertising media.

Standards and Practices A network department that evaluates programs and commercials and approves them for broadcast. See *continuity acceptance*.

standard streamliner bulletin A painted outdoor advertising bulletin, 14 to 15 feet high by 46 to 48 feet wide.

standard structure An outdoor advertising structure built in accordance with the specifications of the Outdoor Advertising Association of America, Inc.

standby space An unscheduled periodical advertising space, offered to an advertiser at a discount with the understanding that the advertisement will appear only when the space happens to be available.

standing order (SO) An order for a certain quantity of merchandise or advertising space, filled automatically at regular intervals on repeated occasions.

standing type Matter that is retained in type because it is used frequently, such as advertisements, tables, etc. Also **constant**.

stand of paper The sheets of paper needed to compose a complete outdoor poster advertisement.

Starch & Associates A research firm that specializes in syndicated sales of measures of consumer recognition of and response to periodical advertising.

star commercial A radio or television commercial presented in a program by the star of the program. See *cast commercial*.

star truck See *satellite news vehicle*.

stat See *Photostat*.

Stat Can See *Statistics Canada*.

state count The number of names and addresses in a given mailing list for each state.

state farm paper A periodical for farm families in a particular state of the United States.

statement stuffer A small, printed advertising piece designed to be inserted in an envelope carrying a customer's statement of account.

state of the art Pertaining to equipment that is the most up-to-date available; not outmoded.

station A facility licensed by the Federal Communications Commission to broadcast original television or radio signals. See *relay station*.

station break An interruption in a radio or television program or the time between programs utilized for station or network identification, commercials, etc.

station format See *format*.

station ID See next.

station identification (SI) The identification of a television or radio station by its call letters or channel number and its location. Also **identification announcement, station ID**.

Station Index See *Nielsen Station Index*.

station log See *log*.

station logo See *logotype*.

station option time See *option time*.

station panel A standard outdoor advertising poster panel erected on the property of a gasoline station.

station poster See *railroad showing*.

station produced program A television or radio program prepared completely by a station.

station rating A rating calculated for a radio or television program.

station reach listing A county-by-county listing of the radio or television stations that can be received there. The listing is based on previous diary history and is updated with recent diary information and changes in power or antenna height.

station rep See next.

station representative An individual or agency that represents a radio or television station and is paid a fee or a commission for the sale of air time to regional or national advertisers or agencies. Also **station rep**.

Station Representatives Association (SRA) A trade association promoting the use of spot advertising.

station time The time on a television or radio station that is not available for network programs.

station total area A station's total audiences based on viewing data obtained from counties both within and outside a station's NSI area.

statistic A sample fact in a collection made from sampling units. See *parameter*.

statistical error (SER) See *standard error*.

statistical population The complete set of elementary units that are deemed pertinent for a given problem. Also **universe**. See *population*.

statistical significance The observed differences between sets of numbers or test results not produced by sampling errors, and therefore representing real differences. Also **significance level, significant difference**.

statistics The mathematical techniques used in the description and analysis of quantifiable data and their interrelationships.

Statistics Canada (Stat Can) The Canadian government agency for collection of population statistics.

status See *social class*.

std See *standard*.

stencil 1. A sheet of paper or the like from which portions have been removed to form designs, letters, etc.; ink, paint, etc., run over the stencil and pass through these areas to mark the surface over which it is laid. 2. A fibrous, waxed sheet used in mimeographing, etc.; a stylus, typewriter, etc., removes the wax to leave designs or lettering, and ink can pass through these areas to a sheet of paper beneath.

step 1. An arbitrary division of a continuous range of statistical data, made for the sake of simplicity and often presented as a bar graph. 2. A single instruction in a computer routine.

step up To use special premiums to get mail order buyers to increase their quantity of purchase.

stereo See *stereophonic, stereotype*.

stereo mat A mold, usually of papier-mâché, for a stereotype.

stereo matrixing See *matrix*.

stereophonic Pertaining to the use of two simultaneously recorded, parallel audio channels to create the auditory illusion of live sound. Also **stereo**. See *monaural, quadraphonic*.

stereo plate See *stereotype*.

stereoscopic Pertaining to a television system that is capable of producing images that appear three-dimensional.

stereotype A printing plate cast in metal from a papier-mâché mold. Also **stereo, stereo plate**.

stet To "let it stand"; an instruction to a typesetter or printer to ignore an alteration called for in a proof.

still 1. A photograph of a scene in a play, motion picture, television show, etc. 2. A publicity photograph of a performer. 3. A slide or other non-moving image used in a television show.

still background An animation background that does not move.

still frame A single shot held for a number of television or motion picture frames.

sting An emphatic, sudden musical chord or phrase used to accentuate or emphasize a dramatic moment, serve as a bridge, and so on. Also **stab, stinger**.

stinger See previous.

stock art See *syndicated art*.

stock close See *standard close*.

stock cut A ready-made decorative or explanatory cut, kept in stock by a printer, publisher, or type house for occasional use.

stock footage A film clip from already exposed and processed film or from a commercial film library. Also **library footage, library material, stock material. See** *stock shot*.

stock format A direct mail format with preprinted illustrations or headings, to which an advertiser adds only the copy.

stock house See *photo agency*.

stock material See *stock footage*.

stock music A library of musical intros, bridges, backgrounds, and so on, usually purchased; often a charge is made for each use. Also **library music**.

stock open See *standard open*.

stock poster A standard outdoor advertising design that covers a specific category of business. It may be purchased and used by advertisers in that category merely by adding their trade names.

stock shot A motion picture or television shot of special effects, scenes, actions, etc., that is kept in a library for repeated use in cases where special filming of such subjects is unnecessary. Also **library shot**.

stock size A standard width for film or tape, such as 35mm, 16mm, 1 inch, and 2 inch.

stop action See *freeze frame.*

stop frame See *freeze frame.*

stop leader The blank leader between two film or tape segments.

stop motion photography A technique by which objects can be animated by adjusting their positions or changing drawings before shooting the next frame in a sequence. See *animation, freeze frame.*

stopper A striking headline or illustration intended to attract immediate attention.

stop set A group of commercials and/or announcements aired between sets of music.

Storage Instantaneous Audimeter (SIA) A microcomputer developed by A.C. Nielsen and used by both NTI and NSI for metered measurement of television tuning.

store audit A measurement of consumer sales made at point of sale, establishing profit or loss.

store bulletin A communication from the main office of a store to its personnel.

storecast A radiolike presentation of music, advertisements, announcements, etc., through loudspeakers in a retail store.

store check An examination of the stock carried by a retail store by persons not on the store's staff, and usually not a salesperson; done as a means of sales or marketing intelligence gathering.

store count basis See *distribution.*

store-distributed magazine A magazine sold primarily at retail stores, especially supermarkets.

store door delivery See *direct store delivery.*

store engineering A branch of design concerned with the proper layout and functioning of retail stores, often provided as a service by wholesalers.

store panel A group of stores used periodically for market research purposes.

store redeemable coupon A coupon issued by a manufacturer that can be redeemed at any store where the product is sold.

store test A test of retail product sales rates, using a panel of cooperating retail stores, usually in a single market, under controlled conditions.

storyboard A presentation panel containing illustrations in sequence of the various shots proposed or planned for a television commercial, with caption notes regarding filming, audio components, and script.

strategy See *creative strategy.*

stratified sample A statistical sample representing all the categories into which the total population has been divided, each of which is measured separately.

stratify To divide a population statistically into a number of nonoverlapping categories, each of which is represented in a sample proportionately or disproportionately to its actual importance.

strip programming The airing of a television or radio series at the same hour on each weekday.

strobe A high-speed electronic flash, often used to stop the action or give multiple exposures, on a single photograph, of rapidly moving objects.

structured interview An interview that requires the interviewer to ask the questions exactly as written. See *unstructured interview.*

structured question See *fixed-alternative question.*

studio 1. The workplace of an artist. 2. An enclosed space for the taking of photographs or the production of television or radio programs and commercials. 3. A firm that specializes in producing artwork, graphics, photographs, or commercials. 4. A place from which television or radio programs originate.

stuffer An advertising piece enclosed in an envelope, newspaper, magazine, and so on.

STV See *subscription television*.

subhead 1. A secondary headline for an advertisement. 2. A display line within the body copy, serving as a subtitle for a portion of the following text.

subjective research See *qualitative research*.

subject to nonrenewal (SNR) A radio or television spot that is available only if a sponsor or advertiser does not exercise renewal rights.

subliminal advertising An advertising message presented below the threshold of perception, as a visual message that is too brief to be consciously recognized.

subsample A selected portion of a sample, such as men between age 39 and 54, or households with income over $30,000.

subscriber A person who has contracted for the purchase of delivered copies of, or programs from, a medium such as a periodical or pay television.

subscriber study A demographic or psychographic study of the subscribers to a periodical, usually commissioned by the publisher.

subscription television (STV) The provision of pay television service on a monthly fee basis.

substantiation The requirement that advertisers have a reasonable basis for making claims about products or services.

success rate See *response rate*.

sudser See *soap opera*.

suggested retail price (SRP) A retail price suggested, but not imposed, by a wholesaler.

Sunday ghetto A time period in which the networks and local stations air public service programs.

Sunday supplement A section included with a Sunday newspaper: comics, television schedules, general interest magazines, etc.

super 1. See *superimpose*. 2. The graphic material that is superimposed.

superette A small, self-service food store operated in the manner of a supermarket; must have an annual business of $75,000–375,000 to be so labeled, according to U.S. Department of Commerce.

superimpose To place over, as one camera image on another, so as to create a composite image. Also **super**.

supermarket A large, departmentalized self-service food store, often with a large variety of nonfood items. A warehouse to supply the store regularly and a large parking lot for patrons are generally regarded as characteristics of a true supermarket.

super slide A slide used in a television superimposition.

supplement A separately printed publication or section added to the main editorial section of a newspaper. See *Sunday supplement*.

Supplemental Register A register for certain marks not eligible for entry in the *Principal Register* under the Trademark Act of 1946.

supplier 1. A graphic arts firm, film or art studio, engraver, printer, etc., that prepares material for an advertising agency or advertiser. 2. A person or organization furnishing merchandise to a retail store. See *vendor*.

support See *advertising weight*.

surface printing Printing by any method, such as lithography, that uses a flat printing surface. See *intaglio*.

surprint See *overprint*.

survey A method of estimating audience size, habits, viewing patterns, and so on, by using a sample selected from a statistical population. See *census*.

survey area The geographic area from which a sample is developed for a study. See *coverage*.

sustainer See *sustaining program*.

sustaining advertising Advertising for the purpose of maintaining the demand for a product rather than creating or increasing it.

sustaining program A television or radio program supported by a commercial station or network, without sponsorship by an advertiser; usually scheduled in the public interest. Also **sustainer, noncommercial program**.

sweep A period, usually of four weeks' duration, during which all local television markets are simultaneously measured and reported by a ratings service. Traditional sweep months are November, February, and May. In addition, *Nielsen Station Index* measures and issues complete *Viewers in Profile* reports on all Designated Market Areas (DMAs) in July.

sweeps The radio ratings taken at various times.

sweepstakes A promotional scheme involving the giveaway of products and services of value to a randomly selected group of those who have submitted qualified entries. To prevent infringement of lottery laws, such schemes typically do not require qualifying entrants to provide a monetary consideration, such as a purchase. See *contest*.

swipe A compilation or file of artwork, designs, photographs and so forth, used as an inexpensive source of illustration for an advertisement or brochure.

Swiss design A layout system that uses grids and is characterized by clean, flowing lines and spaces. Also **international design**.

switch pitch An attempt by a television or radio station to persuade an advertiser to place a spot announcement or schedule using funds currently employed for advertising on a competing station.

symbiotic marketing See *horizontal marketing system*.

symbol compatibility The similarity between the advertiser's intended significance of a symbol and that which the public actually attributes to it.

syndicate 1. To distribute a newspaper column, Sunday supplement, etc., to a number of periodicals for simultaneous publication in exchange for payment made by the periodicals. 2. To sell a television or radio program service as a package to a number of independent stations. 3. To sell a research service's survey results to contracted buyers.

syndicated art A collection of art, illustrations, photographs, and so on, supplied, generally for one-time use, by a commercial art service to advertisers and advertising agencies. Also **standard art, stock art**. See *scrap art*.

syndicated program A program sold, licensed, distributed, or offered to television station licensees in more than one market in the United States, other than network programming.

Syndicated Program Analysis (SPA) An Arbitron term for a special rating and share analysis of syndicated programs to aid in programming decisions.

syndicated supplement   A newspaper supplement sold on a syndicated basis.

syndicator   See *packager*.

synergy   The mutual strengthening of and by the various elements of an integrated advertising campaign or marketing effort.

synopsis   See *scenario*.

synthesizer   A device for producing original audio signals artificially, either by programming pure waveforms using a keyboard or control console or by manipulation of recorded material.

synthetic sound   Sound that is created by drawing, computer input, and so on, as opposed to live sound.

systematic sample   See next.

systematic selection sample   A survey sample that consists of taking every kth element after a random start, where k is the sampling interval, as in the number of elements in the frame divided by the desired sample size. This is the equivalent of selecting a single cluster consisting of k elements. See *probability sample*.

T See *time*.

TA See *total audience*.

TAB See *Traffic Audit Bureau*.

tabloid 1. A newspaper of less than standard page size, normally 14½ inches high by 12 inches wide, with five or six columns and between 1,000 and 1,200 agate lines per page. 2. A small format newspaper characterized by extensive pictorial matter and sensational stories. 3. A preprinted advertising insert of four or more pages, usually about half the size of a regular newspaper page, designed for insertion into a newspaper.

tachistoscope A device used to expose an object to respondents for a brief, precisely measured time interval, e.g., a tenth of a second; used in advertisement and package recognition tests. Also **T-scope**.

tag A voice or musical ending added to a commercial.

tail The last sequence of a radio or television show or commercial.

take-one A transit car card used inside a vehicle and bearing a pouch or pad of leaflets, reply cards, etc., intended for passengers to take.

talent A generic term for all persons who perform, including actors, musicians, announcers, and so on.

talent cost The cost for the talent of a television or radio commercial or program, including residuals.

talk format See *format*.

talk show A television or radio show organized around interviews in the studio or telephone conversations with listeners conducted by the host, sometimes with variety entertainment.

TALO See *total audience listening output*.

T and E See *travel and entertainment*.

tangible product See *product*.

TAP See *total audience plan*.

tare 1. The weight of an empty container. 2. The deduction for container weight, made in computing the cost of things sold by weight. 3. The weight of an unloaded vehicle. 4. A factor of shrinkage applied to the difference between the net weight of a product as shown on a package and the actual weight when sold.

target To design or aim advertising, public relations, and or marketing programs toward a specific audience. See *target audience*, *target market*.

target audience The specific group of individuals, identified by age, sex, or other demographic or psychographic characteristics, for whom an advertiser designs an advertising or public relations campaign. Also **target**. See *target market*.

target consumers See *target market*.

target group See *target market*.

Target Group Index **(TGI)** A syndicated study of national media audiences and their product purchase behavior.

target market An occupational, demographic, or psychographic group of consumers designated by a marketer as the best sales prospects; the marketer's most intensive sales, advertising, and promotional efforts are directed at this group. Also **target, target group, target consumers**. See *target audience*.

target price A product price established by a seller who derives it by specifying a desired rate of return on costs or investment at anticipated sales volume.

task method A method for determining a marketing spending appropriation based on the estimated cost of attaining specific marketing goals.

TBA 1. See *Television Bureau of Advertising*. 2. To be announced.

TBD To be determined.

tear sheet A page torn from a publication and sent to an advertiser as proof of insertion. See *checking copy, reprint*.

teaser 1. An announcement or promo designed to arouse curiosity in the audience. Also **hooker**. 2. An advertisement or promotion planned to excite curiosity about a later advertisement or promotion. See *teaser campaign*. 3. A curiosity-arousing device or slogan placed on a direct mail piece. See *corner card*. 4. A headline used to arouse curiosity in a reader. Also **teaser head**.

teaser campaign An advertising campaign using brief announcements meant to stimulate curiosity rather than to impart information; precedes a major announcement revealing the purpose and meaning of the teaser advertisements. See previous.

teaser head See *teaser*.

teen 1. See *daypart*. 2. Pertaining to a product or medium intended to appeal to adolescents.

telecast A television broadcast.

telemarketing The use of telephone communication for the promotion, sale, and solicitation of goods and services.

telephone coincidental survey A type of audience survey conducted by means of telephone interviews. See *coincidental interview*.

Teleprompter™ A visual cueing device for television performers, reproducing the current portion of the script in enlarged letters.

telerecording See *kinescope recording*.

teleshop To purchase goods or services from the home using telephone, interactive videotex, cable television shopping channels, and so on.

televiewer See *viewer*.

televise To transmit pictures and sound by television.

television (TV) A medium by which moving visual images and sounds are transmitted as radio or electrical waves for reconversion to moving visual images and sounds by receiving sets, usually located in consumer households. Also **video**.

Television Advertisers' Report **(TVAR)** A bimonthly report on television audience composition, program selection, and commercial sponsor identification prepared by Trendex, Inc.

Television Bureau of Advertising (TBA) (TvB) An advertising trade development organization that assists member television networks and stations in promoting television broadcasting as an advertising medium.

Television Code A self-regulatory code of program and advertising standards for television stations. First adopted in 1952 and frequently revised by the National Association of Broadcasters, it was abolished by the NAB after a court decision found the advertising standard to be anti-competitive.

television director 1. An advertising agency employee who serves as production manager for television commercials produced by the agency. 2. A television network or station program director.

television household A household that owns one or more television receivers, which may be out of order or not used.

television households (TVHH) An estimated number of households (including those on military bases) with one or more television receivers; an Arbitron term.

Television Index See *Nielsen Television Index*.

television market A geographic area with one or several cities, served by one or more television stations.

television optical See *telopticon*.

television penetration The percentage of households in a specific area with television receivers.

television recording (TVR) See *kinescope recording*.

television survey season The twelve-month period beginning April 1 of one year and ending March 31 of the following year.

telop See next.

telopticon 1. A device for projecting small cards or slides with messages or artwork for television pickup and transmission. Also **television optical, telop**. 2. The slide or card being projected.

temporary allowance See *buying allowance*.

:10 A ten-second television or radio commercial, such as an identification. Also **ten**.

ten See previous.

tent card A display card printed and folded so its message is visible from two directions.

territory A geographic area assigned exclusively to a salesperson or sales organization by a seller.

test 1. An effort to minimize risk in a marketing decision by conducting a miniature simulation of the proposed conditions in order to observe results. 2. To conduct such an effort.

test commercial See *test market commercial*.

test group A selection of individuals for the purpose of measuring reactions to products or services.

testimonial An advertising technique in which a prominent person endorses a commercial product or service. Also **personal endorsement**.

test mailing See *mailing list test*.

test market 1. A single, well-defined geographic area in which a test of an advertisement, advertising campaign, new product, or packaging is tested. 2. To conduct such a test.

test market commercial A commercial that is used to test a product in a given market. Also **test commercial, test spot**.

test market profile (TMP) A compilation of marketing data by Designated Market Area published annually by A.C. Nielsen.

test market translation 1. A projection of test market results to a larger geographic area. 2. A conversion of a national marketing plan to test market dimensions.

test-retest reliability See *reliability*.

test spot See *test market commercial*.

test store A retail store used for tests of product movement rates, buying habits, selling practices, etc.

text The principal verbal content of an advertisement, booklet, brochure, and so on. See *body copy*.

text size The size of type generally used for the body of printed material. Nine point to twelve point sizes are common for reading matter. Also **text type**. See *display size, display type*.

text type See previous.

TF See *till forbid, to fill*.

TFN Till further notice. See *till forbid*.

TGI See *Target Group Index*.

theater advertising Advertising by film in motion picture theaters, common in Canada but rare in the United States.

theater test A study conducted by exposing a large group of respondents simultaneously to a communication, in order to measure their reactions.

thick market pattern See *market pattern*.

thin Pertaining to an advertising campaign that uses too few spots to be effective.

thin market pattern See *market pattern*.

third class An inexpensive mailing category used for bulk mailings.

third cover (3C) The inside back cover of a periodical; used in ordering magazine advertising. Also **inside back cover**.

:30 A thirty-second radio or television commercial. Also **thirty**.

thirty See previous.

30-sheet poster An outdoor advertising space providing a copy area measuring 21 feet 7 inches by 9 feet 7 inches, usually covered with a single poster printed in sections on 12 paper sheets.

3C See *third cover, three-color*.

three-color (3C) Pertaining to color printing in which yellow, red, and blue are used but not black; lacks the richness of four-color printing.

three-sheet poster 1. An outdoor advertising poster 6 feet high by 12 feet wide. 2. A transit advertising poster, used in train stations, 7 feet high by 3 feet 6 inches wide.

through-the-book method A survey technique in which the researcher leads the respondent through a periodical issue and asks questions section by section to determine whether the respondent has actually read the issue.

throwaway See *handbill, shopping newspaper*.

thumbnail 1. A rough layout sketch containing little detail and often rendered in a smaller size than the final advertisement. 2. A brief verbal or written description or history.

tie in 1. To develop a cooperative marketing effort between products, brands, or marketers. 2. A retail dealer's advertising placed with or near a manufacturer's advertising for the same product line. 3. An advertisement or commercial for two products, which may or may not be from the same manufacturer. See next. 4. A cooperative mailing effort involving two or more advertisers.

tie-in advertisement A periodical advertisement making reference to an advertisement in the same issue run by another advertiser. See previous.

tie-in announcement A commercial announcement for a local retailer who carries the product or products advertised on the network program immediately preceding. Also **trailer**. See *hitchhiker, tag*.

tie-in promotion A single promotion event intended to encourage the sale of more than one product or brand.

tie-in sale A sale in which to purchase one thing the buyer must purchase some other thing as well.

tie-up The use of the name of a well-known person in advertising, especially in a testimonial. See *spokesperson*.

tight 1. Pertaining to a television or radio show or commercial having a running time that threatens to become excessive. 2. Pertaining to a highly detailed advertising layout. 3. Pertaining to a line of copy without adequate spacing.

till forbid (TF) An instruction from an advertiser to a media vehicle for an advertising campaign or spot schedule that runs until canceled by the advertiser. Also **till further notice**.

till further notice See previous.

time (T) 1. The number of repetitions, occasions, or insertions specified in an advertising schedule or rate card. 2. The broadcast occasions available or used for advertising.

time bank A reserve of television or radio station time obtained through barter.

time buyer A person employed by an advertising agency or media buying service to negotiate with television or radio networks or stations or their representatives for the efficient placement and purchase of spot advertising.

time charge The amount a station charges for air time. See *rate card*.

time classification The breakdown of a radio or television rate card into categories for the various time periods, such as AAAA to A, or A to D, from the most expensive time to the least expensive.

time clearance The process of making time available on a station for a program or commercial.

time contract An agreement between an advertising agency and a radio or television station or network, covering all time purchased by the advertiser through all agencies in order to earn the greatest possible discount. See *AAAA spot contract*.

time discount 1. A rate reduction for advertisers who make quantity purchases of time. 2. See *frequency discount*.

time sales The process of selling station time to advertisers, sponsors, or advertising agencies.

time salesperson An individual who sells radio or television station or network time.

time sheet 1. A daily record of agency employee job hours, prepared by the employee by account and, usually, by job number, and used for agency cost control. 2. A record of broadcast media purchases, with pertinent data. Also **buy sheet**.

time slot A specific time period, on television or radio, considered or planned for the broadcast of a program or commercial.

time spent listening (TSL) An estimate of the number of quarter-hours the average person spends listening to radio during a specified period of time.

time spent viewing (TSV) An estimate of the amount of time the average person spends watching television during a specified period of time.

time spent viewing/turnover factor An indicator of relative reach and frequency. Reach aims for broad coverage with minimum duplication (low time spent viewing/high turnover), whereas the goal of frequency is the maximum amount of repetition or duplication (high time spent viewing/low turnover).

timetable See *schedule*.

time zone One of 24 roughly equal longitudinal sections of the earth's surface in which a common hour of the day is conventionally observed. Four time zones cross the continental United States; the hour in each is progressively later by one than in the zone to the immediate west: **Eastern Standard Time (EST), Central Standard Time (CST), Mountain Standard Time (MST), and Pacific Standard Time (PST)**. During daylight saving time (one hour earlier than standard time), the zones are: **Eastern Daylight**

Time (EDT), Central Daylight Time (CDT), Mountain Daylight Time (MDT), Pacific Daylight Time (PDT).

tint   A shade created by mixing white with a color.

tint block   1. A solid area of color used under photographs or text matter. 2. The printing plate used to produce the color background. Also **tint plate.**

tint plate   See previous.

tip-in   1. A preprinted advertising page or card, inserted by glueing into a periodical whose page size is larger. 2. To insert by glueing into a periodical.

tip-on   A coupon, sample, or reply card glued to a page of advertising, by one edge for easy removal.

tissue   1. A sketch, as of a layout or illustration, drawn on translucent paper. 2. A translucent sheet covering finished art and mechanical elements, used to note corrections. 3. A sheet of translucent, often tinted, paper.

title   See *caption.*

title crawl   See *crawl.*

title line   See *flag.*

title music   The theme music that is used with the titles of a motion picture, television program, and so on. See signature.

title roll   See *crawl.*

TM   See *trademark.*

TMA   See *total market coverage.*

TMP   See *test market profile.*

to fill (TF)   An instruction to a typesetter: set to fill space indicated.

token   In direct mail advertising, an involvement device usually consisting of a perforated portion on an order card, or a gummed or self-sticking design of some sort, that can be removed from its original position and then placed in another designated area on the order card or return envelope to signify desire to purchase the product or service offered.

toll television   See *pay television.*

toll video   See *pay television.*

tombstone   1. An informal term for a small print advertisement for a professional person or organization, designed to meet the legal and customary restraints observed in such advertising. 2. A print advertisement that contains text matter only.

tone   See *value.*

tone and manner   A phrase sometimes used to head a section of a creative strategy proposal, describing generally the executional look and feeling of advertisements prepared in accordance with the strategy.

top 40   A radio station format characterized by the most popular music as indicated by current sales charts. See *format.*

top management   See *management.*

top of mind   The first brand or advertising campaign that comes to a respondent's mind in connection with awareness and attitude research. See *share of mind.*

top 100   The one hundred largest metropolitan market areas of the United States, as ranked by population, purchases, or other key indicators.

total audience (TA)   1. A rating that represents the percentage of a given universe that viewed a station for a given interval of time, or a specific program for six minutes or longer. 2. The entire readership of a periodical.

total audience impressions   The total number of exposures to a specific number of issues of a given periodical or to the issues of a given group of periodicals appearing at one time; used for survey purposes.

total audience listening output (TALO) The number of diaries in which a radio or television station is mentioned in a market, a county, or another designated geographic area; a county-by-county printout of the number of mentions in in-tab diaries for each station; can be used to rank stations and to calculate weekly cumes and raw bases.

total audience plan (TAP) A package of radio spots designed to reach the maximum or target audiences by varying the airing time from day to day.

total audience rating A cumulation of instantaneous audiences excluding those that are in the audience for less than a specified time (such as the length of a television or radio program). See *average audience rating*.

total circulation The full number of copies of a publication distributed, including both copies sold to subscribers and single copy buyers, as well as complementary copies.

total distribution 1. A situation in which an item or brand has exhausted all opportunities for enhancing its distribution in retail stores. 2. A condition of an item or brand distributed in all retail outlets that might be expected to carry such products.

total marketable audience The portion of the audience most sought after by radio or television stations, as opposed to the total audience. Generally the group aged 18 to 49 years.

total market coverage (TMA) An advertising concept whereby a newspaper attempts to reach all households in a market by mailing or distributing pamphlets, newspapers, circulars, and so on.

total net paid The total number of purchasers of one issue of a periodical, whether through newsstand sales or subscriptions, according to the standards of the Audit Bureau of Circulations.

Total Prime Time (TPT) A Gallup and Robinson syndicated research service, which measures television audience recollection of paid prime-time commercials, as compared with the potential audience for the programs shown.

total survey area (TSA) A geographic area composed of those counties that, by Arbitron estimates, account for approximately 98 percent of the net weekly circulation of all commercial home market stations, exclusive of counties located outside the MSA or ADI, which are reached solely by communications satellite transmission. It does include all of a market's Metro and ADI counties, plus all other additional counties necessary to account for 98 percent of the viewing.

TPT See *Total Prime Time*.

traceable expenditure An expenditure for media space or time attributed to a specific communications medium and advertiser that is reported by published sources; given usually on a nondiscounted basis. Also **reported spending**.

track See *soundtrack*.

tracking A research study that follows a group or idea over a period of time. Also **trending**. See *benchmark*.

tract A pamphlet, usually religious or political in nature, issued for propaganda purposes.

trade advertising Advertising for consumer products that are intended to appeal to wholesalers and retailers rather than consumers.

trade allowance See *trade discount*.

trade association An organization established to promote the interests of a trade or industry, to establish and enforce standards of quality and practice, and/or to disseminate information among its members.

trade catalog A publication distributed by a manufacturer, dealer, or distributer that describes specific lines of products and provides ordering information.

trade deal See *barter*.

trade discount A discount from an item's retail list or catalog price made by a supplier to a professional or retailer. Also **functional discount, trade allowance**.

trade journal See *trade press*.

trade magazine See *trade press*.

trademark (TM) A word, name, symbol, or device, or any combination of these, adopted and used by a manufacturer or merchant to identify goods and distinguish them from those manufactured or sold by others. The trademark is registered with the U.S. Patent Office. See *brand name*, *logotype*.

trade name 1. A name under which a company or person does business. 2. A name applied to a type of goods furnished by one company that does not have the exclusive character of a trademark. 3. A name by which something is known in the trade, as opposed to its common name or technical description.

trade out See *barter*.

trade paper See next.

trade press A newspaper or magazine that serves the interests of a particular trade or industry. Also **trade journal, trade magazine, trade paper, trade publication, trades**.

trade publication See previous.

trades See *trade press*.

trade spot See *barter*.

trade show A special temporary exhibit of goods or services to trade buyers, often conducted in concert with other exhibitors at a single location.

trading area The geographic area, usually with a central metropolitan market, in which area residents transact most of their retail purchases.

trading stamp A stamp offered as a premium with merchandise purchases, the number given being in proportion to the total sale amount; such stamps, in specific numbers, are redeemable for specific types of goods. This type of promotion has lost its popularity in recent years.

traffic audit An authentication of circulation out-of-doors as applied to outdoor advertising structures.

Traffic Audit Bureau (TAB) An organization of advertisers, advertising agencies, and outdoor companies that establishes traffic circulation figures to determine the value of certain locations for outdoor advertising.

traffic builder A direct mail piece, often featuring some special promotion, intended primarily to attract recipients to the mailer's place of business.

traffic count A recording of the vehicles and pedestrians passing a given outdoor advertising point in order to establish daily effective circulation.

traffic department 1. The department of an advertising agency whose purpose is to coordinate the work of the various departments and to keep it flowing steadily and punctually. 2. The department of a network or station responsible for day-to-day scheduling of programs and announcements.

traffic flow The rate of traffic volume on any system of streets, arteries, or highways relevant to outdoor advertising showings.

traffic flow map A map of traffic densities used in planning outdoor advertising showings.

traffic management The planning and administration of all activities concerned with the physical movement of goods being marketed.

traffic manager An individual who handles the flow of work in an advertising agency.

traffic pattern The general pattern of time and frequency of shopping established by customers.

traffic system A system in an advertising agency for the coordination and continuous surveillance of the physical materials for advertisements and the processes necessary to produce and run them. See *traffic department*.

traffic volume In outdoor advertising, a count of the number of pedestrians and automobiles passing an advertising structure during a specified time period, along with the number of persons passing in mass transit vehicles.

trailer See *tie-in announcement*.

training film A motion picture that is designed to teach the use of equipment, procedures, company policy, and so on.

transfer letters See *rub on*.

transient rate The cost of a single newspaper insertion or radio or television spot. See *one-time rate*.

transit advertising Advertising associated with public transportation, placed inside and outside vehicles and in rail and bus stations. Also **transportation advertising**.

Transit Advertising Association An organization of sellers of transit advertising, formed to provide educational support for members. Formerly National Association of Transportation Advertising.

transition The continuity, action, sound, or device that leads from one scene to another. Transitions may include music, sound effects, dissolves, fades, silence, and so on.

transit radio Radio broadcasting in public transportation.

transit spectacular An advertising display that occupies all of one or both sides on the inside or outside of a public transportation vehicle.

translation See *test market translation*.

translucency A photographic or printed copy of an advertisement used in back-lighted displays.

transparency 1. A transparent photograph, usually positive and in color. 2. A still or graphic on glass, film, or other transparent material for viewing by transmitted light.

transportation advertising See *transit advertising*.

transportation display poster A train or bus station display poster that comes in various sizes: one, two, or six sheets; viewed mainly by commuters.

trap To superimpose cleanly the yellow, red, blue, and black inks used in four-color wet printing, to attain the specific hues and color density desired in the final printed image.

travel and entertainment (T and E) 1. A business expense consisting of employees' expenditures for travel, meals, lodging, and client entertainment for business purposes. 2. A budget established by an employer to pay for such expenses.

traveling display 1. An advertising exhibit that travels from one retail store, mall, or trade show to another. 2. A form of transit advertising in which the display is placed on the outside of buses, taxicabs, and so on. See *car card*.

tray pack A carton that can be converted into a shelf-sized display unit by removing its top.

treatment The general approach to or tone of an advertising campaign or advertisement. See *scenario*.

Trendex, Inc. An audience research firm that takes audience measurements for networks and advertising agencies. See *Television Advertisers' Report*.

trending See *tracking*.

trial A purchase or use of a product or service by a consumer interested in evaluating personally its value, as a step preceding repurchase or regular use.

trial size A product package of small size and consequent price, or given away free, intended or serving to attract product trial.

trial subscriber A person who orders a publication or service on a conditional basis. The condition may relate to delaying payment, the right to cancel, a shorter than normal term, or a special introductory price.

triggyback A trio of 20-second commercials, one after another, each of whose time is sold for one-third that of a 60-second commercial.

trim 1. A border or molding strip used to frame an outdoor advertisement. 2. To cut a publication's pages to their final size. See *trim size*.

trim mark The lines used to indicate the points at which pages or sheets are to be trimmed.

trim size The actual size of a periodical page after trimming.

trine One of three equal parts into which the whole population of a sample is divided, the parts being arranged in some meaningful order.

triple associates method A research technique in which a respondent, being given an advertising campaign theme and product type, is asked to name the brand of product or manufacturer associated with it.

triple-duty envelope An envelope for a mailing piece, so formed as to be the envelope from the advertiser, the reply envelope for the recipient, and the order form.

triple spotting The broadcasting of three consecutive commercials for a single product or service within a single station break.

tri-variant dimension test A ranking order sort test for the importance or desirability, believability, and uniqueness of product features and advertising themes.

Tri-Vision A painted outdoor advertising display embellishment that, through use of a triangular louver construction, permits the display of three different copy messages in a predetermined sequence. Also **Multi-Vision**.

tru-line rate The milline rate of a newspaper based on the circulation in the trading area only.

TSA See *total survey area*.

T-scope See *tachistoscope*.

TSL See *time spent listening*.

TSV See *time spent viewing*.

turnover 1. The ratio of the total number of different persons hearing or viewing a program during a specified period, to the average audience at any one time; used as a measure of the program's holding power. 2. The rate of repetition in the purchase of a product by a consumer.

TV See *television*.

TVA Television Authority. See *American Federation of Television and Radio Artists*.

TVAR See *Television Advertisers' Report*.

TvB See *Television Bureau of Advertising*.

TVHH See *television households*.

TVR Television recording. See *kinescope recording*.

:20 A 20-second television or radio commercial. Also **twenty**.

twenty See previous.

24-sheet panel See *twenty-four sheet poster panel*.

24-sheet poster See next.

twenty-four sheet poster An outdoor advertising space with a copy area of 8 feet 8 inches by 19 feet 6 inches, usually covered with a single poster printed in sections on ten paper sheets. Also **24-sheet poster**.

twenty-four sheet poster panel An outdoor advertising structure 25 feet long and 12 feet high to which outdoor posters are pasted. Also **24-sheet panel**.

twin pack A promotion event calling for two product units to be sold as one, at a discounted price; usually implemented by packaging that physically unites the two units and flags the savings offered. See *bonus pack*.

2C See *second cover, two color*.

two color (2C) Pertaining to printing in black and a single color or two colors other than black.

two-page spread A layout that covers two facing pages.

two-sheet poster A transportation station poster not standardized in dimensions but usually 60 inches high by 42 inches wide.

two-step flow of communication A process by which information, such as an advertising message, is disseminated; the listener, viewer, or reader passes on the information or advertising message received from a mass medium to others. See *word-of-mouth advertising*.

type area See *type page*.

type book A printed book showing the typefaces, rules, ornaments, and so on, available from a particular printer, computer program, and so on.

typeface A designed alphabet cast in metal or photographed for various photographic typesetting processes; metal versions are generally made in a range of point sizes with a complete font in each size. See next.

type family A group of visually related typefaces.

type mechanical See *keyline*.

type page The portion of a page that type or other printed matter will utilize. Also **copy area**, **type area**. See *gutter, margin*.

type series All of the fonts of one typeface.

type style See *typeface*.

typo A typographical error; used to indicate the source of a typographical flaw or mistake in typing.

typography 1. The art of choosing, composing, and setting type for printing. 2. The effect obtained from the style of a printed page.

UC See *uppercase*.

U and LC See *upper and lowercase*.

U&L See *upper and lowercase*.

UL See *Underwriter's Laboratories*.

ultimate consumer The final user; not necessarily the purchaser of the product. Also **final consumer**.

umbrella promotion A promotional method that employs a theme to cover a number of different products sold or manufactured by the same company.

unaided recall A recall interview in which the interviewer gives the respondent no assistance in remembering past behavior. Used extensively in advertising content surveys. See *aided recall*.

uncombined listening estimates See *discrete demographics*.

uncut tape See *raw tape*.

Underwriter's Laboratories (UL) An independent laboratory that tests products to see if they meet certain safety standards.

undisplay advertising Classified advertising without display type or artwork.

unduplicated audience See *reach*.

unfair advertising Advertising prohibited by the FTC under the Magnuson-Moss Warranty-Federal Trade Commission Improvement Act.

unfair competition The misappropriation of that which belongs to a competitor.

unilluminated panel A standard outdoor advertising poster panel not equipped with lighting.

unique selling proposition (USP) The original and unique benefit claimed for an advertised product or service.

unit 1. A sales territory, usually subdivided into several sections, each with its own sales force. See *region, zone*. 2. A standard volume equivalent by which a single product item sale is measured. 3. A single copy of an advertisement or medium.

unitize To dimension cases of merchandise so that they fit evenly into standardized warehouse space.

unit of sale A description of the average dollar amount spent by customers on a mailing list.

unit split A division of a single radio or television commercial unit into two even parts, each with its own announcement. See *piggyback unit*.

universe See *statistical population*.

unlisted sample The telephone numbers that are not in the data bank of numbers listed in telephone directories.

unload To sell merchandise quickly through various promotional expedients.

unpaid copy A copy of a periodical distributed free or at a price lower than the minimum prescribed by the Audit Bureau of Circulations.

unrestricted sample See *random sample*.

unstructured interview An interview in which the interviewer is free to ask questions about the survey subject in a form and manner that seem appropriate. See *structured interview*.

until forbid   See *till forbid.*

unusable diary   A returned diary determined to be unusable according to established Arbitron Ratings diary edit procedures.

unusable sample   A household included in the original designated sample determined to be ineligible for survey participation. Includes households with disconnected telephones and no new listing in the survey area, institutional housing with nine or more occupants, nonresidential listings, and those with a media-affiliated member.

up-cutting   The elimination of part of a network or syndicated program by a television or radio station in order to give more time for local announcements. See *triple spotting.*

upfront   Early in the buying season or planning period; as of a purchase of advertising time or space, especially one of long duration.

upper and lowercase (U and LC) (U&L)   Pertaining to capitals and lowercase letters used in the normal manner; an instruction to a typesetter.

uppercase (UC)   Pertaining to the capital letters of an alphabet of type or lettering, as opposed to small letters. See *lowercase.*

upright   See *standard.*

upscale   Pertaining to the upper end of a range in a demographic analysis in terms of income, education, etc.

upstage   The direction away from the cameras or audience. See *downstage.*

usage pull   The ability of advertising to persuade people to purchase the advertised product or service.

uses and gratifications model   An approach to the mass media that contends that the members of an audience seek gratification rather than being used by the media.

USP   See *unique selling proposition.*

VAC See *Verified Audit Circulation Corporation*.

vac-pack posting A method of collating outdoor advertising posters, treating them with adhesives, and placing them in a sealed plastic container to ensure a uniform, wrinkle-free, brilliant appearance and to eliminate pop-outs, tears, and cracks.

validation A procedure used in surveys to verify the accuracy of an interviewer's methods and to verify that the interviews actually were accomplished. Also **cross-validation, verifying**.

validity The competence of a research technique for measuring or sampling to perform the task for which it is intended.

valuable consideration The receipt by a radio or television station of anything of value other than money or services. "Valuable consideration" is used in connection with the requirement for radio and television sponsor identification.

value 1. The relative lightness of a hue, white having the highest value and black the lowest. Also **tone**. 2. The utility of a product or service to a user or prospect, as measured by the rate of sale of such products or services at varying prices. 3. The usual retail price of a product or service.

value added theory The idea that advertising raises consumers' expectations about products and services.

Vandyke™ A blueline that is brown instead of blue. See *blueline, brownline*.

variance A statistical measure equal to the square of a standard deviation; used to measure the actual differences among the scores of a sample.

vehicle 1. An advertising or communications medium. Also *media vehicle*. 2. A specific newspaper, magazine, and so on, used for advertising. 3. A program used to carry commercial matter. 4. A liquid to which pigment is added to form paint or ink.

Velox™ A screened and highlighted photographic print frequently used in newspaper advertising as an inexpensive substitute for a halftone. Also **screen print**. See *benday*.

vendor A person or organization with products to sell. See *supplier*.

Verified Audit Circulation Corporation (VAC) A corporation that audits periodical circulations.

verifying See *validation*.

vertical buy An advertising schedule wherein time is purchased on radio or television programs that appeal to the same types of listeners or viewers. See *vertical saturation*.

vertical contiguity See *contiguity*.

vertical cume A cumulative rating for two or more radio or television programs broadcast on the same day. See *horizontal cume*.

vertical discount A reduction in price for the purchase of radio or television time at a given frequency during a limited period, such as a week. See *horizontal discount*.

vertical half-page The left or right half of an entire width of the full height of a periodical page purchased for an advertisement. See *horizontal half-page*.

vertical integration The common ownership of more than one level in the traditional multilevel supply and distribution chain of autonomous businesses that create and distribute products to consumers. Also **vertical ownership**. See next.

vertical marketing system A means used by organizations to diminish the traditional autonomy of their suppliers, dealers, or customers; such techniques include vertical integration, franchises, cooperatives, etc. See previous.

vertical ownership See *vertical integration*.

vertical publication A publication edited for persons in a specific trade, profession, interest group, life style, and so on. See *horizontal publication*.

vertical saturation A heavy advertising schedule for a single advertiser, used during one or two days on a station to reach all members of the station's audience. See *horizontal saturation*.

vertical selling Selling to buyers in a limited range of industries. See *horizontal selling*.

vertical spacing The distance between lines in printed matter.

vertigrate To integrate vertically the advertising and promotion efforts of a retail dealer, franchiser, or licensee into the broader advertising and promotion plans of a manufacturer or licensor to permit greater impact and efficiency.

video 1. The visual, as opposed to the audio, part of television. 2. See *television*.

Videoprobe Index, Inc. A cable television audience measurement organization.

viewer An individual who watches television; a member of the audience. Also **televiewer**. See *listener*.

viewer impression study A study conducted by the research firm of Starch & Associates to obtain qualitative data about television commercials through interviews on the messages and significance of the commercials to viewers.

Viewers in Profile **(VIP)** The regularly scheduled television market reports for over 220 markets. See *Nielsen Station Index*.

viewers per household (VPH) The average number of persons viewing a television program in both viewing and nonviewing households.

viewers per set (VPS) The number of persons watching a single television receiver in a household at the same time. See next.

viewers per viewing household (VPVH) (V/VH) The estimated number of viewers, usually classified by age and sex, recorded as comprising the audience in those households tuned to a given station or program or using television during a particular period. See previous.

viewing area See *coverage*.

vignette 1. A photograph or halftone in which the background is faded away gradually. See *silhouette*. 2. A picture that has soft edges; often done using cutouts or masks. 3. To fade or blur the edges of a photograph to give a vignette-like effect. 4. See *spot drawing*.

VIP See *Viewers in Profile*.

virgin tape See *raw tape*.

visible distribution The measured extent to which a given product is visible and readily accessible to the customers of retail stores.

visual 1. See *rough*. 2. Graphic material, such as illustrations, slides, videotape, pictures, and so on.

visual inventory The measured amount of a given product visible and readily accessible to the customers of retail stores;

specifically excludes storeroom inventory. See *visible distribution*.

visualization The process of producing a sketch, layout, and so on, from a mental image.

VMA See *volume merchandising allowance*.

VMA–C See *volume merchandising allowance–contract*.

VO See next.

voiceover (VO) The voice of an unseen narrator or commentator, speaking over film, slides, or other visual material. Also **off screen narration**, **over frame**.

volume discount 1. A discount offered for the purchase of a certain amount of advertising in a medium. 2. A discount offered by a seller for the purchase of a certain amount of merchandise.

volume merchandising allowance (VMA) An allowance offered to a retailer for the purchase of large volumes of wholesale goods; offered to encourage the retailer to merchandise the goods aggressively.

volume merchandising allowance–contract A volume merchandising allowance made in consideration of a contract obligating a retailer to merchandise the goods aggressively.

voluntary chain A group of independent stores that combine under a common trade name for merchandising purposes, often under the sponsorship of a wholesaler.

voluntary store An independent retailer that belongs to a voluntary chain.

VPH See *viewers per household*.

VPS See *viewers per set*.

VPVH See *viewers per viewing household*.

V/VH See *viewers per viewing household*.

waist shot A camera shot of a person from the waist up.

wait order 1. An instruction to set advertising copy in type and hold it for later use. 2. An order to a periodical to hold an advertisement until told to run it.

wall banner 1. A hanging advertisement in a retail store. 2. An outdoor advertising sign; often placed on a wall, but may be hung on a wire across a street.

wallpaper video A generic visual used on television, such as a library stock shot.

warehouse 1. A storage point for merchandise; can be owned by a manufacturer, wholesaler, or retailer. 2. To place merchandise into such storage.

warehouse store A retail store, usually of large size, offering discount prices by means of reducing such services as carryouts, deliveries, price marking of items, shelf stocking, etc.

warranty A supplier's commitment to retail purchasers of a product or service that it will perform as specified, or the supplier will provide a limited compensation or service of a corrective nature. See *guarantee*.

wash See next.

wash drawing An ink or watercolor drawing done mainly in tints or shaded tones, by use of diluted vehicles. Sometimes in black-and-white watercolor, intended for halftone reproduction. Also **wash**.

waste circulation 1. A figure reflecting the readers of a periodical who are unlikely to purchase a certain product or service advertising in it. 2. The advertising of a product or service in an area where the product or service is not available.

watercolor 1. A water-soluble paint, especially one intended for use on paper. 2. A painting made with such paint.

watermark A faint design integrated into paper that can be seen when held up to the light; often used as a papermaker's trademark, an organizational logo, and so on.

wave plan An advertising strategy that programs commercials in intermittent periods, such as two weeks of saturation, two weeks without commercials, two weeks of saturation, etc.

wave posting A concentration of outdoor advertising poster showings in a succession of areas in a market; usually coincides with special promotions in each of these areas.

wearout The point at which an advertisement or advertising campaign loses its sales effectiveness because consumers have been overexposed to it and no longer notice it. See *life*.

weekend special A type of retail merchandise given special displays or sold at a special price from Thursday through Saturday.

weekly A publication issued each week.

weight 1. The amount of advertising in support of a marketing effort; expressed in terms of gross rating points, reach and frequency, impressions, spending levels, etc. 2. The basis on which the thickness of paper is determined and sold; a ream of bond paper 17 by 22 inches weighs 20 pounds, and is referred to as 20 pound bond. 3. An adjustment made in a survey sample to correct for demographic or geographic imbalance.

weighted average A statistical quantity calculated by multiplying each value in a group by an assigned weight, summing those products, and dividing the total by the sum of the weights. Also **weighted mean**. See *weighting*.

weighted in-tab An audience measurement survey that is adjusted for over- or under-representation of the statistical population.

weighted mean See *weighted average*.

weighting 1. The numeric score assigned to a market and used to determine the reuse fees paid to talent. 2. In general, the application of ratio estimation to adjust in-tab sample data from samples so that the weighted sample is in balance with the universe for various household or personal characteristics.

Orson Welles Award An award given by the Radio Advertising Bureau for excellence in local radio commercial production.

wet printing Printing in which each ink color is immediately laid over the previous color printed before it has dried.

wf See *wrong font*.

Wheeler-Lea Act The amendments to the Sherman and Clayton Acts that allowed the FTC to regulate unfair or deceptive acts or practices in commerce, including the forbidding of false advertising of food, drugs, cosmetics, and health devices.

whip pan An extremely fast camera pan.

white audit See *audit report*.

white coat rule An FTC restriction that prohibits advertisers from using individuals who purport or appear to be medical professionals (physicians, dentists, and so on) in commercials and other advertisements.

white good A major household appliance, such as a refrigerator, range, washing machine, dryer, dishwasher, etc.

white mail A mail order request for information or goods that does not indicate the advertisement that prompted the requests.

white space The unprinted areas between blocks of type, illustrations, headlines, and so on. Used to improve the appearance of the printed page.

WICI See *Women in Communications, Inc.*

wide type See *enlarged type*.

widow A one- or two-word line at the end of a paragraph. A widow is not acceptable when it is the first line of a new column or page or when it is contained in a caption.

wild spot A spot commercial for a national or regional advertiser used on a local station.

window banner See *window streamer*.

window card An advertising card used for display purposes in store windows.

window envelope An envelope with a die-cut portion on the front to permit viewing of the name and address printed on an enclosure. The die-cut window may or may not be covered with a transparent material.

window streamer An advertising strip posted in a store window. Also *window banner*.

Women in Communications, Inc. (WICI) An organization of women in journalism, public relations, advertising, broadcasting, and so on.

women's publication A magazine or other publication designed primarily to serve a female audience or cater to women's tastes. Also **service magazine**, **women's service magazine**.

women's service magazine See previous.

word association test A test used for evaluating attitudes, in which respondents are asked to reply to a word spoken to them with the first word that comes to mind.

word jobber See *hack*.

word-of-mouth advertising The advocacy of action regarding a product or service that is passed from one person to another without a sponsor's paid support (hence not truly advertising). See *two-step flow of communication*.

word processing Using a computer program to write, edit, format, and print text.

word slinger See *hack*.

wordsmith See *hack*.

wordspacing The increase or decrease of units between words in a line of type to justify it. See *letterspacing*.

work order See *job ticket*.

work print (WP) A film print used for final editing to produce the answer print.

WP See *work print*.

wrap To conclude a rehearsal, taping, or filming session.

wraparound 1. A decorative or promotional printed sheet wrapped around a case of retail items for display purposes. Also **wrapper**. 2. See *donut*.

wrapper See previous.

writer 1. A creative and professional individual employed by a company to write literary or technical material or make revisions, modifications, or changes. 2. An advertising or continuity writer who works on staff, as a commissioned writer, or as a freelance writer for an advertising agency, public relation firm, network, broadcast station, and so forth. See *copywriter*.

wrong font (wf) A notation indicating a printer's error in using one or more type characters in a different size or type font.

X-axis See *abscissa*.

XCU See *extreme close-up*.

X-dissolve A cross-dissolve. See *dissolve*.

xerography A patented electrostatic process for reproducing printed matter; a negatively charged powder is fused to the paper by heat. Now loosely applied to the function of all copying machines.

x height 1. The standard height of lower-case letters in a given font. 2. The distance between the base line and the mean line of a line of type. 3. A type character without ascenders or descenders. Also **ex height**.

y-axis See *ordinate*.

yellow good A good that is seldom consumed and replaced; usually requires relatively high levels of service, is not broadly distributed, and has a relatively high gross margin (e.g., a washing machine). See *orange good*, *red good*.

yield The ratio of the number of usable questionnaires in a survey to the number obtained by the interview.

yuppie A term coined for young, urban professionals; an upwardly mobile group of people who are the target of extensive advertising.

zero correlation   See *correlation*.

Zip-A-Tone™   A brand of shading sheet with a pattern of dots or lines; used to create gray values in artwork without the use of a standard halftone screen.

ZIP code count   The number of names and addresses on a mailing list, arranged by ZIP code.

ZIP code selection   A process carried out by computer that selects individuals to receive promotional mail by ZIP code.

ZIP code sequence   The arrangement of names and addresses in a list according to the numeric progression of the ZIP code in each record. This form of list formatting is mandatory for mailing at bulk third class

mail rates based on the sorting requirements of the U.S. Postal Service regulations.

zone   1. A geographic subarea, used to define sales territories, mailing areas, and so on. See *region*, *unit*. 2. A geographic area that is covered by different editions or sections of newspapers.

zone plan   An advertising and marketing plan wherein a product or service is experimentally introduced into a limited geographic area.

zoom lens   A camera lens capable of rapid changes of magnification and range, and, hence, scene scale.

zoom shot   A camera shot during which the focal length of a zoom lens is changed.